Contributions to Finance and Accounting

The book series 'Contributions to Finance and Accounting' features the latest research from research areas like financial management, investment, capital markets, financial institutions, FinTech and financial innovation, accounting methods and standards, reporting, and corporate governance, among others. Books published in this series are primarily monographs and edited volumes that present new research results, both theoretical and empirical, on a clearly defined topic. All books are published in print and digital formats and disseminated globally.

Ioana Ignat • Liliana Ionescu-Feleagă

Transfer Pricing in Manufacturing

An Analysis of the OECD Guidelines

Springer

Ioana Ignat
Department of Accounting and Auditing
Bucharest University of Economic Studies
Bucharest, Romania

Liliana Ionescu-Feleagă
Department of Accounting and Auditing
Bucharest University of Economic Studies
Bucharest, Romania

ISSN 2730-6038 ISSN 2730-6046 (electronic)
Contributions to Finance and Accounting
ISBN 978-3-030-93888-8 ISBN 978-3-030-93889-5 (eBook)
https://doi.org/10.1007/978-3-030-93889-5

This Springer imprint is published by the registered company Springer Nature Switzerland AG
The registered company address is: Gewerbestrasse 11, 6330 Cham, Switzerland

Preface

Immediately after the Second World War, developed countries began to make massive investments in rebuilding their economies. Subsequently, more and more companies began to operate in several countries. Moreover, since then and until now, the number of these companies is constantly growing, a fact which determines a significant increase in the number of transactions between multinationals. Therefore, in this context, more and more groups of companies are formed, and the fact that these groups set up subsidiaries in different countries has led to issues related to the taxation of results at group level and has led to the shaping of the transfer pricing concept.

Going further, transfer pricing is considered a new and complex concept in terms of guidelines and regulations. In this context, more and more academics and tax professionals are interested in understanding the mechanism of a transfer pricing analysis. Therefore, this book is addressed to professionals from the accounting and taxation area, tax inspectors, academics, professors, and students interested in understanding the transfer pricing concept and which is the mechanism of a transfer pricing analysis. In this respect, the main objective of the book is to help them in this process by presenting in a practical approach (using case studies and schemes) and in accordance with the OECD Transfer Pricing Guidelines for Multinational Enterprises and Tax Administrations ("OECD Transfer Pricing Guidelines") the way in which the basic transfer pricing elements operate and also the steps needed to follow in order to perform a transfer pricing analysis. It is important to mention that the transfer pricing concept has relevance even in organizations operating within a single tax jurisdiction. This book does not address this aspect (i.e., the book is rather addressed to analyze aspects related to the transfer pricing concept in the context of multinational organizations). Moreover, the book presents the transfer pricing concept only from a tax perspective.

Considering all the above, the book was structured in the following way:

- *Chapter 1. Short History of the Transfer Pricing Concept and Interesting Concerns in Relation to It*—this chapter provides a short presentation regarding the history of the "transfer pricing" concept, starting from the moment that triggered the shaping of the transfer pricing notion and continuing with the appearance of the first transfer pricing regulations, including also a short presentation regarding the involvement of the Organisation for Economic Co-operation and Development ("OECD") in the transfer pricing field. Furthermore, based on the literature reviewed, the chapter includes some concerns in relation to the transfer pricing concept. In this respect, previous studies on transfer pricing regulations are presented, but also studies related to the transfer pricing manipulation phenomenon.
- *Chapter 2. Transfer Pricing Regulations: An International Approach*—this chapter, through practical case studies, presents the way in which the basic transfer pricing elements operate (i.e. arm's-length principle, double taxation, advanced price agreement, transfer pricing documentation, functional analysis, transfer pricing methods, and comparability analysis). In addition, the chapter contains a short presentation of the Base Erosion and Profit Shifting Action Plan related to the transfer pricing subject and of the transfer pricing regulations applicable at the level of the European Union.
- *Chapter 3. How to Perform a Transfer Pricing Analysis in Case of Manufacturing Entities*—considering that the manufacturing sector is the chief wealth-producing sector of the global economy, this chapter illustrates complete transfer pricing analyses applicable for manufacturing transactions. The analyses are performed based on concrete case studies and in accordance with the OECD Transfer Pricing Guidelines provisions. Moreover, the comparability analysis (one of the steps needed to be followed in order to perform a transfer pricing analysis) is performed using Orbis database. In terms of transfer pricing, manufacturing entities are classified in toll manufacturer, contract manufacturer, and fully-fledged manufacturer, the transfer pricing analysis having certain particularities for each type. Given this, the chapter also provides a picture of how the transfer pricing analyses are changing over the different type of manufacturer.
- *Chapter 4. Recent Disputes from the Manufacturing Industry Regarding the Transfer Pricing Analysis*—in the end, the book presents some recent disputes between manufacturing entities and tax authorities in relation to the transfer pricing analysis for manufacturing transactions. The issues identified in each dispute are outlined. The scope is to help the readers avoid making the same errors when preparing a transfer pricing analysis.

Concluding, the main particularity of this book consists in the usage of a simple language sustained by practical case studies, tables, figures, and schemes in order to also ensure an easy understanding by the readers without significant expertise in the transfer pricing field.

In the end, given that the subject of transfer pricing is a relatively new concept, the authors are open to any suggestions for supplementing or improving this material so that it meets the needs of readers.

Bucharest, Romania

Ioana Ignat
Liliana Ionescu-Feleagă

Contents

1 Short History of the Transfer Pricing Concept and Interesting Concerns in Relation to It 1
1.1 History (the Origins) of the "Transfer Pricing" Concept 1
1.2 Short History Regarding the OECD's Involvement in Transfer Pricing 3
1.3 Interesting Concerns Regarding the Transfer Pricing Subject 6
References 16

2 Transfer Pricing Regulations: An International Approach 21
2.1 OECD Transfer Pricing Guidelines 21
2.1.1 Arm's Length Principle 24
2.1.2 Double Taxation 26
2.1.3 Advance Price Agreement 29
2.1.4 Transfer Pricing Documentation 30
2.1.5 Functional Analysis 34
2.1.6 Transfer Pricing Methods 37
2.1.7 Comparability Analysis 43
2.2 BEPS Actions Plan 46
2.2.1 Actions 8–10 "Aligning Transfer Pricing Outcomes with Value Creation" 48
2.2.2 Action 13 "Guidance on Transfer Pricing Documentation and Country-by-Country Reporting" 48
2.3 Regulations at the Level of the European Union 50
2.4 Preliminary Conclusions 51
References 56

3 How to Perform a Transfer Pricing Analysis in Case of Manufacturing Entities 59
3.1 Toll Manufacturing Entity 60
3.2 Contract Manufacturing Entity 73

3.3 Fully-Fledged Manufacturing Entity 86
3.4 Conclusions Regarding the Differences Among the Analyses 99
References 101

4 Recent Disputes from the Manufacturing Industry Regarding the Transfer Pricing Analysis 103
4.1 Case No. SKM2020.224.VLR 104
4.2 Case No. KHO:2020:34 108
4.3 Case No. SKM2018.173.LSR 110
4.4 Case No. 5 Afs 194/2015 – 34 112
4.5 Case No. I SA/Sz 115/20 114
4.6 Case No. IT(TP)A No. 1915/Bang/2017 118
4.7 Case No. TS-580-ITAT-2020(MUM)-TP 119

Appendices 121

Abbreviations

APA	Advance price agreement
BEPS	Base erosion and profit shifting
CPM	Cost plus method
CUPM	Comparable uncontrolled price method
EU	European Union
MAP	Mutual Agreement Procedure
NCP	Net cost plus
OECD Transfer Pricing Guidelines	OECD Transfer Pricing Guidelines for Multinational Enterprises and Tax Administrations
OECD	Organisation for Economic Co-operation and Development
PSM	Profit split method
RPM	Resale price method
TNMM	Transactional net margin method

Chapter 1
Short History of the Transfer Pricing Concept and Interesting Concerns in Relation to It

This chapter provides a short presentation regarding the history of the "transfer pricing" concept, starting from the moment that triggered the shaping of the transfer pricing notion and continuing with the appearance of the first transfer pricing regulations, including also a short presentation regarding the involvement of the Organization for Economic Co-operation and Development ("OECD") in the transfer pricing field.

Furthermore, based on the literature reviewed, the chapter includes some concerns in relation to the transfer pricing concept. In this respect, there are presented previous studies on transfer pricing regulations, but also studies related to the transfer pricing manipulation phenomenon. There are identified researches where the transfer pricing regulations are compared at the level of various countries in order to evaluate the strictness of the regulations from those countries. Researches presented in relation to the transfer pricing manipulation are divided on three pillars: definition of the transfer pricing manipulation concept; identification of the transfer pricing manipulation phenomenon impact at global level; identification of ways to prevent this phenomenon.

1.1 History (the Origins) of the "Transfer Pricing" Concept

According to Satapathy (2001: 1689) transfer prices are those prices invoiced by the parent company to its affiliates or by the affiliates to the parent company, as well as prices invoiced between affiliates or between divisions of the same group of companies, for the transfer of goods or services.

Rollinson (2001: 150) states that the subject of transfer pricing is considered more and more important in the context of an increase in the volume of intra-group transactions. First of all, the attention comes from governments who are aware that transfer prices can affect the revenue they collect. Multinational companies focus on

I. Ignat, L. Ionescu-Feleagă, *Transfer Pricing in Manufacturing*, Contributions to Finance and Accounting, https://doi.org/10.1007/978-3-030-93889-5_1

the subject of transfer pricing for a number of reasons, including the amount of taxes and fees they pay.

Therefore, it is noted that the main concern that has led to the shaping of the "transfer pricing" concept is increasingly active at global level. More exactly, the history of the "transfer pricing" concept is closely linked to the concern of states related to the revenue collection, and although this concern arose more than 100 years ago, it continues to be a topic of great interest to states of the whole world.

Returning to the outline of the "transfer pricing" concept, it can be considered that a history of this concept began in the interwar period, immediately after the First World War, when tax rates began to rise, and in this context countries such as the US put emphasis on how to allocate profits between entities. Moreover, in 1930 the USA became the first state to use and adopt the notion of *arm's length principle*. Based on this principle, entities should ask themselves *what price an independent entity would charge to provide services or deliver comparable goods*.

Subsequently, after the Second World War, having as a starting point the arm's length principle, the USA developed and adopted the first regulations in the field of transfer pricing (Mirjam, 2015). Furthermore, other countries such as Australia, Germany, Indonesia, Italy and Japan have expressed their interest in transfer pricing and have adopted a legislation in this regard (Lohse et al., 2012). Moreover, for the development of global regulations in the field of transfer pricing, in 1979 OECD published a report on the allocation of profit and expenditures between affiliated entities. More details on this report can be found in Sect. 2.1—OECD Transfer Pricing Guidelines.

On the other hand, other researchers (Adams & Coombes, 2003) consider that the history of transfer pricing is closely linked to the emergence of multinational companies. Thereby, Adams and Coombes (2003) point out that economists have often mentioned that the origin of multinational companies can be found in the sixteenth or even fifteenth century. During this period, there was noticed the appearance of the largest companies, which were predominantly from Great Britain and which traded very large quantities of goods in the colonies. However, it was not until the twentieth century when companies began to engage in significant production activities outside their country of origin. Some historians claim that these activities took place immediately after the Second World War, as developed countries began to make massive investments in rebuilding their economies. Moreover, since then and until now the number of companies operating in several countries is constantly growing, this aspect being due primarily to the desire of multinational companies to increase their production activities in the context of some lower labor costs and opportunities to expand the product range.

Going further, given that the number of companies operating in several countries is constantly increasing, aspect which leads to a significant increase in the number of transactions between multinational companies, the tax authorities have begun to pay particular attention to the prices at which these transactions take place and to be aware that a transfer of profits can be made through these transfer pricings. In this context, regulations on transfer pricing have begun to be adopted.

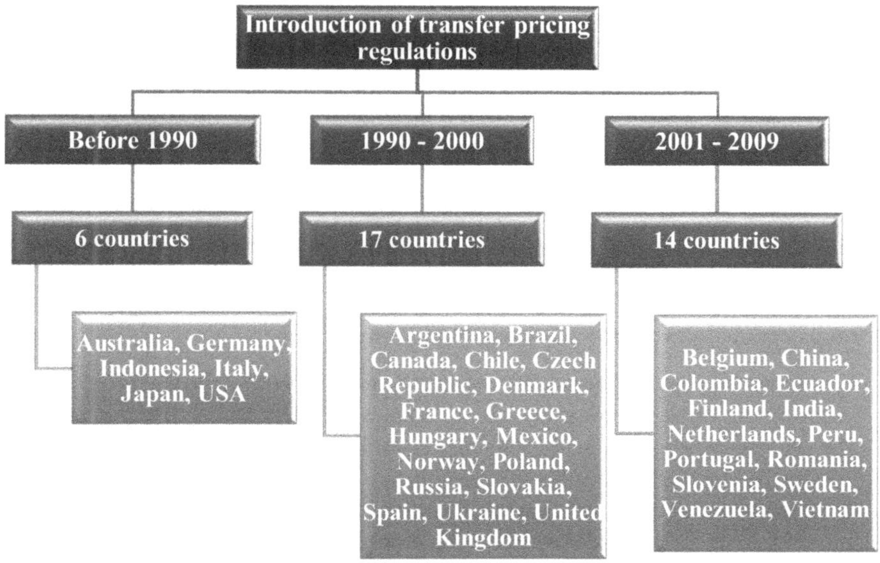

Fig. 1.1 Evolution of regulations in the field of transfer pricing. Source: Lohse et al. (2012: 7)

Lohse et al. (2012) conducted a study to capture the international evolution of the times when countries have adopted regulations in the field of transfer pricing. The study of the authors was carried out until 2009, its results being summarized in Fig. 1.1 below. As can be seen, most countries adopted regulations on transfer pricing after 1990, specifically between 1990 and 2000. This could support the novelty of the transfer pricing concept.

1.2 Short History Regarding the OECD's Involvement in Transfer Pricing

OECD is an international organization where governments work together in order to find solutions related to social, economic and environmental challenges. OECD work is also concentrated on the development of global standards and sharing of experiences for the promotion of better polices for better lives.

OECD was established in 1961 based on the transforming of the Organization for European Economic Co-operation (OEEC)—an organization which was formed in order to administer the Canadian and American aid in the context of the Europe's reconstruction after the Second World War.

The tax area, including the transfer pricing subject, is covered by OECD through the Committee on Fiscal Affairs (i.e. the main tax policy body of the OECD). Based on the actual mandate which is in force until the end of 2024, the Committee on Fiscal Affairs has the following main objective: *"to contribute to the shaping of globalization for the benefit of all through the promotion and development of effective and sound tax policies, international tax standards and guidance that will allow governments to provide better services to their citizens while maximizing economic growth and achieving environmental and social objectives. Its work is intended to enable OECD and Partner (i.e. non-Member) governments to improve the design and operation of their national tax systems, to promote co-operation and co-ordination among them in the area of taxation and to reduce tax barriers to international trade and investment"* (https://oecdgroups.oecd.org/Bodies/ShowBodyView.aspx?BodyID=963&Lang=en).

In order to achieve the above mentioned objective, the Committee on Fiscal Affairs is in charge with the following main actions:

- supporting the development of an equitable and efficient tax system through the comparative statistics, comparisons regarding the experience of other countries in the tax system's design, analysis of issues concerning the tax policy, sponsoring/conducting research about the tax design;
- facilitation of the bilateral tax treaties' negotiations;
- promotion the adoption of policies in order to avoid an international double taxation or a tax evasion, as well as the communication among countries;
- encouraging the elimination of those tax measure that distort the investment flow;
- encouraging mutual assistance between countries;
- improving of the effectiveness and efficiency of tax administrations;
- supporting the integration of Partners (i.e. non OECD Members) into the international economy.

In the light of the above actions, the Committee on Fiscal Affairs delivers the following outputs:

- standards, best practices and guidelines;
- a discussion forum dedicated to tax administrators and senior policymakers;
- internationally comparable tax statistics.

Regarding the transfer pricing subject, during the time, the work of OECD through the Committee on Fiscal Affairs was materialized in the following main aspects (https://www.oecd.org/tax/transfer-pricing/):

- 1979—the issuance of the first version of the OECD Transfer Pricing Guidelines under the name "Transfer Pricing and Multinational Enterprises";
- 1995—amendment and revision of the 1979 version of the OECD Transfer Pricing Guidelines;
- 1996—the issuance of a report which envisages the intangible assets and intra-group services;
- 1997—the issuance of a report on cost contribution arrangements;
- 1999—the work of OECD envisages the advance price agreements;
- 2006—issuance of the "Report on the attribution of profits to permanent establishments";
- 2008—update of the OECD Transfer Pricing Guidelines;
- 2010—the issuance of a new version for the OECD Transfer Pricing Guidelines;

do not have or have limited legislation on transfer pricing, where there are no documentation requirements, in the second category countries where the documentation requirement is not introduced in their national tax law but such documentation is required during a tax audit, and in the third category the countries where the documentation requirements are implemented in the national tax legislation. In addition, the two authors mention that when conducting an analysis of transfer pricing regulations, in addition to the documentation requirement, other features could be taken into account (such as methods for determining transfer pricing, penalties for non-compliance with transfer pricing rules and the possibility to apply an advance price agreement).

In another study, Lohse et al. (2012) noted that in order to measure the strictness of transfer pricing legislation, additional factors could be taken into account such as: the definition of related parties, the deadline for documenting transfer pricing, the limitation period and the penalties applied. According to these researchers, stricter transfer pricing regulations are determined by lower threshold used to determine the affiliation relationship, shorter deadlines for submitting transfer pricing documentation, longer statute of limitations and higher penalties. Moreover, in this study, the authors examined the rules on transfer pricing in 44 countries over a 9-year period (2001–2009) and found that transfer pricing regulations are less stringent in European countries than in countries outside Europe.

Marques and Pinho (2016) designed an index to measure the strictness of the legislative framework in the field of transfer pricing. This index was built on two fundamental pillars: rules on transfer pricing (legal rules and documentation requirements) and law enforcement mechanisms (issues related to sanctions, issues regarding the tax authorities involved in the transfer pricing audit, presentation of information on transfer pricing in the annual corporate income tax return etc.). The value 1 was assigned when a certain element was found in the legislative framework, and the value 0 otherwise. The study carried out by these two authors focused on the legislative framework on transfer pricing existing in certain European countries during the period 2001–2009. Marques and Pinho noted that the index increased significantly during the period under review, indicating a particular focus by European governments on related party transactions. In addition, the results of their study show that tightening the legislative framework on transfer pricing may discourage the practice of multinational companies to move profits from high-tax countries to lower-tax countries.

Riedel et al. (2015) investigated whether the strictness of transfer pricing regulations is effective in reducing profit shifting between multinational companies. This study was conducted in 26 European countries. The authors concluded that the provisions on transfer pricing documentation have some effectiveness in limiting the opportunistic practices of multinationals. However, regarding the transfer pricing regulations, the authors examined, in addition to the documentation requirement, other issues such as the existence of specific penalties, the availability of advance price agreement and the methods used to assess the arm's length principle.

Nicolay et al. (2016) measured the strictness of transfer pricing regulations using as an indicator the existence of formal or informal requirements for transfer pricing documentation. Specifically, the authors considered that a country has strict transfer pricing regulations if that country requires (in practice or as a legislative requirement) the submission of the transfer pricing documentation at the request of the tax authorities or the submission of such documentation together with the annual corporate income tax return. The authors used the requirement to document transfer pricing as an indicator of stringency, as they considered this requirement as a crucial element in increasing the transparency in determining transfer pricing.

Beer and Loeprick (2013) analyzed the relationship between the introduction of the transfer pricing documentation requirement and the phenomenon of profit shifting between multinational companies. The authors concluded that over 4 years since the introduction of mandatory transfer pricing documentation, the transfer of profits between the subsidiaries of a multinational group has decreased by 60%.

Lohse et al. (2012) considered that in order to have a transfer pricing legislation, countries should implement, in addition to the arm's length principle, key concepts such as related parties, controlled transactions, transfer pricing methods and requirements related to the transfer pricing documentation. Moreover, these authors compared the regulations on transfer pricing in 44 countries over a 9-year period (2001–2009). In order to show the differences between the existing transfer pricing regulations at the level of the countries analyzed, the authors classified these regulations as follows:

- category 0—there are no regulations on transfer pricing;
- category 1—the arm's length principle exists in the national tax legislation, but there are no requirements regarding the transfer pricing documentation;
- category 2—the arm's length principle exists in the national tax legislation, the requirement regarding the transfer pricing documentation is not implemented in the national tax legislation, but the documentation is required in practice (during a tax audit);
- category 3—the arm's length principle exists in the national tax legislation, the requirement regarding the transfer pricing documentation is implemented in the national tax legislation, but the complete documentation is available only on request;
- category 4—the arm's length principle exists in the national tax legislation, the requirement regarding the transfer pricing documentation is implemented in the national tax legislation and a short presentation/transmission of the documentation is required;
- category 5—the arm's length principle exists in the national tax legislation, the requirement regarding the transfer pricing documentation is implemented in the national tax legislation and a more detailed presentation/transmission of the documentation is necessary.

In addition to presenting the various concepts of transfer pricing regulations (e.g. the arm's length principle, transfer pricing methods, comparability analysis, advance price agreement etc.), the literature also examines how the states and companies apply these regulations, respectively use the key concepts. Eden et al.

(2001) point out that the setting of global transfer pricing standards/regulations may lead countries to adopt such regulations at the local level, however, there will be some differences between the existing global and local standards due to the institutional and socio-political environment from each country.

Thereby, Bremer and Engler (2004) consider that the global existence of requirements for transfer pricing documentation is beneficial, but these requirements should be adapted at the level of each country according to their specific legislation. The authors also note that entities do not consider the requirement to document transfer pricing a priority, but rather an issue for compliance with the tax authorities' requests.

McLure (2008) considers that the process of setting transfer pricing causes certain difficulties in practice, such as:

- lack of comparable transactions between independent entities;
- given that transfer pricing tax regulations offer entities the possibility of an analysis in order to perform the comparability analysis by reference to a range of values, multinationals may consider this as an opportunity to manipulate transfer pricing;
- in order to mitigate the phenomenon of transfer price manipulation, governments have adopted various requirements for transfer pricing documentation, these requirements becoming costly for entities;
- intra-group transactions between multinationals involve rules on transfer prices existing at the level of several countries. Thus, the tax authorities of those countries may not reach a final conclusion on compliance with the arm's length principle, which results in the occurrence of double taxation or double non-taxation.

Stevenson and Cabell (2002) consider that the determination of the "correct" transfer price is influenced by many factors, including market conditions, economic conditions, competition in the foreign market, and the level of corporate income tax in different countries. The role of corporate income tax is particularly important because in a transaction involving transfer pricing, several tax authorities may be involved, which often involves different levels of taxation and different tax rules. Non-compliance with the tax authorities in one of the countries involved can have significant consequences, in the sense of triggering a tax audit that could lead to double taxation at group level. For example, if a US entity sells goods to a subsidiary in Japan, the transfer pricing regulations that apply to this transaction are both those from US and those from Japan. In this context, it is likely that the tax authorities in the two jurisdictions will both disagree on how the transfer price will be set. Thus, entities face the risk of being in an insecure tax position (Borkowski & Gaffney, 2012).

A study of top Fortune 500 firms found that cost-based transfer pricing methods are the most widely used in practice (Tang, 2002 in Matsui, 2013: 261). On the other hand, Chan and Chow (2001) consider that cost-based transfer pricing methods (e.g. the cost plus method) are often used by multinationals that intend to use transfer pricing as a tool to maximize profits. This recital is based on the fact that these methods are much more flexible compared to methods that use existing market prices (such as the comparable uncontrolled price method).

B. Transfer pricing—a tool for manipulating results

The transfer pricing subject has been presented in detail below as a tool for shifting profits, a process referred to in the literature as the phenomenon of transfer pricing manipulation. In this sense, the analysis focused on the following aspects:

- defining the phenomenon of transfer pricing manipulation and identifying the ways in which such manipulation can be performed;
- identifying the impact that the phenomenon of transfer price manipulation has globally;
- identifying ways to prevent the phenomenon of transfer price manipulation.

B.1. Defining the phenomenon of transfer pricing manipulation and identifying ways in which such manipulation can be performed

According to Keuschnigg and Devereux (2013), collecting corporate income tax from multinational companies has become a difficult task for the tax authorities. Unlike national companies, these companies can minimize the value of corporate income tax by transferring profits to locations with low tax rates. One tool used by multinationals in this regard is the transfer pricing manipulation.

Therefore, the phenomenon of transfer price manipulation is considered to be the main tool used by multinationals to move profits from a jurisdiction with high taxation to a more relaxed jurisdiction from a fiscal point of view (Eden et al., 2005: 400).

According to Styron (2007) in Lin and Chang (2010: 1218), in order to obtain a maximum level of profit after taxation, multinational groups manipulate the transfer prices practiced between the parent company and subsidiaries or between subsidiaries. For example, when products are exported from a country where the tax rate is high to subsidiaries located in jurisdictions with a lower tax rate, the transfer price is set at a lower level than the market so that the taxable profit of the export subsidiaries to be reduced. Similarly, when exports of products are made to countries with a high tax rate, the transfer price is set at a higher level than the market price. Thus, the manipulation of transfer pricing is done in order to maximize the profit at group level by reducing the amount of corporate income tax paid within the group.

In the context of transfer pricing manipulation, some researchers considered that entities organize their operations so that they can benefit from differences in taxable revenues, adjusting the taxable base so that most of the profit generated at group level is taxed in countries with favorable tax regimes (Egger et al., 2010; Bauer & Langenmayr, 2013). Devereux (2006) studied the impact that taxation has on the location of capital, companies and profits and concluded that the value of the corporate income tax rate plays an important role in the decision taken by multinationals regarding the location of taxable profit. Olibe and Rezaee (2008) pointed out that the rate of profitability and that of effective taxation increase with the increase in the volume of intra-group transactions, which means that those companies that have high values of indicators on taxes due, assets and profitability, have a greater ability to manipulate transfer prices compared to companies with low values for the aforementioned indicators.

Madan (2000: 53–54) mentions that the prices of goods sold by a division of a group of multinational enterprises to another division of the same group are in fact transfer prices. The author states that in the context in which the operations carried out by a multinational enterprise include intra-group transactions between divisions located in different countries, at that enterprise there will be an incentive to manipulate transfer pricing in order to move profits from one jurisdiction to another. The author also states that the reasons behind the profit manipulation phenomenon will influence the group's decision regarding the location of the entities (e.g. the location of the production unit). In this context, Rawlings (2017) considers that tax havens are the most used for manipulating transfer pricing and shifting profits. In addition, regarding the location of entities, Gravelle (2013) in Rawlings (2017: 665) noted that one of the ways in which companies can move their profits and thus reduce tax debts is represented by "double Irish-Dutch sandwich". Using this strategy, for example, Google has registered intellectual property rights in Ireland. It then set up a subsidiary, which made sales in the rest of Europe. The "sandwich" between the Irish parent company and the European sales affiliate was a subsidiary incorporated in the Netherlands, which collected royalty payments from the European sales company and forwarded them to the Irish parent company. Finally, the Irish entity claimed that it was not actually managed in Ireland, but rather in Bermuda, where the tax rate was 0%.

Schwarz (2009: 450–451) identified the following ways in which multinationals can manipulate transfer pricing:

- over-invoicing of the transfer price for goods exported to countries with high taxation. The over-invoicing of the exported goods determines an increase of the expenses with the purchased good, respectively a reduction of the result of the affiliate in the region with a high level of taxation;
- underestimation of the price of the traded good when that good is exported to subsidiaries located in jurisdictions with low taxation or in tax havens. The underestimation of the transfer prices determines the decrease of the expenses with the purchased good, respectively an increase of the affiliate result in the region with low level of taxation;
- financing affiliates in regions with a high level of taxation, with an amount as high as possible, as the payment of interest earned by those affiliates is deductible from the tax base, reducing the tax result, respectively the corporate income tax paid;
- another more complicated option, but also more promising, is to finance affiliates through a holding structure;
- the use of royalty payments as patents as well as trademarks have the advantage of being inhomogeneous products. Thus, compared to other goods, it is more difficult for tax authorities to investigate whether prices are in line with the arm's length principle.

Smith (2002: 162) analyzed how multinational companies can manipulate transfer pricing. Thus, the author concluded that a firm can move profits in two ways, as follows:

- in the context in which it is difficult to identify independent comparables for the transactions carried out, the tax authorities can only determine an acceptable range of transfer prices. Therefore, tax authorities cannot always detect deviations from the arm's length principle. Smith called this situation *ex post discretion*;
- another way of moving profits can be materialized by distorting investments, a situation called by Smith *ex ante discretion*.

Richardson et al. (2013) applied a statistical model to study the main determinants of transfer pricing aggressiveness. The authors defined the aggressiveness of transfer pricing as a means by which firms can significantly reduce their corporate tax obligations. The aggressive activity of setting transfer prices is reflected in transactions with related parties without respecting the arm's length principle. The study was conducted on the basis of a sample of 183 entities listed on the Australian stock exchange in 2009. The results of the study show that the size of companies, their profitability, leverage, intangible assets and whether or not they are part of a group of multinationals are associated with the aggressiveness of transfer pricing. The results also indicate that firms are increasing their aggression in terms of transfer pricing through intangible assets and in the context in which they are part of a group of multinationals.

According to Lin and Chang (2010), the literature deals to a very small extent with the methods and theories used by companies to manipulate transfer prices.

B.2. The impact of the transfer pricing manipulation at global level

Gresik (2001: 809) points out that most of the distortions regarding transfer pricing are generated by the largest companies in the USA. Thus, these companies end up reducing their US tax debt by 52% through transactions with subsidiaries located in a low-tax country. The author also notes that the extent to which a multinational company could distort transfer pricing depends on both the differences in tax rates and the expected penalties.

Klassen and Laplante (2012) analyzed the extent to which US multinationals engage in actions related to the transfer of profits through the transfer pricing mechanism. The two authors applied a statistical model using a sample of 380 companies and concluded that in the period 2005–2009 the value of the profit moved by these companies was each year in this period higher by 10 billion.

Clausing (2000) analyzed the impact of corporate income tax reduction on intragroup transactions. The author took into account the transactions made between 1982 and 1994 between the US parent companies and their subsidiaries in other countries and noted that there is a clear link between the level of taxes and intragroup transactions. The results showed that during the analyzed period the balances of the US trade balances were less favorable than those of the countries with lower taxes. According to the author, this aspect supports the theoretical premises according to which US multinationals that intend to minimize their global tax burden will charge lower prices for exports to affiliates in countries with low tax rates, respectively will charge higher prices for imports from affiliates located in those countries.

In May 2013, the case of Apple Inc. was investigated in the US, a case in which the US lost $10 billion annually as a result of tax avoidance schemes, which included establishing divisions in low-tax countries and manipulating transfer pricing (Gao & Zhao, 2015).

Bernard et al. (2006) observed that the export prices of US multinationals for intra-group transactions are significantly lower than the prices for the same good exported to an independent customer. The authors concluded that on average, a price that respects the arm's length principle and invoiced to an independent customer is 43% higher than the price invoiced in exports to affiliates.

Langli and Saudagaran (2004) conducted a study on multinationals in Norway operating in the production and distribution sectors and following the application of a regression model concluded that except for very small entities in the production sector (with a lower turnover $1 million), the analyzed companies recorded certain deviations of taxable income suggesting the existence of a potential phenomenon of transfer pricing manipulation.

Chang et al. (2013) conducted a study applying a statistical model and using a sample of 1346 companies in the electronics sector in Taiwan. The study was conducted for the period 2000–2005 and its results show that operating revenues in tax havens decreased after the amendment of the regulation on the audit of transfer pricing in Taiwan in 2004.

In the context of using transfer pricing as a tool for shifting profits, according to Sikka and Willmott (2010) the UK tax authorities made transfer pricing adjustments for 1724 cases between 2005 and 2006. The authors also mention that in the period 2003–2007 the adjustments of the transfer prices determined the registration of additional revenues of £ 1134 million, and by 2009 the value of these revenues increased by £2114 million.

Pak et al. (2003) conducted a study to estimate the economic impact of over-invoicing/under-invoicing in exports/imports from/to Greece. The results obtained by the authors show that through transfer pricing, in 1995, profits worth $5.5 billion were moved from Greece. Boyrie et al. (2005) conducted a similar study and concluded that through transfer prices in the period 1995–1999 were transferred from Russia to the US profits in the maximum amount of $8.92 billion.

Bartelsman and Beetsma (2003) analyzed some OECD member countries to see if the corporate income tax rate causes changes in profits that are not influenced by the company's activity. The results of the study show that a 1% increase in the tax rate in a country reduces the taxable profits of multinationals by 3% in that country. The two authors presented the BMW case as a model for shifting profits outside Germany, a company whose corporate income tax paid in Germany, as a percentage of the corporate income tax paid globally, fell from 88% in 1998 to 5% in 1991, and subsequently increased to 16% in 1993.

B.3. Prevention of the transfer pricing manipulation phenomenon

Haufler and Schjelderup (2000: 320) consider that when a state introduces incentives for foreign investment, that state should also consider reducing the corporate income tax rate so as to ensure that the phenomenon of transfer pricing manipulation and transfer of profit is minimized.

Azémar (2010) considers that a low level of enforcement of transfer pricing legislation is associated with a high level of profit shifting. The author also considers that developing countries are more vulnerable to abuse in terms of transfer pricing because these countries have a weaker system that amplifies the difficulty of setting transfer pricing, carrying out tax audits and imposing sanctions. Thus, Azémar points out that countries with low taxation lose their attractiveness in the context in which they have a solid transfer pricing system, which contributes to a very large extent to the prevention of the profits shifting.

Raimondos-Møller and Scharf (2002: 230) consider that the topic of taxing multinational corporations has grown in political circles, this being a consequence of a differentiated taxation at each country level that could lead multinationals to shift profits from one jurisdiction to another. In this context, the shift of profits could be achieved through the transfer pricing mechanism. Thus, the two authors mentioned that in order to temper the initiative of companies to use transfer pricing to move profits from a high-tax jurisdiction to a low-tax one, governments have developed rules to assess the fairness of transfer pricing. The standard used for this purpose by most states is called the arm's length principle and assumes that the transfer price applied in intra-group transactions is the same as the price charged between independent entities, in similar transactions, carried out under comparable conditions.

Regarding the reduction of the phenomenon of transfer price manipulation, Blonigen et al. (2014: 5) consider that governments should impose regulations on transfer pricing. Chan (2005) conducted a study to determine whether regulations in the field of transfer pricing can prevent the phenomenon of manipulation. The results of the study showed that the regulations adopted by the countries influence the decision to set transfer prices within a multinational company. Finally, the author pointed out that the authorities should establish rules and penalties if they are interested in solving the problems related to the manipulation of transfer prices. Also, Eden et al. (2005) applied a statistical model based on which they concluded that the introduction of transfer pricing penalties could reduce the initiative of multinationals to manipulate these prices.

On the other hand, Hindriks et al. (2014) highlight the possibility of applying solutions to blur the phenomenon of transfer price manipulation and profit shifting, namely:

- setting limits for the level of transfer pricing;
- the application of the solution proposed by the European Commission on the common consolidated tax base, according to which the taxable profit is consolidated at group level and allocated to each jurisdiction according to certain fixed rules.

At the same time, Hindriks et al. (2014) consider that setting limits for the level of transfer pricing would be difficult to implement, and the solution proposed by the European Commission is very likely not to be accepted by all jurisdictions. In this context, the author proposes a third solution which consists of an income allocation scheme.

Peralta et al. (2006) analyzed the phenomenon of profit shifting in 16 OECD member countries and concluded that:

- there is an obvious situation regarding the correlation between the manipulation of transfer prices and the differences related to corporate income tax rates;
- the phenomenon of profit shifting decreases simultaneously with the degree of implementation of regulations in the field of transfer pricing.

Huang et al. (2011) consider that in order to prevent the phenomenon of transfer pricing manipulation by multinationals and the shift of profits to more tax-relaxed jurisdictions, tax authorities should implement two opposing strategies: first to impose penalties and in the second phase to reimburse those taxes that have been overpaid at group level.

Holtzman and Nagel (2014) argue that in the context of the phenomenon of profit shifting by multinationals, tax authorities have begun to become increasingly aggressive in terms of transfer pricing, introducing stricter penalties and new documentation requirements, adopting various rules to increase the degree of information exchange, improving the training offered to tax inspectors and increasing the number of tax audits performed. For example, the US intends to propose stricter tax rules for transactions conducted by US entities with foreign affiliates (Paletta & Mckinnon, 2014 in Zheng, 2017: 48).

Researchers (Sikka & Willmott, 2010; Urquidi & Thompson, 2010) argue that the loss of tax revenue from the aggressive use of transfer pricing by multinational corporations has led tax authorities to pay increasing attention to how tax audits are conducted. They point out that tax authorities around the world are beginning to challenge the calculation of corporate income tax, especially in the case of related party transactions. In addition, the authors note that tax authorities may impose high tax penalties and transfer pricing documentation requirements to discourage aggressive transfer pricing manipulation practices and to encourage increased transparency in related party transactions.

Wong et al. (2011) argue that, in order to protect their tax base, governments in many countries often give tax authorities the right to conduct audits and adjust corporate income tax in the case of related party transactions, as well as to charge various penalties.

Moreover, in order to prevent the phenomenon of transfer price manipulation, jurisdictions have implemented the provisions of the OECD Transfer Pricing Guidelines in the national tax law. In addition, in order to prevent and blur the phenomenon of profit shifting between multinationals, in 2013 the OECD initiated the Action Plan on base erosion and profit shifting—the BEPS Action Plan (Lamers et al., 2014). Details of the actions concerning the subject of transfer pricing can be found in Sect. 2.2—BEPS Actions Plan.

Going further, Lo et al. (2010) applied a statistical model at the level of entities listed in 2004 on the Shanghai Stock Exchange and concluded that the level of quality of corporate governance is important in order to discourage the phenomenon of transfer price manipulation. In this context, the authors considered the directors 'earnings as the cause of the transfer price manipulation phenomenon. Specifically, the cause is that directors are rewarded based on the financial performance of the entities they lead. Thus, it was found that directors representing the interests of unlisted parent companies are associated with the use of non-market prices in related party transactions. Finally, in order to increase the level of quality of corporate governance in order to prevent transfer price manipulation, the authors suggested the following:

- involvement of a larger number of independent directors in companies that frequently conduct transactions with related parties;
- the presence of financial experts in the audit committee.

On the other hand, Cheung et al. (2009) applied a statistical model using a sample of 254 transactions performed between Hong Kong affiliates between 1998 and 2000 and concluded that in terms of preventing transfer price manipulation, corporate governance would have an impact in this regard only through the audit committee. In addition, the authors noted that entities with audit committees pay lower prices to related parties for purchases and receive higher prices from related parties for sales.

References

Journal Articles

Azémar, C. (2010). International corporate taxation and U.S. multinationals' behaviour: An integrated approach. *The Canadian Journal of Economics, 43*(1), 232–253.

Bartelsman, E. J., & Beetsma, R. M. W. J. (2003). Why pay more? Corporate tax avoidance through transfer pricing in OECD countries. *Journal of Public Economics, Elsevier, 87*(9–10), 2225–2252.

Bauer, C., & Langenmayr, D. (2013). Sorting into outsourcing: Are profits taxed at a gorilla's arm's length? *Journal of International Economics, 90*(2), 326–336.

Bird, F., Vance, T., & Woolstencroft, P. (2009). Fairness in international trade and investment: North American perspectives. *Journal of Business Ethics, 84*(3), 405–425.

Blonigen, B. A., Oldenski, L., & Sly, N. (2014). The differential effects of bilateral tax treaties. *American Economic Journal: Economic Policy, 6*(2), 1–18.

Borkowski, S. C., & Gaffney, M. A. (2012). FIN 48, uncertainty and transfer pricing: (Im)Perfect together? *Journal of International Accounting, Auditing and Taxation, 21*(1), 32–51.

Boyrie, M. E., Pak, S. J., & Zdanowicz, J. S. (2005). Estimating the magnitude of capital flight due to abnormal pricing in international trade: The Russia–USA case. *Accounting Forum, 29*(3), 249–270.

Bremer, C. S., & Engler, G. (2004). Tightening of the German transfer pricing documentation requirements. *International Tax Journal, 30*(2), 17–30.

Chan, C. (2005). Do government regulations prevent transfer pricing manipulations? *International Business & Economics Research Journal, 4*(10), 1–9.

Chan, K., & Chow, L. (2001). Corporate environments and international transfer pricing: An empirical study of China in a developing economy framework. *Accounting and Business Research, 31*(2), 103–118.

Chang, L.-L., Hsiaob, F. D., & Tsaic, Y.-C. (2013). Earnings, institutional investors, tax avoidance, and firm value: Evidence from Taiwan. *Journal of International Accounting, Auditing and Taxation, 22*(2), 98–108.

Cheung, Y.-L., Qi, Y., Rau, P. R., & Stouraitis, A. (2009). Buy high, sell low: How listed firms price asset transfers in related party transactions. *Journal of Banking & Finance, 33*(5), 914–924.

Clausing, K. A. (2000). The impact of transfer pricing on intrafirm trade. *International Taxation and Multinational Activity, January*, 173–200.

Eden, L., Dacin, M., & Wan, W. P. (2001). Standards across borders: Crossborder diffusion of the arm's length standard in North America. *Accounting, Organization and Society, 26*(1), 1–23.

Eden, L., Juarez Valdez, L. F., & Li, D. (2005). Talk softly but carry a big stick: Transfer pricing penalties and the market valuation of Japanese multinationals in the United States. *Journal of International Business Studies, 36*(4), 398–414.

Egger, P., Eggert, W., & Winner, H. (2010). Saving taxes through foreign plant ownership. *Journal of International Economics, 81*(1), 99–108.

Gao, L., & Zhao, X. (2015). Determining intra-company transfer pricing for multinational corporations. *International Journal of Production Economics, 168*, 340–350.

Gresik, T. A. (2001). The taxing task of taxing transnationals. *Journal of Economic Literature, 39*(3), 800–838.

Haufler, A., & Schjelderup, G. (2000). Corporate tax systems and cross country profit shifting. *Oxford Economic Papers, 52*(2), 306–325.

Hindriks, J., Perlata, S., & Weber, S. (2014). Local taxation of global corporation: A simple solution. *Annals of Economics and Statistics, 113*(114), 37–65.

Holtzman, Y., & Nagel, P. (2014). An introduction to transfer pricing. *Journal of Management Development, 33*(1), 57–61.

Huang, C.-J., Kao, C.-J., Shyu, S.-D., & Yu, C.-H. (2011). Transfer pricing of Taiwan's listing/OTC enterprises between mainland China and Taiwan: Quantile regression analysis. *Review of Pacific Basin Financial Markets and Policies, 14*(1), 129–151.

Hung Chan, K., Agnes, W. Y. L., & Phyllis, L. L. M. (2015). An empirical analysis of the changes in tax audit focus on international transfer pricing. *Journal of International Accounting, Auditing and Taxation, 24*, 94–104.

Keuschnigg, C., & Devereux, M. P. (2013). The arms length principle and distortions to multinational firm organization. *Journal of International Economics, 89*(2), 432–440.

Klassen, K. J., & Laplante, K. S. (2012). Are U.S. multinational corporations becoming more aggressive income shifters? *Journal of Accounting Research, 50*(5), 1245–1285.

Langli, J., & Saudagaran, S. (2004). Taxable income differences between foreign and domestic controlled corporations in Norway. *European Accounting Review, 13*(4), 713–741.

Lin, C.-W., & Chang, H.-C. (2010). Motives of transfer pricing strategies – systemic analysis. *Industrial Management & Data Systems, 110*(8), 1215–1233.

Lo, A. W. Y., Wong, R. M. K., & Firth, M. (2010). Can corporate governance deter management from manipulating earnings? Evidence from related-party sales transactions in China. *Journal of Corporate Finance, 16*(2), 225–235.

Madan, V. (2000). Transfer prices and the structure of intra-firm trade. *The Canadian Journal of Economics, 33*(1), 53–68.

Marques, M., & Pinho, C. (2016). Is transfer pricing strictness deterring profit shifting within multinationals? Empirical evidence from Europe. *Accounting and Business Research, 46*(7), 703–730.

Matsui, K. (2013). Entry deterrence through credible commitment to transfer pricing at direct cost. *Management Accounting Research, 24*(3), 261–275.
McLure, C. E. (2008). Harmonizing corporate income taxes in the European community: Rationale and implications. *Tax Policy and the Economy, 22*, 151–195.
Mirjam, K. (2015). Transfer pricing in a BEPS era: Rethinking the e– Part I. *International Transfer Pricing Journal, 3*, 141–144.
Neighbour, J. (2002). *Transfer pricing: Keeping it at arm's length.* OECD Observer No. 230, OECD Center for Tax Policy and Administration. Accessed March 2017, from http://oecdobserver.org/news/archivestory.php/aid/670/Transfer_pricing:_Keeping_it_at_arms_length.html
Nicolay, K., Nusser, H., & Pfeiffer, O. (2016). *On the interdependency of profit-shifting channels and the effectiveness of anti-avoidance legislation.* Accessed February 2017, from http://www.sbs.ox.ac.uk/sites/default/files/Business_Taxation/Events/conferences/2016/Doctoral_mtg_2016/nusser-final.pdf
Olibe, O. K., & Rezaee, Z. (2008). Income shifting and corporate taxation: the role of cross-border intrafirm transfers. *Review of Accounting and Finance, 7*(1), 83–101.
Pak, S. J., Zanakis, S. H., & Zdanowicz, J. S. (2003). Detecting abnormal pricing in international trade: The Greece-USA case. *Interfaces, 33*(2), 54–64.
Peralta, S., Wauthy, X., & van Ypersele, T. (2006). Should countries control international profit shifting? *Journal of International Economics, 68*, 24–37.
Raimondos-Møller, P., & Scharf, K. (2002). Transfer pricing rules and competing governments. *Oxford Economic Papers, 54*(2), 230–246.
Richardson, G., Taylor, G., & Lanis, R. (2013). Determinants of transfer pricing aggressiveness: Empirical evidence from Australian firms. *Journal of Contemporary Accounting & Economics, 9*(2), 136–150.
Rollinson, B. (2001). Review of the "Taxing Multinationals: Transfer Pricing and Corporate Income Taxation in North America" by Lorraine Eden. *Journal of Economic Literature, 39*(1), 150–151.
Sansing, R. (2014). International transfer pricing. *Foundations and Trends® in Accounting, 9*(1), 1–57.
Satapathy, C. (2001). Transfer pricing: Impact on trade and profit taxation. *Economic and Political Weekly, 36*(20), 1689–1692.
Schwarz, P. (2009). Tax-avoidance strategies of American multinationals: An empirical analysis. *Managerial and Decision Economics, 30*(8), 539–549.
Sikkaa, P., & Willmottb, H. (2010). The dark side of transfer pricing: Its role in tax avoidance and wealth retentiveness. *Critical Perspectives on Accounting, 31*, 342–356.
Smith, M. J. (2002). Ex ante and ex post discretion over arm's length transfer prices. *The Accounting Review, 77*(1), 161–184.
Stevenson, T. H., & Cabell, W. E. (2002). Integrating transfer pricing policy and activity-based costing. *Journal of International Marketing, 10*(4), 77–88.
Urquidi, A. J., & Thompson, J. (2010). The challenge of transfer pricing in the Asia Pacific region. *Asian Journal of Public Affairs, 3*(1), 60–75.
Wong, H., Nassiripour, S., Mir, R., & Healy, W. (2011). Transfer price setting in multinational corporations. *International Journal of Business and Social Science, 2*(9), 10–14.
Yao, J. T. (2013). The arm's length principle, transfer pricing, and location choices. *Journal of Economics and Business, 65*(January–February), 1–13.
Zheng, S. (2017). Can corporate diversification induce more tax avoidance? *Journal of Multinational Financial Management, 41*, 47–60.

Working Papers/Papers Published in Conferences Volumes

Beer, S., & Loeprick, J. (2013). *Profit shifting: Drivers and potential countermeasures*. WU International Taxation Research Paper Series, No. 2013-3. Accessed February 2017, from http://epub.wu.ac.at/3893/1/SSRN-id2271539.pdf

Bernard, A. B., Bradford, J., & Schott, P. K. (2006). *Transfer pricing by US-based multinational firms*. NBER Working Paper 12493.

Devereux, M. (2006). *The impact of taxation on the location of capital, firms and profit: A survey of empirical evidence*. European Tax Policy Forum Conference "The Impact of Corporation Taxes across Borders".

Lamers, I., Mcharo, P., & Nakajima, K. (2014). *Tax base erosion and profit shifting (BEPS) and international economic law*. CTEI working papers. The Graduate Institute, Centre for Trade and Economic Integration.

Lohse, T., & Riedel, N. (2012). *The impact of transfer pricing regulations on profit shifting within European multinationals*. FZID Discussion paper, Nr. 61-2012. Accessed March 2017, from https://www.econstor.eu/bitstream/10419/67717/1/732536626.pdf

Lohse, T., Riedel, N., & Spengel, C. (2012). *The increasing importance of transfer pricing regulations – a worldwide overview*. Oxford University Centre for Business Taxation working paper 12/27.

Riedel, N., Zinn, T., & Hofmann, P. (2015). *Do transfer pricing laws limit international income shifting? Evidence from Europe*. University of Bochum, CESinfo Munich, DIW Berlin, NoCet & Oxford University CBT.

Book Chapter

Ito, J., & Komoriya, Y. (2015). The impact of transfer pricing regulations on the location decisions of MNEs. In T. Ishikawa (Ed.), *Firms' location selections and regional policy in the global economy* (pp. 81–106). Springer.

Rawlings, G. (2017). Shifting profits and hidden accounts: Regulating tax havens. In P. Drahos (Ed.), *Regulatory theory: Foundations and applications* (pp. 653–674). ANU Press.

Book

Adams, C., & Coombes, R. (2003). *Global transfer pricing: Principles and practice*. LexisNexis-K.

Chapter 2
Transfer Pricing Regulations: An International Approach

The transfer pricing concept is considered a new and complex one in terms of guidelines and regulations. In this context, more and more academics and tax professionals are interested in understanding the transfer pricing mechanism. The main objective of this chapter is to help them in this process by presenting in a practical approach (using case studies and schemes) and in accordance with the OECD Transfer Pricing Guidelines (version from 2017, updated in the context of the BEPS Actions Plan) the way in which are operating the basic transfer pricing elements.

The chapter is focused on the following elements: arm's length principle, double taxation, advance price agreement, transfer pricing documentation, functional analysis, transfer pricing methods and comparability analysis.

In addition, the chapter contains a short presentation of the BEPS Actions Plan related to the transfer pricing subject and of the transfer pricing regulations applicable at the level of the European Union.

2.1 OECD Transfer Pricing Guidelines

The OECD Transfer Pricing Guidelines contain guidelines on the application of the arm's length principle to related party transactions. Multinational companies are encouraged to follow the OECD Transfer Pricing Guidelines in order to ensure compliance with the arm's length principle when setting transfer prices.

The first version of the OECD Transfer Pricing Guidelines was issued in **1979** under the name "Transfer Pricing and Multinational Enterprises". This version was developed in the context in which the United States had already developed a transfer

I. Ignat, L. Ionescu-Feleagă, *Transfer Pricing in Manufacturing*, Contributions to Finance and Accounting, https://doi.org/10.1007/978-3-030-93889-5_2

pricing legislation, and OECD member countries[1] considered that such a legislation would be useful to implement at their level in order to avoid the impact which could have the double taxation on international trade.

The 1979 version of the OECD Transfer Pricing Guidelines was amended and revised, with the OECD publishing a new version in **1995**. The 1995 version contained five chapters on: the arm's length principle, transfer pricing traditional transactional methods, other transfer pricing methods, administrative issues to avoid and resolve disputes in the field of transfer pricing; transfer pricing documentation. Subsequently, the 1995 version was supplemented by the incorporation of additional chapters, as follows:

- a report on intangible assets and intra-group services was prepared in **1996** and incorporated into Chapters VI and VII of the OECD Transfer Pricing Guidelines;
- in **1997**, a report on cost contribution arrangements was incorporated into Chapter VIII of the OECD Transfer Pricing Guidelines. Also in 1997, a report on the monitoring of the procedures and the involvement of the business community was incorporated in the annexes;
- in **1999**, guidelines regarding the issuance of advance price agreements based on the amicable procedure were incorporated in the annexes;
- in **2008** Chapter IV was updated.

In **2010** a revised version of the OECD Transfer Pricing Guidelines was published, which compared to the updated 1995 version contained the following updates/additions:

- a new chapter, namely Chapter IX related to the transfer pricing implications on business restructuring;
- updating of the Chapters I–III;
- updating the sections Foreword, Preface, Glossary, Chapters IV–VIII and annexes.

One of the most important changes made by the 2010 version of the OECD Transfer Pricing Guidelines, compared to the 1995 version, is the elimination of the hierarchy of transfer pricing methods. Therefore, the preference for the use of traditional methods is eliminated and the expression "the most appropriate method" is introduced.

In the context of the elaboration by the OECD of the BEPS Actions Plan, in **July** 2017 a new version of the OECD Transfer Pricing Guidelines was published, which compared to the 2010 version presents the following changes/updates:

---

[1]Currently, OECD member countries are: Australia, Austria, Belgium, Canada, Chile, Colombia, Costa Rica, Czech Republic, Denmark, Estonia, Finland, France, Germany, Greece, Hungary, Iceland, Ireland, Israel, Italy, Japan, South Korea, Latvia, Lithuania, Luxembourg, Mexico, Netherlands, New Zealand, Norway, Poland, Portugal, Slovakia, Slovenia, Spain, Sweden, Switzerland, Turkey, United Kingdom, United States of America.

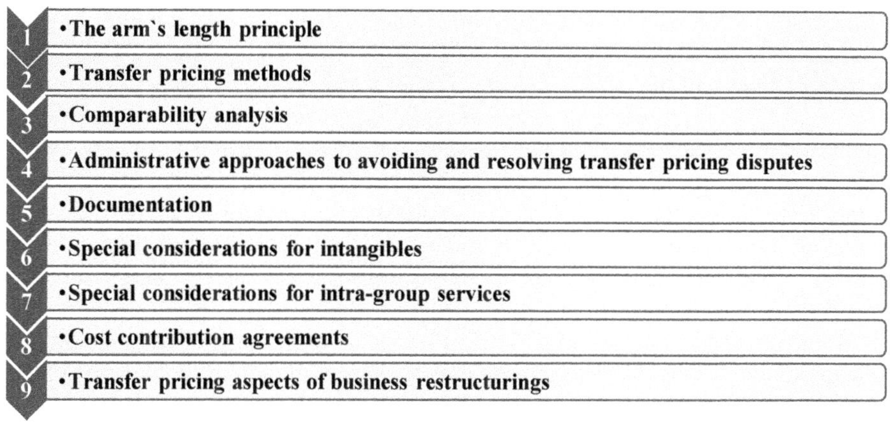

Fig. 2.1 Structure of the OECD Transfer Pricing Guidelines, July 2017 version. Source: Own processing based on the table of contents of the OECD Transfer Pricing Guidelines, July 2017 version

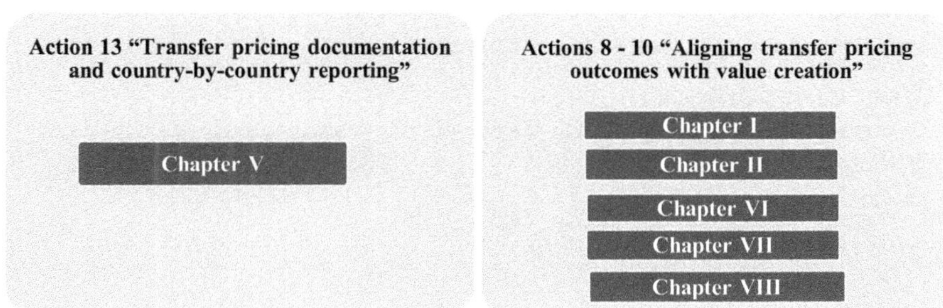

Fig. 2.2 OECD Transfer Pricing Guidelines and BEPS actions. Source: Own processing

- revision of Chapter IV and some annexes according to a report issued in 2013;
- revision of Chapters I, II, V–VIII according to Action 13 "Transfer pricing documentation and country-by-country reporting" and Actions 8–10 "Aligning transfer pricing outcomes with value creation" of the BEPS Actions Plan;
- revision of Chapter IX, approved in 2016.

Considering the above, it can be concluded that the report regarding the OECD Transfer Pricing Guidelines developed in 1979 has been updated and revised three times so far, in 1995, 2010 and 2017.

The OECD Transfer Pricing Guidelines published in 2017 is structured in nine chapters according to Fig. 2.1 below. These chapters describe and present certain key concepts from the point of view of a transfer pricing analysis. These key concepts have been detailed and analyzed in the following sections of the paper.

In addition, Fig. 2.2 shows a correlation between the chapters of the OECD Transfer Pricing Guidelines, July 2017 version and Action 13 "Transfer pricing documentation and country-by-country reporting", respectively Actions 8–10

"Aligning transfer pricing outcomes with value creation" from the BEPS Actions Plan. More exactly, it sets out the provisions whose actions have been incorporated into each chapter of the OECD Transfer Pricing Guidelines.

The OECD Transfer Pricing Guidelines do not contain rules on transfer pricing applicable to permanent establishments. This topic was addressed separately by the OECD in the paper "Report on the attribution of profits to permanent establishments". The first parts of this paper were published by the OECD in 2006.

In addition, in February 2020, OECD published a report including transfer pricing recommendations for financial transactions (i.e. *Transfer Pricing Guidance on Financial Transactions*).

Moreover, the impact of the COVID-19 pandemic on the economic conditions and government decisions determined challenges in relation to the application of the arm's length principle. In this context, on 2020 December 18th OECD published a report entitled *Guidance on the transfer pricing implications of the COVID-19 pandemic*.

It is important to note that this report should be applied in connection with the OECD Transfer Pricing Guidelines and does not represent a replacement or a revision of the later. Guidance on the transfer pricing implications of the COVID-19 pandemic envisages four issues as follows:

- comparability analysis;
- losses and the allocation of COVID-19 specific costs;
- government assistance programs;
- advance pricing agreements.

2.1.1 Arm's Length Principle

The OECD Transfer Pricing Guidelines contain guidelines on the application of the arm's length principle and present this principle as the method that provides the best approximation of free market conditions in cases where goods and other tangible and intangible assets are transferred or services are provided between affiliated entities (OECD Transfer Pricing Guidelines, July 2017 version, paragraph 1.14: 38).

According to the arm's length principle, transactions between affiliated persons must be carried out under conditions/circumstances that must not differ from the commercial or financial relations established between independent parties. The principle is based on comparing all the circumstances in which the controlled transactions (i.e. those transactions performed between affiliated entities) were carried out with the circumstances of the uncontrolled transactions performed between independent entities (OECD Transfer Pricing Guidelines, July 2017 version, paragraph 1.33: 43–44).

Regarding the situation in which the affiliated entities do not respect the arm's length principle, the OECD Transfer Pricing Guidelines refers to paragraph 1 of Article 9 from the Model Tax Convention, according to which when the conditions

Fig. 2.3 Transactions flow. Source: Own processing

established between two affiliated persons in financial or commercial relations differ from the conditions which would have been established between independent entities, any profit that could have been recorded at the level of any of the affiliated entities, but due to these conditions was not recorded, should be included in the profits of that entity and taxed accordingly.

A practical approach of the arm's length principle can be illustrated starting from the following example.

Case study: the arm's length principle
Alfa RO produces model Y shoes in Romania, which it sells to its affiliate Alfa BG, a Bulgarian company. Alfa RO incurs costs of EUR 100 for the production and delivery of a pair of shoes. Furthermore, the selling price of a pair of shoes from Alfa RO to Alfa BG is of EUR 130. Alfa BG sells shoes on the Bulgarian market at a price of EUR 150/pair, with a distribution cost of EUR 5/pair. Therefore, the flow of transactions could be represented according to Fig. 2.3 below:

If independent companies producing model Y shoes sell a pair of such shoes at a price between EUR 125 and EUR 145, then the price charged by Alfa RO to Alfa BG is in line with the arm's length principle. The range of values practiced by independent entities is determined on the basis of comparability studies, as detailed in the following chapters of the paper.

According to Table 2.1, as a result of the transactions presented above, at the level of the Group to which the Alfa RO and Alfa BG entities belong, a profit of EUR 45 was recorded, of which EUR 30 was taxed in Romania and EUR 15 in Bulgaria.

Considering the above, through transfer pricing it was determined which part of the profit realized at Group level will be taxed in Romania and which part in Bulgaria. Taking into account the fact that in Bulgaria the corporate income tax rate of 10% is lower compared to 16% in Romania, there could be tried a movement of profits from Romania to Bulgaria in order for the Group to reduce the value of the corporate income tax. In this respect, Alfa RO could sell to Alfa BG the shoes at a price of EUR 110/pair, otherwise diminishing the profit registered by the Group in Romania. On the other hand, the acquisition cost recorded by Alfa BG would decrease from EUR 130 to EUR 110, which would lead to an increase in the Group's profit in Bulgaria. According to Table 2.2, the gross profit recorded at Group level would still remain at EUR 45/pair, but the transfer price would determine how much of this profit would be taxed in each of the two countries. In other words, the transfer pricing would influence the total value of the corporate income tax that would be paid at Group level.

Table 2.1 Transfer pricing mechanism—compliance with the arm's length principle

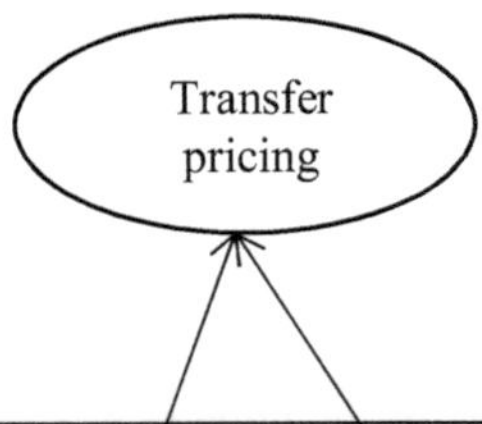

Indicator (EUR)	Alfa RO	Alfa BG	Total
Sales revenues	130	150	280
Production and delivery costs	(100)	-	(100)
Acquisition cost	-	(130)	(130)
Distribution costs	-	(5)	(5)
Gross result	30	15	45
Corporate income tax	4.8 (30*16%)	1.5 (15*10%)	6.3
Net result	25.2	13.5	38.7

Source: Own processing

Table 2.2 Transfer pricing mechanism—non-compliance with the arm's length principle

Indicator (EUR)	Alfa RO	Alfa BG	Total
Sales revenues	110	150	260
Production and delivery costs	(100)	–	(100)
Acquisition cost	–	(110)	(110)
Distribution costs	–	(5)	(5)
Gross result	10	35	45
Corporate income tax	1.6 (10 × 16%)	3.5 (35 × 10%)	5.1
Net result	8.4	31.5	39.9

Source: Own processing

As could be observed, the movement of profits to Bulgaria was achieved by using a transfer price that does not fall within the range of values practiced by independent entities (i.e. a transfer price which is not in compliance with the arm's length principle). Given this, the tax authorities may adjust the transfer pricing, situation which would lead to an additional corporate income tax and interest and penalties for delay at the level of Alfa RO. Also, as detailed in Sect. 2.1.2—Double Taxation, this situation could lead to a double taxation of results at Group level.

2.1.2 *Double Taxation*

Double taxation involves taxing the same profit in the hands of different taxpayers. Double taxation can be national (i.e. profit is taxed twice in the same country) or

Table 2.3 Double taxation of results

Indicator (EUR)	Alfa RO Before adjustment	After adjustment	Alfa BG
Sales revenues	110	135	150
Costs	(100)	(100)	(115)
Result	10	35	35

Source: Own processing

internationally. Lefter and Chirica (2010) state that in the case of double taxation at international level, companies are taxed twice: once in the state where the revenue is generated (i.e. in the source state) and once in the state of residence.

Double taxation should be eliminated whenever possible, as it constitutes a potential obstacle to the development of international trade and investment flows (OECD Transfer Pricing Guidelines, July 2017 version, paragraph 4.2: 171).

For the elimination of a national double taxation, states have established their own regulations in this regard. In order to eliminate an international double taxation, various measures and instruments have been developed, which are detailed below, in this chapter.

In order to illustrate the way in which the double taxation of results operates at Group level, there was continued the case study presented above in Sect. 2.1.1—Arm's Length Principle. Therefore, it will be assumed that Alfa RO was subject to a tax audit which envisaged the transfer pricing and the tax authorities found that the price charged by Alfa RO to the affiliated entity Alfa BG for the sale of a pair of shoes does not respect the arm's length principle. In this respect, the tax authorities noted that the price of EUR 110/pair is lower than the market price of independent entities producing model Y shoes. In these circumstances, the tax authorities decided to adjust the price invoiced by Alfa RO to Alfa BG in the sense of increasing it from EUR 110/pair to EUR 135/pair.

The impact of this adjustment on Alfa RO's results is shown in Table 2.3 below.

After adjusting the transfer price from EUR 110/pair of shoes to EUR 135/pair of shoes, the result recorded by Alfa RO increased from EUR 10 to EUR 35, this situation leading to the registration at Alfa RO level of an additional corporate income tax, as well as to the payment of interest and late payment penalties. The result obtained by the Group before the adjustment was EUR 45 (10 + 35), which becomes EUR 70 (35 + 35) after adjusting the transfer price. Therefore, the Group finds itself in the situation of taxing twice the amount of EUR 25 (the value of the adjustment made by the tax authorities, in the sense of increasing the transfer price from EUR 110 to EUR 135)—once in Romania and the second time in Bulgaria. Therefore, the Group faces a double taxation of results. In order to avoid this double taxation of results, the Bulgarian tax authorities should make a corresponding adjustment, i.e. to reduce for tax purposes the tax base of Alfa BG by EUR 25 (Luca, 2009a).

According to the OECD Transfer Pricing Guidelines, a first step in this direction is to initiate a Mutual Agreement Procedure ("MAP"). Practically, based on this

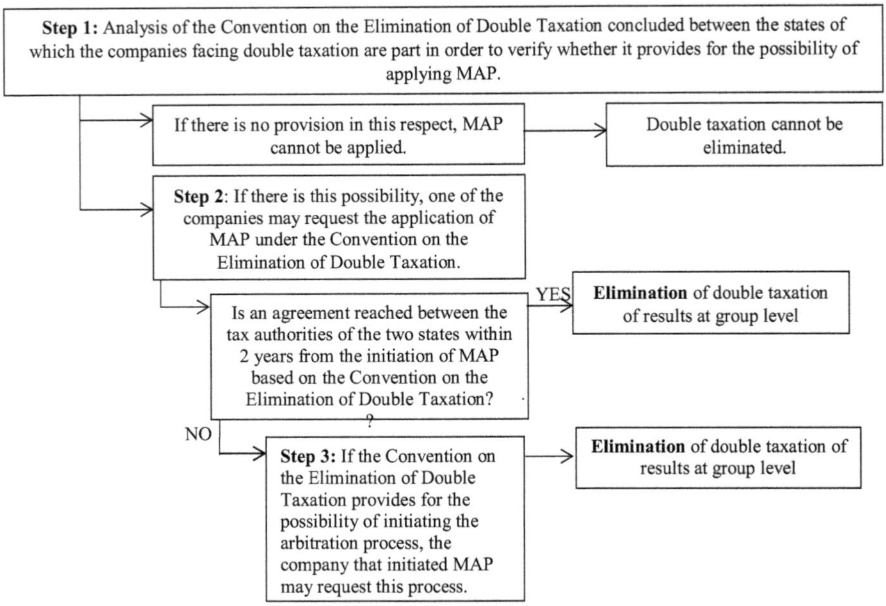

Fig. 2.4 Steps regarding the elimination of the double taxation based on MAP. Source: Feleagă and Neacşu (2016: 134)

procedure the tax authorities of the two states examine the circumstances that led to the double taxation of the results at Group level and try to find a solution to eliminate this double taxation. This procedure is initiated on the basis of the following legislative acts:

- *Article 25 of the Convention on the Elimination of Double Taxation* concluded between the two states. The MAP is required under the Convention on the Elimination of Double Taxation only if that Convention provides for the possibility of initiating such a procedure. Also, the MAP under the Convention on the Elimination of Double Taxation may be requested only within 3 years from the date of issuance of the taxation decision on the basis of which the adjustment of transfer pricing has been established.

  Moreover, if within 2 years from the initiation of the MAP the tax authorities of the two states do not reach to a common agreement on the elimination of double taxation, at the request of the company that initiated the MAP, the situation may be subject to an arbitration process. Within this process, an arbitration commission is established and the decision of this commission is binding for both states, respectively both companies. The arbitration process shall take place only on condition that there is a provision in this respect in the Convention for the Elimination of Double Taxation concluded between the two states.

Figure 2.4 below illustrates the steps involved in initiating the MAP under the Convention on the Elimination of Double Taxation.

- *Convention on the Elimination of Double Taxation in connection with the adjustment of profits of associated enterprises* (also called the EU Arbitration Convention), applicable only to EU Member States. Also, as in the case of MAP initiated under the Convention on the Elimination of Double Taxation, the MAP initiated under the EU Arbitration Convention may be requested within 3 years from the date of the decision regarding the transfer adjustment.

  If within 2 years the tax authorities do not reach to a common agreement for the elimination of double taxation, then the arbitration process may be requested. The difference between requesting MAP under the Convention on the Elimination of Double Taxation and the one under the EU Arbitration Convention is that in the latter case the arbitration process can be requested in all situations where the tax authorities have not reached a common agreement, while in the first case the initiation of the arbitration process is conditioned by the existence of a provision in this respect within the Convention on the Elimination of Double Taxation concluded between the two states.

  Further, after the end of the arbitration process, the tax authorities of the two states have 6 months to discuss the measures established by the arbitration commission and to reach a common agreement. If no joint agreement is reached after 6 months, the decision of the arbitration panel becomes binding on the tax authorities and taxpayers.

  The EU Arbitration Convention does not apply if one of the two companies involved in the transaction subject to transfer pricing adjustments is also subject to a "severe penalty". Severe penalty means any action of tax evasion or any action that contravenes the accounting, tax legislation, as well as the law of companies. Also, the severe penalty includes any administrative sanctions such as refusal to submit certain tax returns/accounting records at the request of tax authorities, etc.

2.1.3 Advance Price Agreement

On the other hand, a double taxation of results at group level could also occur, for example, if during a tax audit the tax authorities adopt an aggressive position and do not agree with certain transfer pricing analysis presented by the taxpayer.

In order to avoid facing such a situation, companies have the possibility to apply for the issuance of an Advance Price Agreement ("APA"). This is also supported by the literature, for example Lohse and Riedel (2012) considering that companies could reduce the risk associated with double taxation of results through APA applications.

The concept of APA is defined in paragraph 4.134 of the OECD Transfer Pricing Guidelines, July 2017 version as an agreement between a taxpayer and the tax

Table 2.4 Advantages and disadvantages of APA

Advantages	Disadvantages
An APA removes the uncertainty in relation to the tax treatment of the transfer pricing applied with the transaction subject to APA. Moreover, due to the certainty provided, the taxpayer could make an accurate forecast of his tax debts. From this point of view, an APA provides a favorable tax environment for investments.	The process of issuing an APA by the tax authorities can take a long time, this affecting the activity of the taxpayer.
The APA can be an opportunity for both tax administrations and taxpayers to consult and work in a less competitive work environment. The possibility to discuss complex tax issues in a less competitive working environment (compared to the situation of a tax audit) could stimulate a free flow of information between all parties involved, in order to reach a fair legal outcome.	In order to issue APAs, the tax authorities may request more detailed information compared to the information presented in a transfer pricing documentation file.
An APA can prevent costly and time-consuming examinations, as well as future litigations.	The application for the issuance of an APA can be rejected by the tax authorities after examining the information provided by the taxpayer.
An APA can reduce or eliminate the risk of double taxation.	Applying for an APA can be quite expensive for a small business and that is why in most of the time the requests for APA come from large companies.

Source: Own processing based on the provisions of OECD Transfer Pricing Guidelines, July 2017 version

authorities for the purpose of determining in advance, for a transaction that will be performed between affiliates, a certain set of criteria necessary to determine the transfer price (e.g. the transfer pricing method to be applied, the set of comparable companies used to determine an interval for profitability indicator, etc.).

More exactly, the APA sets out in advance the transfer pricing methodology to be applied to a future transaction between affiliates (Becker et al., 2017). Depending on the number of tax authorities involved in the negotiations, an APA can be unilateral, bilateral or multilateral. Table 2.4 below shows the advantages/disadvantages of an APA.

2.1.4 *Transfer Pricing Documentation*

The subject of transfer pricing documentation is addressed in Chapter V of the OECD Transfer Pricing Guidelines, July 2017 version. The main objectives of a transfer pricing file are to support and document whether transactions made by a company with its affiliates comply with the arm's length principle and to provide the tax authorities with the basis for the information necessary to verify this aspect in the context of a transfer pricing audit.

Following the incorporation into the OECD Transfer Pricing Guidelines of the provisions of Action 13 "Transfer pricing documentation and country-by-country reporting"[2] of the BEPS Actions Plan, section C of Chapter V of the OECD Transfer Pricing Guidelines, July 2017 version presents three levels for the preparation of the transfer pricing documentation, as follows:

- *the master file* (i.e. a documentation prepared at group level)—the purpose of this documentation is to provide an overview of the entire group of companies. The main recommendations of the OECD Transfer Pricing Guidelines, July 2017 version, on the structure of a master file are presented in Table 2.5 below.
- *the local file*—this documentation is prepared at the level of each entity of the group that carries out transactions with affiliates. The preparation of this documentation is done according to the transfer pricing legislation from the country where the entity preparing the documentation is located. Some of the information that should be presented in the local file can be taken from the master file. The main recommendations of the OECD Transfer Pricing Guidelines, July 2017 version on the structure of a local file are presented in Table 2.6 below.
- *the country-by-country report*[3]—this report is prepared by multinational groups that meet certain criteria and aims to provide the following categories of information for each tax jurisdiction in which the group operates:
  - information on the allocation of profit, taxes and economic activity in each tax jurisdiction. Therefore, for each tax jurisdiction, data will be presented on revenues from related-party transactions, revenues from independent transactions, total revenues, profit (or loss) before corporate income tax, corporate income tax paid, corporate income tax accumulated in the reporting year, declared social capital, undistributed profit, number of employees, fixed assets (other than cash or cash equivalents);
  - a list of the constituent entities of the multinational group, prepared for each fiscal jurisdiction separately. For each constituent entity, information is required regarding the economic activity performed (for example, production activity, distribution activity, provision of administrative services, etc.).

The country-by-country report is useful for tax administrations to analyze the transfer pricing risk of the multinational groups. The report is prepared at group level by a reporting entity, the other entities having only the obligation to notify the tax authorities of the jurisdiction in which they operate regarding the name of the reporting entity that prepares at group level the report for each country.

---

[2] A detailed presentation of Action 13 "Transfer pricing documentation and country-by-country reporting" is provided in Sect. 2.2—BEPS Actions Plan.

[3] Further details on this type of documentation can be found in Sect. 2.2—BEPS Actions Plan.

Table 2.5 Structure of a master file

Type of information	Details
Organizational structure	This structure should be presented as a diagram illustrating the legal structure of the whole group, including the holding percentages applicable to each entity, as well as the geographical location of the entities.
Description of the group's activity	The information that should be detailed regarding the activity of the group is the following: • description of the group's value chain; • description of the most important categories of services provided intra-group, including the description of the transfer pricing methodology applied for the provision of these services; • description of the main sales markets for the group's products and services; • presentation of a functional analysis performed at group level (i.e. detailing the main functions performed, risks incurred and assets used at group level); • description of the business restructurings that took place at group level.
Presentation of the group's intangible assets	This presentation should include information such as: • a general description of the group's strategy regarding the research-development activities; • a list of the group's intangible assets, which are important in terms of transfer pricing. This list should also show which entities within the group hold those intangibles; • presentation of the main contracts concluded between the entities within the group in relation to the intangible assets (for example licensing contracts, research contracts, etc.); • general description of the transfer pricing policy applied for transactions involving intangible assets and research and development activities.
The financial activities of the group	Information on the group's financial activities concerns the following: • a general description of the financing method used within the group, including the presentation of financing contracts concluded with non-affiliated entities; • identification of those entities within the group that fulfill the financing function of the other entities; • presentation of transfer pricing policies applied at group level in relation to the financing activities.
Presentation of the financial and fiscal position of the group	The information provided in relation to the financial and fiscal position of the group refers to: • consolidated financial statements at group level; • advance price agreements concluded at group level.

Source: Own processing based on the provisions of Appendix I, Chapter V of the OECD Transfer Pricing Guidelines, July 2017 version

Table 2.6 Structure of a local file

Type of information	Details
Information regarding the entity which performs the preparation of the local file	The information from this section refers to: • presentation of the management structure; • presentation of the organizational structure; • presentation of the activity carried out; • presentation of the business strategy; • presentation of business restructuring; • presentation of the main competitors, etc.
Information regarding the related-party transactions performed by the entity which prepares the local file	The following information should be provided for each material related-party transaction: • description of the respective transaction and of the context in which it takes place; • presentation of the amounts related to the payments/receipts made within the respective transaction; • copies of the contracts concerning the respective transaction; • a detailed presentation of the functional analysis[a] of the parties involved, from the perspective of each transaction analyzed; • indication of the most appropriate transfer pricing method[b] selected in order to perform the transfer pricing analysis of the transaction, indicating the reasons for selecting that method; • comparability analysis[c] of the transaction; • indication of the entity (from those participating in the transaction) that was selected as a tested party, as well as the reasons for its selection; • the list of independent entities considered comparable with the tested entity from the perspective of the analyzed transaction, mentioning the financial indicators of these entities, as well as the methodology applied for searching for comparable independent entities and the information source, etc. Regarding the determination of material transactions, the OECD Transfer Pricing Guidelines recommend that each country should set its own materiality thresholds in this respect.

(continued)

Table 2.6 (continued)

Type of information	Details
Financial information	Information from this category refers to: • the financial statements of the entity that prepares the local file; • financial information of comparable entities and their source, etc.

Source: Own processing based on the provisions of Appendix II, Chapter V of the OECD Transfer Pricing Guidelines, July 2017 version

[a]The presentation of the concept of functional analysis can be found in Sect. 2.1.5—Functional Analysis

[b]The presentation of transfer pricing methods can be found in Sect. 2.1.6—Transfer Pricing Methods

[c]The presentation of the comparability analysis concept can be found in Sect. 2.1.7—Comparability Analysis

2.1.5 *Functional Analysis*

According to the OECD Transfer Pricing Guidelines, the purpose of the functional analysis is to identify the main activities performed, assets used and risks incurred by the entities involved in a transaction. Also, according to paragraph 1.51 of the OECD Transfer Pricing Guidelines, version July 2017, in transactions between two independent entities, the remuneration established by them will reflect the functions performed by each one, taking into account the assets used, respectively the risks incurred in those transactions (OECD Transfer Pricing Guidelines, July 2017 version, paragraph 1.51: 51). In other words, the functional analysis influences the price that will be paid in a transaction.

At the level of the literature, Herksen (2009) considers that from the point of view of functional analysis, companies could be divided into three main categories, namely manufacturers, distributors and service providers. The author further mentions that each of these three categories could be divided into subcategories as follows:

- the manufacturers can be: toll manufacturer, contract manufacturer and fully-fledged manufacturer;
- distributors can be grouped into four main categories: commission agent, commissionaire classic buy-sell distributor and fully-fledged distributor;
- service providers can be: shared service center, contract service provider and complex service provider.

Table 2.7 below presents the functions performed, the risks incurred and the assets used, specific to each category of manufacturer and distributors. Practically, this table does not include all the functions performed, the risks incurred and the assets used by each subcategory, but only those on the basis of which the differentiation between each subcategory is made. More exactly, those functions, risks and assets common to all subcategories were not presented in the table below.

Table 2.7 Functions, risks and assets for manufacturers and distributors

Manufacturer			
Functions/risks/assets	Toll manufacturer	Contract manufacturer	Fully-fledged manufacturer
Functions performed			
Raw materials acquisition	n/a	✓	✓
Custody of raw materials	✓	n/a	n/a
Research and development activities	n/a	n/a	✓
Ownership of finished products	n/a	✓	✓
Marketing and promotion activities	n/a	n/a	✓
Sale to independent customers	n/a	n/a	✓
Warranty and repair	n/a	n/a	✓
Risks incurred			
Research and development risk	n/a	n/a	✓
Market risk	n/a	n/a	✓
Inventory risk	n/a	✓	✓
Product liability risk	n/a	✓	✓
Assets used			
Intangible assets related to production (e.g. manufacturing recipes, patents)	n/a	n/a	✓

Distributors				
Functions/risks/assets	Commission agent	Commissionaire	Classic buy-sell distributor	Fully-fledged distributor
Functions performed				
Ownership of the goods	n/a	n/a	✓	✓
Warehousing and logistics	n/a	n/a	✓	✓
Procurement planning	n/a	n/a	n/a	✓
Quality control	n/a	n/a	n/a	✓
Warranty and repairs	n/a	n/a	n/a	✓
Risks incurred				
Inventory risk	n/a	n/a	n/a	✓
Product liability risk	n/a	n/a	✓	✓
Assets used				
Intangible assets related to distribution activity (e.g. trademarks)	n/a	n/a	n/a	✓

Source: Own processing, based on the classification performed by Herksen (2009)
✓—function is performed/risk is incurred/assets are used; n/a—function is not performed/risk is not incurred/assets are not used

Radolovic (2012) considers that remuneration should reflect the functions performed, the risks incurred and the assets used by each company. For example, the profit made by a contract manufacturer should be higher than the profit made by a toll manufacturer, and the profit made by a fully-fledged manufacturer should be higher than the profit made by a contract manufacturer.

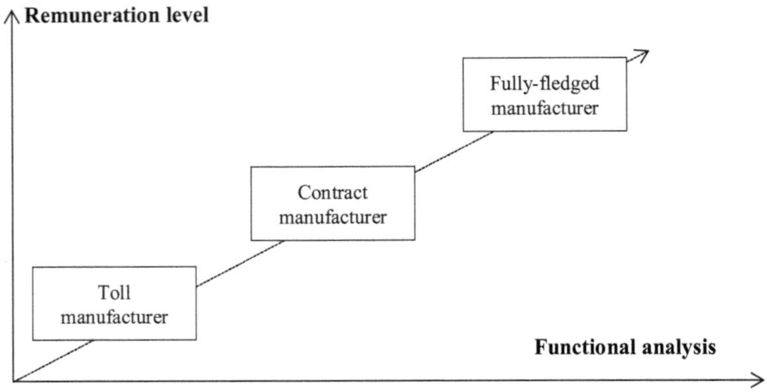

Fig. 2.5 Remuneration level of manufacturer. Source: Own processing

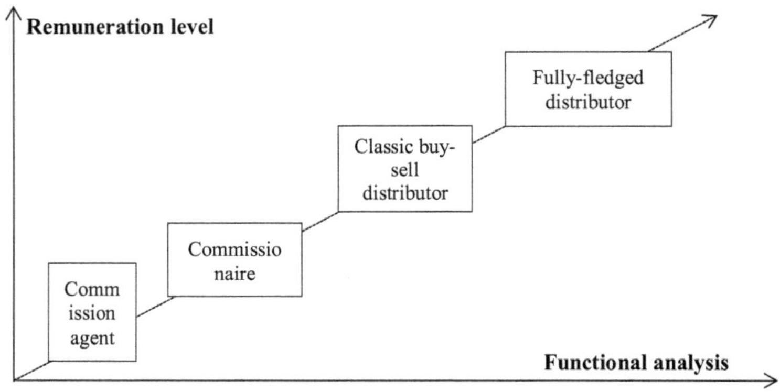

Fig. 2.6 Remuneration level of distributors. Source: Own processing

Figure 2.5 below shows the correlation between the level of remuneration and the functional analysis of the manufacturing companies, according to Radolovic (2012).

Figure 2.6 below shows the correlation between the level of remuneration and the functional analysis of the distribution companies, according to Radolovic (2012).

A functional analysis has a significant impact on the decision regarding the selection of the transfer pricing method, as well as on the comparability analysis. This aspect is due to the fact that the functional analysis should determine which company is the tested party (i.e. the part from the perspective of which the transfer pricing analysis will be performed).

Thereby, according to the OECD Transfer Pricing Guidelines, the tested party should be the company with the simplest functional profile, as the most reliable comparables can be found for this company (OECD Transfer Pricing Guidelines, July 2017 version, paragraph 3.18: 153).

Concrete and complete functional analyses are provided within Chap. 3. How to perform a transfer pricing analysis in case of manufacturing entities.

2.1.6 *Transfer Pricing Methods*

The OECD Transfer Pricing Guidelines present five transfer pricing methods, dividing them into two categories as follows:

- Traditional transaction methods:
  - Comparable uncontrolled price method;
  - Cost plus method;
  - Resale price method;
- Transactional profit methods:
  - Transactional net margin method;
  - Profit split method.

Comparable uncontrolled price method ("CUPM")
CUPM compares the price invoiced between affiliates for the provision of services or transfer of goods with the price practiced between independents who carry out (in comparable circumstances) comparable transactions. If there are identified material differences between the transactions that should be compared (i.e. related-party transactions vs. transactions performed between independents) CUPM cannot be used. Examples of material differences could be: differences regarding the type of goods traded or services provided, differences between the quantities traded by affiliates vs. quantities traded by independents, different markets sales etc.

However, according with the OECD Transfer Pricing Guidelines it is difficult in practice to identify perfect comparable transactions. In this situation, in order to eliminate the impact of the differences on the price, certain adjustments should be performed (OECD Transfer Pricing Guidelines, July 2017 version, paragraph 2.16: 101–102).

According with the provisions of the OECD Transfer Pricing Guidelines, the comparison requested by the CUPM can be performed as follows:

- an internal comparison of prices—this type of comparison could be used when one of the affiliates involved in the related-party transaction analyzed performs similar transactions (in comparable conditions) with independents;
- an external comparison of prices—if there are not meet the conditions to apply an internal comparison, but there are identified (using public sources) the prices practiced on market by independents for transactions comparable with the related-party transition analyzed, then an external comparison could be applied.

The way in which the CUPM operates in practice is illustrated in the below case study.

Case study
Ball Production and Ball Distribution are both part of the Ball Group, being considered affiliated entities. The main activity performed by Ball Production is

represented by the production of soccer balls, while the main activity of Ball Distribution is the distribution of the balls produced by its affiliated entity.

Ball Productions sells 100 soccer balls to Ball Distribution at a price of EUR 99/ball. In the same time, Ball Production sells to an independent entity, in comparable circumstances, 50 soccer balls to a price of EUR 110/ball. Therefore, between the two transactions carried out by Ball Production is identified a difference in relation to the quantity traded. Based on a commercial policy, Ball Production grants a 10% discount for sells higher than 70 soccer balls.

In this case study, the sale of soccer balls from Ball Production to Ball Distribution is a related-party transaction, while the sale of balls from Ball Production to the independent entity is an independent transaction. Given this, in order to apply the CUPM there could be performed an internal comparison between the price invoiced by Ball Production to Ball Distribution and the price charged by Ball Production to the independent entity. However, given the fact that between these two transactions is identified a difference regarding the traded quantity, there should be performed an adjustment in order to eliminate the impact of this difference on the price.

The adjustment means to apply the 10% discount to the price charged by Ball Production to the independent entity (EUR 110/ball). After this adjustment, there is obtained a price of EUR 99/ball, this meaning that the price charged by Ball Production to Ball Distribution complies with the arm's length principle.

Cost plus method ("CPM")

CPM is used for the analysis of transactions which involve the provision of services or the production of goods. According to CPM, the comparison is performed at the level of the gross mark-ups practiced by the service provider/the manufacturer and added to the costs related to the provision of the services/production of goods.

Similar to CUPM, the comparison could be an internal or an external one. An internal comparison involves the comparison of the gross mark-up applied within the analyzed related-party transaction with the gross mark-up applied within independent transactions performed by one of the affiliated entity with independent entities. In this case, the two transactions compared should involve similar goods/services.

An external comparison involves the preparation of a benchmark study in order to obtain a range of gross mark-ups applied by independent entities with a functional profile similar to that of the tested party. If the mark-up applied within the related party-transaction is situated in this range, then the related-party transaction complies with the arm's length principle.

Comparing the CPM with the CUPM, there should be mentioned that in case of CPM the services/goods traded should not be identical, but should have the same functions in order to include them in the same category. In the case of CPM, the accent is put on the circumstances in which the transactions are performed.

Regarding the profitability indicators (e.g. gross mark-ups), the OECD Transfer Pricing Guidelines (July 2017 version, paragraph 2.94: 126) recommends to compute them as a ratio between the operational result and a denominator which should not be impacted by related-party transactions. Considering the example of a service provider which records revenues from the provision of services to affiliates, the costs related to this provision being recorded from independent transactions, the value of the denominator should be represented by these costs.

Going further, according to the OECD Transfer Pricing Guidelines (July 2017 version, paragraph 2.54: 114) the difference between a gross profitability indicator and a net one is represented by the costs structure. More exactly, a gross indicator is computed based on the direct and indirect production costs, while the net indicator includes also other operational expenses (e.g. general administration expenses).

Considering the above, the gross mark-up compared within the CPM method is computed based on the following formula:

$$Gross\ mark-up = \frac{Turnover - Costs\ of\ goods\ sold/services\ provided}{Costs\ of\ goods\ sold/services\ provided} * 100$$

In addition, when applying the CPM there should be checked the comparability at the level of the base costs on which the mark-up is added. Therefore, if there are identified differences among the cost base from related-party transaction and the cost base from independent transactions, the CPM cannot be applied. For example, the financial statements prepared according to the Romanian accounting legislation do not present separately the costs of goods sold/services provided and the other operational expenses (this is due to the fact that the Profit and Loss account presents the expenses based on their nature, rather than on their destination). Given this, in the lack of an internal comparison, the CPM could be difficult to apply (Luca, 2009b).

The way in which the CPM operates in practice is illustrated in the below case study.

Case study

Ball Production manufactures two types of soccer balls: type A and type B. The production cost of a ball type A is of EUR 79, while the production cost of a ball type B is of EUR 32. Balls type A are sold to the affiliated entity Ball Distribution to a price of EUR 99/ball, while balls type B are sold to an independent client to a price of EUR 40/ball. Conditions in which these transactions are performed are similar.

Even if the two types of balls are not identical, these could be included in the same category and therefore the CPM could be applied (there could not be applied the CUPM as the products are not identical). In order to apply the CPM there should be compared the gross mark-up obtained by Ball Production from the sale of balls to Ball Distribution with the gross mark-up obtained by Ball Production from the sale of balls to the independent client.

The gross mark-up obtained by Ball Production from the sale of balls to Ball Distribution is 25% (i.e.$((99–79)/79 \times 100)$, while the gross mark-up obtained by Ball Production from the sale of balls to the independent client is also 25% (i.e. $((40–32)/32) \times 100$).

Considering the above, there could be concluded that the price invoiced by Ball Production to Ball Distribution complies with the arm's length principle.

Resale price method ("RPM")

The RPM is applied when there is analyzed a related-party transaction that involves the acquisition of goods from affiliates and the distribution of them to independent entities. Practically, the RPM applies when the tested party is a distributor. However, according to the OECD Transfer Pricing Guidelines (July 2017, paragraph 2.35: 108), RPM should be applied only if the distributor does not perform substantial changes on the goods acquired from affiliates and resold to independents.

Regarding the transfer pricing analysis that should be performed under the RPM, it starts from the price at which the goods acquired from affiliates are further sold to independents, i.e. the resale price (OECD Transfer Pricing Guidelines, July 2017 version, paragraph 2.27: 105). In the next step, this resale price is diminished with the gross margin obtained by the distributor from the goods resold, the result being represented by the price at which the goods were traded between affiliates. Further on, the gross margin obtained by the distributor is compared with gross margins obtained by independent entities performing similar transactions to that analyzed. If this gross margin complies with the arm's length principle, then also the price at which the goods were traded between the affiliated entities complies with this principle.

Similar to CPM and CUPM, the RPM can be applied using either internal comparables or external ones.

Considering the provision of the OECD Transfer Pricing Guidelines related to the profitability indicators (presented above within the section dedicated to the CPM), when applying the RPM the gross margin is computed based on the below formula:

$$Gross\ margin = \frac{Turnover - Costs\ of\ goods\ sold/services\ provided}{Turnover} * 100$$

When applying the RPM (similar to the CPM) the product comparability is not an essential condition. Products should not be identical, but should be included in the same category of products. An essential condition to apply the RPM is a high degree of comparability between the functional profiles of the entities.

Moreover, considering the differences between the accounting treatments of the costs classification, RPM could be difficult to apply in the lack of internal comparables.

The way in which the RPM operates in practice is illustrated in the below case study.

Case study

Ball Distributions acquires soccer balls from its affiliated entity, ball Productions, in order to resale them to independent entities. The price invoiced by Ball Production is of EUR 100/ball. Ball Distribution further sells the balls to a price of EUR 120/ball.

Ball Distribution does not acquire soccer balls from independent entities, neither Ball Production sells the balls to independents. Therefore, the RPM based on an internal comparison could not be applied.

Based on a benchmark study, there was identified that independent distributors (i.e. distributors which are not part to a related-party transaction) which a similar functional profile to that of Ball Distribution and which distribute similar products obtain a gross margin of 10%.

In order to check if the price of EUR 100/ball complies with the arm's length principle, there will be diminished the resale price of EUR 120/ball with the gross margin of 10%. After this, the result obtained indicate a price of EUR 108/ball which is different from the price charged by Ball Production to Ball Distribution. Therefore, the price charged by Ball Production does not comply with the arm's length principle.

Transactional net margin method ("TNMM")

The TNMM operates in a similar approach to CPM and RPM, the difference between them being the fact that the TNMM uses net profitability indicators, while the other two methods use gross ones (OECD Transfer Pricing Guidelines, July 2017 version, paragraph 2.64: 117). The difference between a gross profitability indicator and a net one is represented by the costs structure. The gross indicators use only the costs of goods sold/services provided, while the net indicators include also other operating expenses (e.g. general administration expenses).

Given the fact that in practice companies faces with lack of information (i.e. costs classification) in order to compute gross profitability indicators for comparable independent entities, the TNMM is most often used in practice.

Based on the functional analysis it is determined if the TNMM will be applied in an approach similar to CPM or to RPM and what profitability indicator will be used. According to Luca (2009b), the profitability indicators are:

- operational margin—applied when the tested party is a distributor and the TNMM is applied in a similar approach to RPM;
- return on assets and net cost plus—applied when the tested party is a manufacturer or a service provider and the TNMM is applied in a similar approach to CPM;

The above mentioned profitability indicators are computed based on the following formulas:

$$Operational\ margin\ (OM) = \frac{Operational\ result}{Operational\ turnover} * 100$$

$$Return\ on\ assets\ (ROA) = \frac{Operational\ result}{Operational\ assets} * 100$$

$$Net\ cost\ plus\ (NCP) = \frac{Operational\ result}{Operational\ costs} * 100$$

Where

The *Operational result* is the result obtained by the distributor/service provider/manufacturer from the related-party transaction under analysis, being determined as a difference between the turnover, the cost of goods sold/services provided and other operational expenses related to this transaction.

The way in which the TNMM operates in practice is illustrated in the below case study.

Case study

Ball Production manufacturers and sells soccer balls to Ball Distribution, obtaining from this transaction a net cost plus indicator of 7%. Based on a benchmark study, there was concluded that independent entities with a functional profile similar to that of Ball Production obtain an average net cost indicator between 5% and 10%.

Given the fact that the NCP obtained by Ball Production (7%) is situated between the market interval, there could be concluded that the transaction performed between Ball Production and Ball Distribution complies with the arm's length principle.

Profit split method ("PSM")

The PSM is used when the activities carried out within a related-party transaction are interconnected and a separate analysis of them could not be performed or when the affiliated entities bring unique contributions to the transaction (e.g. unique intangible assets). Given the fact that independent companies would choose to share the profit generated by the transaction based on the contribution of each of them in the transaction, the PSM could be considered the most appropriate transfer pricing method to be applied in this situation.

According with the OECD Transfer Pricing Guidelines (July 2017 version, paragraph 2.124: 136), the PSM could be applied using two approaches: contribution analysis or residual analysis. The contribution analysis involves the fact that the cumulated profit generated by the related-party transaction and allocated to each participating entity reflects the functions performed, risks incurred and assets used by each of these entities. This analysis is based on the market conditions related to the ways in which independent parties would share the profit generated in similar conditions. The residual analysis involves a sharing of the cumulated profit in two steps. In the first step the profit is allocated to each entity so to ensure a "normal" profitability indicator (i.e. a profitability indicator that would have recorded by independent entities if, for example, there were not used unique intangible assets). In the second step, the residual profit (what remained after the first step) is allocated to each entity based on the contribution to the transaction and the market conditions. For example, if one of the entity owns a unique intangible assets which significantly contributes to the profit generation, then that entity is entitled to receive a considerable share from the residual profit.

The way in which the PSM operates in practice is illustrated in the below case study.

Case study
Ball Production owns a unique manufacturing technology for the soccer balls, these balls being appreciated by the public due to a superior quality compared with the balls of other competitors from the market. The soccer balls are sold exclusively to Ball Distribution.

Ball Distribution owns the "BallBall" brand under which the balls are traded on the market, being a brand known an international level as a leader on the market. In addition, Ball Distribution owns a list with the customers who acquire the balls.

The production cost of a ball is of EUR 80, while the resale price is of EUR 120. The marketing expenses recorded by Ball Distribution for the promotion of balls is of EUR 10/ball. The cumulated profit generated by the related-party transaction for the sale of a ball is of EUR 30 (EUR 120 − EUR 80 − EUR 10).

Based on a market study, there was concluded that the cumulated profit should be allocated 60% to Ball Production and 40% to Ball Distribution. Therefore, based on the PSM the price invoiced by Ball Production to Ball Distribution for the sale of a ball should be EUR 90.8 (EUR 80 + 60% × EUR 30).

Summarizing the information presented above in relation to the transfer pricing methods, Figure 2.7 below shows the steps that should be followed to perform the analysis necessary to choose the most appropriate transfer pricing method.

2.1.7 Comparability Analysis

According to the OECD Transfer Pricing Guidelines, the comparability analysis is the "heart" of the arm's length principle (OECD Transfer Pricing Guidelines, July 2017 version, paragraph 1.6: 35). In general, a comparability analysis involves examining the analyzed transaction that takes place between affiliates and the transactions between independents, considered potentially comparable.

Performing a comparability analysis involves the following steps (OECD Transfer Pricing Guidelines, July 2017 version, paragraph 3.4: 148–149):

Step 1 Determining the period to be analyzed;

Step 2 Analysis of the taxpayer's economic circumstances. This step can be represented by an analysis of the industry in which the taxpayer operates, including a presentation of the competitors or of the economic and legislative factors that impact the environment in which the taxpayer operates;

Step 3 Understanding the analyzed transaction. This step involves the performance of the functional analysis, which is the basis for selecting the tested party, the transfer pricing method and the profitability indicator, as well as the basis for identifying comparability factors that should be further considered;

Step 4 Checking whether internal comparable can be used;

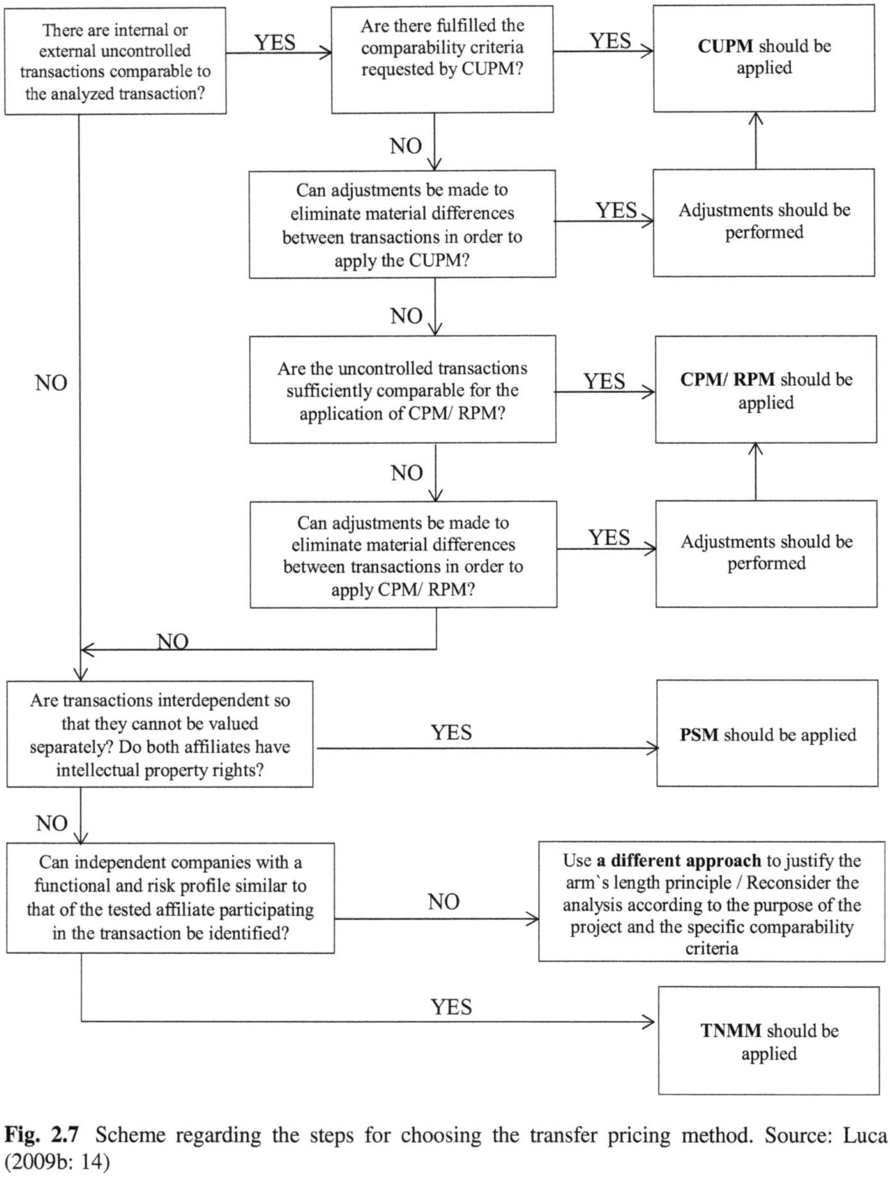

Fig. 2.7 Scheme regarding the steps for choosing the transfer pricing method. Source: Luca (2009b: 14)

Step 5 If internal comparable cannot be used, there should be identified the sources of information needed to apply an external comparability. The most used such sources are represented by certain databases that contain information for certain categories of companies. The information contained in these databases is that submitted by companies to the Trade Register of the country in which they operate. Examples of such databases are Amadeus, Orbis, TP Catalyst etc. The search for external comparables in these databases is done by applying qualitative criteria (e.g. on the activity code, independence status, geographical area in which the potentially comparable entity operates, etc.) and quantitative (e.g. on the volume sales, number of employees, etc.). This process of searching and identifying external comparables is called a benchmark study or comparability study;

Step 6 Selecting the most appropriate transfer pricing method, as well as the profitability indicator;

Step 7 In order to determine whether or not an uncontrolled transaction (conducted between independents) is comparable to the transaction analyzed, the following five comparability factors should be considered: the contractual terms of the transaction; the functions performed, the risks incurred and the assets used by the entities (i.e. the functional analysis); the characteristics of the transferred goods or services provided; the economic circumstances and business strategies of the entities;

Step 8 Performance of comparability adjustments, where necessary;

Step 9 Interpretation and use of the information collected, as well as determination of remuneration that complies with the arm's length principle. As the transfer pricing analysis is not an exact science, following the comparability analysis in most of the times a comparability interval is obtained (a price interval or an interval of profit margins applied/obtained by independent companies). If the price/profit margin from the analyzed transaction is within this comparability range, then the arm's length principle was applied within the analyzed transaction. Moreover, the OECD Transfer Pricing Guidelines recommends that the profitability indicators of comparable entities and on the basis of which the comparability interval is determined be calculated as an average over several years. In this respect, the last years for which the necessary financial information is available should be taken into account. The justification for using a multi-year average is to neutralize the negative influences caused by changes in economic conditions, changes in the exchange rate, seasonal activities, etc. Dessatniuk and Cherevko (2015) mention that, as a rule, transfer pricing specialists use an average over the last 3 years. For example, if the analyzed transaction took place in 2015, depending on when the analysis is actually performed, the last 3 years may be 2013, 2014, 2015 or 2012, 2013, 2014. More exactly, if the analysis is performed at the beginning of 2016 when the database used to identify comparable companies has not been updated with the information related to 2015, the period included in the analysis is 2012–2014. If the analysis is performed at the end of 2016, when the database contains data for 2015, the analyzed period is 2013–2015. In practice, there are also rarer situations when an average of profitability indicators over a period of 5 years is used.

In practice, the above described steps are not applied in a linear way step by step. In fact, the comparability analysis is a complex process which contains all the steps, certain steps being repeated until the final results are obtained. Concrete and complete comparability analyses are provided within Chap. 3. How to perform a transfer pricing analysis in case of manufacturing entities.

Moreover, in relation to the comparability analysis, the OECD Transfer Pricing Guidelines provide certain useful recommendations, as follows:

- In relation to the comparability range, if after the performance of the comparability analysis is obtain a sizeable number of comparables (in the practice of many countries, this meaning the identification of minimum five comparables), there should be used a statistical tool which is based on a central tendency (like the interquartile range).
- Regarding the quantitative criteria applied in order to perform a benchmark study, the OECD Transfer Pricing Guidelines provide the following examples:
  - Criteria regarding the size: the volume of the sales registered, the assets value or the employees' number;
  - Criteria regarding the intangibles applied in order to exclude those companies which have valuable intangibles or perform research and development activities: ratio between the Net Value of Intangibles and Total Net Assets Value, or ratio between Research and Development (R&D) and Sales;
  - Criteria regarding the inventories;
  - Criteria related to the export sales;
  - Other criteria in order to exclude companies that are in a special situation (e.g. bankruptcy, start-ups).
- Regarding the geographical criterion, even if the OECD Transfer Pricing Guidelines do not provide a preference for a certain hierarchy (e.g. first should be searched local comparables and if these are not identified to extend the search on other regions), it is mentioned that "the requirement to use the most reliable information will usually, but not always, require the use of local comparables over the use of regional comparables where such local comparables are reasonably available" (OECD Transfer Pricing Guidelines, July 2017 version, paragraph 5.46: 242).

2.2 BEPS Actions Plan

Over the time, with the increase of the international trade and of the number of multinationals, it has been found that multinational entities develop various tax strategies that result in the payment of lower taxes. In this context, there was

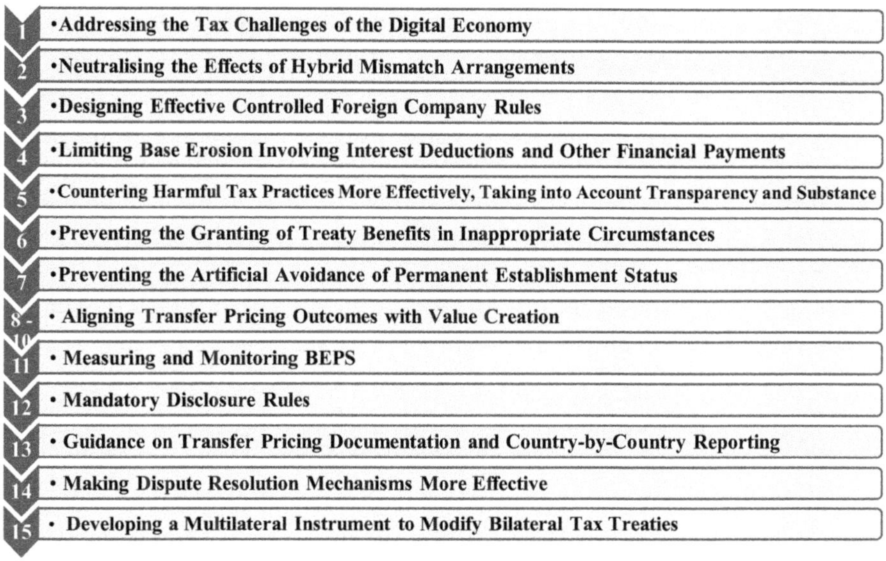

Fig. 2.8 BEPS Actions Plan. Source: http://www.oecd.org/tax/beps/beps-actions.htm

identified the phenomenon of base erosion and profit shifting (BEPS). To combat this phenomenon, at the initiative of G20[4] leaders, the OECD presented in February 2013 the report "Addressing Base Erosion and Profit Shifting", which addressed the main causes of the erosion of the tax base and the shift of profit. Subsequently, in July 2013, the OECD published the report "Action Plan on Base Erosion and Profit Shifting" which presents a series of 15 actions to combat the phenomenon of tax base erosion and profit shifting, covering three major areas: double taxation avoidance treaties, information exchange and transfer pricing rules. In 2015, the OECD published a detailed report on each action. Figure 2.8 below presents the 15 actions of the BEPS Actions Plan.

Of the 15 actions mentioned in the figure above, a direct impact on transfer prices has Actions 8–10 "Aligning Transfer Pricing Outcomes with Value Creation", respectively Action 13 "Guidance on Transfer Pricing Documentation and Country-by-Country Reporting". These actions were integrated into the OECD Transfer Pricing Guidelines published in July 2017. A presentation of the provisions of these actions is presented below.

[4]An international forum for the governments and governors of central banks in Argentina, Australia, Brazil, Canada, China, France, Germany, India, Indonesia, Italy, Japan, Mexico, the Russian Federation, Saudi Arabia, South Africa, South Korea, Turkey, United Kingdom, United States of America and European Union.

2.2.1 Actions 8–10 "Aligning Transfer Pricing Outcomes with Value Creation"

Actions 8–10 "Aligning transfer pricing outcomes with value creation" of the BEPS Actions Plan aimed at developing transfer pricing rules to ensure that the profit generated by a transaction that involves transfer prices is in line with the value generated by that transaction. Therefore, the actions address the following issues (OECD, 2015a):

- Action 8 establishes rules that prevent the erosion of the tax base and the transfer of intangible assets between the group entities. These rules aimed at:
  - establishing special measures for the transfer of intangible assets;
  - adopting a clear definition of intangible assets, ensuring that the profit associated with the transfer and use of intangible assets is allocated in accordance with value creation.
- Also, through Action 8, updates are made on the cost contribution agreements concluded between the member entities of a group.
- Action 9 establishes rules that prevent the erosion of the tax base and the transfer of profits through the transfer of risks or the excessive allocation of capital between group entities;
- Action 10 establishes rules that prevent the erosion of the tax base and the transfer of profits by carrying out transactions that independent entities would not normally carry out (called risky transactions). Action 10 also sets out rules for the application of a simplified analysis for low value-added intra-group services. Moreover, Action 10 provides clarifications on the application of the transfer pricing methods, in particular on the PSM.

2.2.2 Action 13 "Guidance on Transfer Pricing Documentation and Country-by-Country Reporting"

The main purpose of Action 13 "Guidance on transfer pricing documentation and country-by-country reporting" of the BEPS Actions Plan is to help increase transparency for tax administrations and to ensure the provision of relevant information on overall revenue allocation, activity and the taxes paid by multinationals in each country in which they operate. To achieve this goal, Action 13 requires the preparation of three types of reports:

- a group level report—this report is called a "master file" and should contain general information about the activity of the whole group, as well as about the transfer pricing policies applied at group level;
- a local report—this report should be prepared at local level by each entity part of the group, according to the transfer pricing regulations from the jurisdiction in

which it operates. The local report should provide detailed information on the analysis of the entity's related party transactions;

- a country-by-country report—this reporting requirement applies to tax periods beginning on or after January 1, 2016. The obligation to prepare this report exists only for multinational groups that recorded in the fiscal year preceding the reporting year, a consolidated revenue equal to or greater than EUR 750 million. In the country-by-country report the groups should present for each fiscal jurisdiction in which they operate information related to the reporting year on: the revenues obtained, the profit before tax, the corporate income tax paid, the corporate income tax accumulated in the reporting year, declared share capital, retained earnings, number of employees and the fixed assets (other than cash or cash equivalents). The country-by-country report should also contain a list of the constituent entities of the multinational group, presented for each tax jurisdiction.

Regarding the responsibility for the preparation and submission of the country-by-coutry report, Action 13 of the BEPS Actions Plan presents the following aspects (OECD, 2015b):

- each Ultimate Parent Entity of a multinational group should prepare and submit the country-by-country documentation in the country where it is tax resident. A company is considered to be an Ultimate Parent Entity if it is part of a group of multinational companies and if the following criteria are cumulatively met:

  (a) has, directly or indirectly, a sufficient interest in one or more constituent entities of the multinational group, so that it is required to prepare consolidated financial statements in accordance with the accounting principles generally applied in the jurisdiction in which has its tax residence, or would be obliged to do so if its holdings in equity were traded on a public stock exchange in the jurisdictions in which it has its tax residence;
  (b) there is no other constituent entity in that multinational group that has, directly or indirectly, an interest such as that described in letter a) above.

- another company within the multinational group, called a Constituent Entity (i.e. a company that is not an Ultimate Parent Entity) should prepare and submit the country-by-country documentation if the following criteria are cumulatively met:

  (a) that company is a tax resident in a certain jurisdiction;
  (b) one of the following criteria is applicable:

    – the Ultimate Parent Entity is not obliged to prepare and submit the country-by-country documentation in the jurisdiction in which it is a tax resident;
    – the jurisdiction in which the Ultimate Parent Entity is a tax resident has an International Agreement (i.e. a multilateral convention on mutual administrative assistance in tax matters, any multilateral or bilateral tax convention, or any agreement for the exchange of information for tax purposes), but has not signed Qualifying Competent Authority Agreement for the exchange of country-by-country documentation;

  - there is a systematic failure of the jurisdiction in which the Ultimate Parent Entity is a tax resident, which has been notified by the tax authorities in its country of tax residence. Systematic failure implies that a jurisdiction has a qualification agreement as the competent authority, but has suspended or failed to exchange the country-by-country documentation.

- if the above criteria were met so that another company within the multinational group is responsible for preparing and submitting the country-by-country documentation (i.e. the Constituent Entity), this company would not have this responsibility if the multinational group appointed a substitute parent company, i.e. a Surrogate Parent Entity and whether a set of criteria set out in Action 13 of the BEPS Actions Plan are met cumulatively.

According to Action 13 of the BEPS Actions Plan, local and group level documentation (master file documentation) should be made available to the local tax authorities by each entity of the multinational group. Country-by-country documentation is submitted only to the tax authorities of the country of residence of the entity that is responsible for preparing this documentation (Ultimate Parent Entity, Constituent Entity or Surrogate Parent Entity depending on the situations presented above). Subsequently, on the basis of an instrument for the automatic exchange of information (e.g. a multilateral convention on mutual administrative assistance in tax matters), the country-by-country documentation is also transmitted to the tax authorities of the jurisdictions in which the constituent entities of the multinational group operate.

Also, Action 13 of the BEPS Actions Plan stipulates the obligation of the entity in charge of preparing the country-by-country documentation, to notify in this respect the tax authorities of the jurisdiction in which it is resident for tax purposes. The other entities of the group have the obligation to notify the tax authorities, from the jurisdiction in which they are tax residents, regarding the entity that has the responsibility of preparing and submitting the country-by-country documentation.

Analyzed together, the three types of documentation provide tax administrations with useful information for assessing the risks related to transfer pricing. Therefore, the tax authorities can identify whether the companies have engaged in transactions that result in the artificial relocation of considerable amounts to more relaxed jurisdictions.

2.3 Regulations at the Level of the European Union

Regarding the EU transfer pricing regulations, these are based on the OECD recommendations. Thus, the European Union's concerns about transfer pricing transpose the provisions of the OECD's work in this area. Moreover, research conducted at European Union level in the field of transfer pricing is not intended to duplicate the work done at OECD level, but rather to provide clarifications and solutions to some practical issues on the subject of transfer pricing. The main concerns of the European Union on the subject of transfer pricing are:

1. ***European Union Directive 2016/881 as regards the mandatory automatic exchange of information in the field of taxation***

   This directive contains provisions for regulating at EU level the automatic exchange of information related to the country-by-country documentation. The directive also transposes at EU level the provisions of Action 13 of the BEPS Actions Plan.
2. ***Convention on the Elimination of Double Taxation in Relation to the Adjustment of Profits of Associated Enterprises (i.e. the Arbitration Convention)***

   The Arbitration Convention establishes the procedure for resolving disputes related to double taxation caused by transfer pricing adjustments of the intra-group transactions performed between companies located in European Union countries.

   The origin of the Arbitration Convention is represented by the proposal of the European Commission from 1976 to issue a directive for the elimination of double taxation in case of transfer of profits between associated companies in the European Union. After lengthy negotiations, the Commission proposal was transformed from a Directive into an Intergovernmental Convention which was signed on 23 July 1990.

   Details on how to apply the Arbitration Convention have been presented in Sect. 2.1.2—Double Taxation.
3. ***EU Joint Transfer Pricing Forum***

   The EU Joint Transfer Pricing Forum was established in 2002. The work of this Forum is based on the provisions of the OECD Transfer Pricing Guidelines and aims to propose to the European Commission non-legislative solutions to the transfer pricing issues encountered in EU practice. The EU Joint Transfer Pricing Forum consists of a representative of the tax authorities of each EU country, 18 non-governmental organizations and observers of the OECD member states or of the states intending to join the European Union, being administered by an independent person.

   Table 2.8 below shows the works developed by the EU Joint Transfer Pricing Forum.

2.4 Preliminary Conclusions

The chapter presented the main transfer pricing regulations existing at international level and at the level of the European Union.

Thus, at international level, the basis of the transfer pricing regulations was laid in 1979 through the elaboration of the OECD Transfer Pricing Guidelines. These Guidelines are used and recognized by most states, being the most important tool in terms of a transfer pricing analysis. The OECD Transfer Pricing Guidelines have

Table 2.8 Works of the EU Joint Transfer Pricing Forum

Work	Description
Code of conduct for the effective implementation of the Arbitration Convention	The purpose of this code is to ensure the efficient and uniform application by the EU member countries of the Arbitration Convention provisions. The Code was approved in 2004 and revised in 2009. In 2015, the EU Joint Transfer Pricing Forum prepared the Report for Improving the Functioning of the Arbitration Convention, which includes a revision of the Code of Conduct for the effective implementation of the Arbitration Convention. Both the report and the revised code are the result of a monitoring exercise carried out by the EU Joint Transfer Pricing Forum and provide clarifications on the following issues: • application of the Arbitration Convention when a non-payment of taxes is noticed or when changes of the taxpayer's status are noticed; • transparency in cases where the application of the Arbitration Convention is rejected; • the implications of Article 7 of the 2010 OECD Model Convention; • clarifications regarding the 3-year period provided in the case of the Arbitration Convention; • severe penalties, tax collection and collection of interest.
Code of conduct on transfer pricing documentation for associated enterprises in the EU	This code was adopted by the European Commission in 2006 and aims to standardize the documentation that multinationals should provide to tax authorities for intra-group transactions. According to this code, the transfer pricing documentation prepared by companies operating within the European Union should be structured in two main parts: • a documentation that includes information about the group of companies (i.e. the master file documentation); and • local documentation.
Guidelines for Advance Pricing Agreements (APAs) in the EU	These guidelines were adopted by the European Commission in 2007, with the aim of preventing disputes over transfer pricing and, implicitly, double taxation. Thus, these guidelines contain the general framework on how an APA application process should work effectively. Examples are also provided of the time frame required and the areas that should be covered by an APA.

(continued)

Table 2.8 (continued)

Work	Description
Guidelines on low-value-adding intra-group services	These guidelines were adopted in 2011 and provide details on routine intra-group transactions (represented by the provision of routine services) and propose an analytical approach to these services through the involvement of fewer resources. Also, aspects regarding shareholder costs, cost base, allocation keys, etc. are analyzed.
Potential approaches to non-EU triangular cases	These approaches were issued in 2011. The EU Joint Transfer Pricing Forum defined triangular cases involving companies outside the European Union as cases in which two states involved in a MAP cannot resolve double taxation caused by transfer pricing issues, as an affiliated entity located in a third country is identified as the source for non-compliance with the arm's length principle in a chain of transactions or commercial/financial relations.
Report on Small and Medium Enterprises (SMEs) and Transfer Pricing	This report was adopted in 2012 and examines specific issues for small and medium-sized enterprises. The report also provides a number of recommendations on access to information, documentation requirements, tax audits, etc.
Report on Cost Contribution Arrangements on Services not creating Intangible Property (IP)	The report was adopted in 2012 and provides a list of requirements that should be considered when determining whether a cost contribution arrangement for services that do not create intangible assets complies with the arm's length principle. Recommendations are also provided so that the analysis of these types of transactions is carried out in a uniform manner at the level of the European Union.
Report on Secondary Adjustments	This report was issued in 2014 and contains general provisions on secondary adjustments in the context of transfer pricing. At the same time, it contains recommendations aimed at avoiding double taxation.
Report on Transfer Pricing Risk Management	This report was issued in 2014, recognizing the need of tax administrations and taxpayers to allocate efficiently the transfer pricing resources. The report also contains an example of a work plan in the event of a tax audit.
Report on Compensating Adjustments	This report was issued in 2014 and provides practical recommendations on the avoidance of double taxation or double non-taxation in the application of compensating adjustments, in the context in which the EU Member States have different practices on compensating adjustments.

(continued)

Table 2.8 (continued)

Work	Description
Study on Comparable data used for Transfer Pricing in the EU	The European Commission adopted this study in December 2016. The study provides an overview and assessment of the availability and quality of ("comparable") market data used to establish transfer prices in the EU. In addition, the study presents the situations that characterize the unreliability of comparable data, as well as the situation of the search for comparable at pan-European level.
Study on the Application of Economic Valuation Techniques for Determining Transfer Prices of Cross Border Transactions between Members of Multinational Enterprise Groups in the EU	The European Commission adopted this study in December 2016. The study provides an overview of how valuation techniques can be used practically and more effectively in order to set transfer prices in the EU, especially for transactions involving intangible assets
Report on the Use of Comparables in the EU	The report was issued by the EU Joint Transfer Pricing Forum in May 2017 and sets out best practices and pragmatic solutions by issuing recommendations to both taxpayers and EU tax administrations, with the aim of increasing the objectivity and transparency of comparable searches for the transfer pricing analysis.
Report on the use of economic valuation techniques in transfer pricing	The report was issued in September 2017 containing a description of valuation techniques and presentation what should be considered when these techniques are used for transfer pricing purposes.
Report on a Coordinated approach to transfer pricing controls within the EU	The report was agreed in October 2018 and contains best practices in the context of transfer pricing audits.
Report on the application of the profit split method within the EU	The report was agreed in March 2019, clarifying certain aspects in relation the profit split method.

Source: Own processing based on information published on https://ec.europa.eu/taxation_customs/business/company-tax/transfer-pricing-eu-context/joint-transfer-pricing-forum

been updated three times so far, respectively in 1995, 2010 and 2017, and contain the main key concepts in the field of transfer pricing. The most important concept that constitutes the engine of a transfer pricing analysis is the arm's length principle according to which transactions between affiliates must be carried out under conditions/circumstances that must not differ from the commercial or financial relations established between independent companies.

In order to test whether a transaction between affiliates complies with the arm's length principle, according to the OECD Transfer Pricing Guidelines, a transfer pricing analysis should be performed. The main steps in this regard are represented by the functional analysis, the choice of the transfer pricing method and the comparability analysis. Functional analysis means identifying the main functions performed, risks incurred and assets used by the entities involved in the analyzed transaction. Based on the functional analysis, it is determined which company will be the tested party, i.e. the part from the perspective of which the transfer price analysis will be performed further. Specifically, the OECD Transfer Pricing Guidelines recommend that the tested party be the company with the simplest functional profile, as the most reliable comparables can be found for this company. Subsequently, the choice of the tested party influences the decision on the selection of the transfer pricing method. The transfer pricing methods provided by the OECD Transfer Pricing Guidelines are CUPM, CPM, RPM, TNMM and PSM. Depending on the applied transfer pricing method, in the next main step is compared the price or the gross/net profitability indicator of the tested party with the price or the gross/net profitability indicator practiced by independent companies that perform similar transactions to that analyzed. In order to make this comparison (i.e. the comparability analysis), the existence of internal comparables is firstly checked (i.e. the existence of similar transactions carried out in comparable circumstances by the entities involved in the transaction analyzed with independent entities). In the absence of internal comparables, external comparables are used, which are usually identified in special databases and following the application of a set of criteria. Finally, the comparability analysis results in obtaining a comparability interval that represents the range of prices or gross/net profitability indicators obtained by comparable independent companies, i.e. by companies that have a functional profile similar to that of the tested party and which carry out transactions similar to the one analyzed. If the price or the gross/net profitability indicator applied in the transaction analyzed and carried out between affiliated entities is within this range, then the analyzed transaction complies with the arm's length principle.

If the affiliated entities carry out transactions without respecting the arm's length principle, then they are subject to the risk of double taxation of the results. In order to eliminate the double taxation of results at group level, entities may request the initiation of MAP. Also, in order to avoid that during a tax audit the tax authorities adopt an aggressive position and make adjustments of the transfer prices that determine a double taxation of the results, the entities can either request the issuance of an APA or prepare a transfer pricing documentation. Obtaining an APA, compared to preparing a transfer pricing file, is more likely to reduce the risk of double taxation.

Regarding the transfer pricing documentation, the OECD's concerns were directed towards the development of the BEPS Actions Plan. Therefore, Action 13 "Guidance on transfer pricing documentation and country-by-country reporting" of the BEPS Actions Plan focuses on transfer pricing documentation requesting its preparation on three levels: a master file, a local file and a country-by-country report.

Other actions from the BEPS Actions Plan that envisage the transfer pricing subject are represented by Actions 8–10 "Aligning transfer pricing outcomes with value creation". The main scope of these actions is to ensure that the profit generated in transactions involving transfer pricing is in line with the value generated by those transactions.

At EU level, the European Commission recognizes the OECD Transfer Pricing Guidelines and supports the arm's length principle as the engine of a transfer pricing analysis. The research carried out at European Union level in the field of transfer pricing is not intended to duplicate the work done at OECD level, but rather to bring clarifications and solutions to some practical issues on the subject of transfer pricing. A first concern of the European Commission in the field of transfer pricing was materialized by the issuance of the Arbitration Convention in 1990. Subsequently, in order to establish solutions regarding the practical application of the Arbitration Convention, in 2002 the EU Joint Transfer Pricing Forum was established. Over time, this Forum has addressed other issues regarding transfer pricing, proposing to the European Commission non-legislative solutions to transfer pricing issues encountered in the EU practice. The EU Joint Transfer Pricing Forum also issued certain reports on transfer pricing issues, as well as two codes of conduct. In 2016, in the context of the BEPS phenomenon and in order to respond to international concerns, the European Union Directive 2016/881 was issued regarding the mandatory automatic exchange of information in the tax field. This directive contains provisions for regulating at EU level the automatic exchange of information related to the country-by-country documentation.

As a general conclusion, it is important to mention that the field of transfer pricing is a dynamic one, the regulations in this field being constantly modified and updated to respond to the needs generated by the increase and complexity of transactions between related parties.

References

Journal Articles

Becker, J., Davies, R. B., & Jakobsa, G. (2017). The economics of advance pricing agreements. *Journal of Economic Behavior & Organization, 134*, 255–268.

Dessatniuk, O., & Cherevko, O. (2015). Practical application of the methodology for calculating the arm's length range of prices/profitability for transfer pricing purposes. *European Journal of Economics and Management Sciences, 4*, 30–33.

Feleagă, L., & Neacşu, I. (2016). Transfer pricing documentation – An efficient measure for combating the base erosion and profit shifting? *Audit Financiar, XIV*(2(134)/2016), 183–194.

Lefter, C., & Chirica, S. (2010). Evitarea dublei impuneri internationale (Reglementări legale interne şi convenţii fiscale încheiate de România). *Economie teoretică şi aplicată, XVII*(9), 38–51.

Luca, A. (2009a). Preţurile de transfer pe înţelesul tuturor. *Consultantul Fiscal, March*, 34.

Radolovic, J. (2012). Transfer pricing model based on multiple-factor transfer pricing model using the transactional net margin method. *Ekonomska Istrazivanja-Economic Research, 25*(1), 34–50.

Book Chapter

Herksen, M. (2009). Business models. In A. Bakker (Ed.), *Transfer pricing and business restructurings: Streamlining all the way* (pp. 13–48). IBFD.

Online Publications

Convention on the elimination of double taxation in relation to the adjustment of profits of associated enterprises (i.e. the arbitration convention). Accessed January 2021., from https://eur-lex.europa.eu/resource.html?uri=cellar:ba007830-4ed1-43f9-8c98-c397c79373d8.0008.02/DOC_1&format=PDF

European Union Directive 2016/881 as regards the mandatory automatic exchange of information in the field of taxation. Accessed January 2021., from https://eur-lex.europa.eu/legal-content/EN/TXT/PDF/?uri=CELEX:32016L0881&from=en

http://www.oecd.org/tax/beps/beps-actions.htm

https://ec.europa.eu/taxation_customs/business/company-tax/transfer-pricing-eu-context/joint-transfer-pricing-forum

Lohse, T., & Riedel, N. (2012). *The impact of transfer pricing regulations on profit shifting within European multinationals.* FZID Discussion paper, Nr. 61-2012. Accessed March 2021, from https://www.econstor.eu/bitstream/10419/67717/1/732536626.pdf

Luca, A. (2009b). *Prețurile de transfer – metode de stabilire.* Accessed March 2021, from http://www.transferpricing.ro/articole/c5bc27284c7c6b4fb67d1fd3f34294e5.pdf

OECD. (2015a). *Aligning transfer pricing outcomes with value creation, Actions 8-10 – 2015 Final Reports.* OECD/G20 Base Erosion and Profit Shifting Project. OECD. Accessed June 2021, from https://doi.org/10.1787/9789264241244-en

OECD. (2015b). *Transfer pricing documentation and country-by-country reporting, Action 13 – 2015 Final Report.* OECD/G20 Base Erosion and Profit Shifting Project. OECD. Accessed June 2021, from https://doi.org/10.1787/9789264241480-en

OECD. (2017). *OECD transfer pricing guidelines for multinational enterprises and tax administrations 2017.* OECD. Accessed June 2021, from https://doi.org/10.1787/tpg-2017-en

Chapter 3
How to Perform a Transfer Pricing Analysis in Case of Manufacturing Entities

Manufacturing entities are performing the oldest business model (comparing with the distributors or service providers), they representing the most important link in the economic chain. Moreover, according to the Transfer Pricing Industry Guide published by Deloitte "the manufacturing sector continues to be the chief wealth-producing sector of the global economy and involves a large volume and variety of complex cross-border transactions" (Deloitte 2014). Given this, the main scope of this chapter is to present the steps that should be followed in order to perform a transfer pricing analysis for manufacturing entities (i.e. for manufacturing transactions). The analysis is performed based on concrete case studies and in accordance with the OECD Transfer Pricing Guidelines provisions, July 2017 version.

In terms of transfer pricing, manufacturing entities are classified in various categories, the transfer pricing analysis having certain particularities for each type of manufacturer. Given this, the chapter provides also a picture on how the transfer pricing analyses are changing over the different type of manufacturer.

More exactly, for each type of manufacturing entity there are presented the main steps that should be followed in order to perform a transfer pricing analysis. In this regard, there were conducted case studies which provide an overview of how the key transfer pricing concepts should be correlated so as to obtain an analysis based on which to determine whether the transfer price applied in a transaction complies with the arm's length principle.

The steps followed in the transfer pricing analysis are presented below:

- description of the transaction carried out between affiliated parties, subject of the transfer pricing analysis and presentation of the economic circumstances in which it takes place;
- performing the functional analysis based on the comparison of the functions performed, the risks incurred and the assets used by each entity participating in the transaction mentioned above. In this stage, depending on the results of the functional analysis, the tested party is selected, i.e. the company from the perspective of which the transfer pricing analysis is further performed;

I. Ignat, L. Ionescu-Feleagă, *Transfer Pricing in Manufacturing*, Contributions to Finance and Accounting, https://doi.org/10.1007/978-3-030-93889-5_3

- presenting the arguments regarding the selection of the most appropriate transfer pricing method, as well as the arguments regarding the rejection of the other methods. At this stage, the profitability indicator used to perform the comparability analysis was also selected;
- performing the comparability analysis itself (i.e. identifying comparable companies, from the point of view of the analyzed transaction, with the entity selected as a tested party, a process also called comparability study or benchmarking study). In this last stage of the case study, the online version of the Orbis database was used. The criteria applied in the Orbis database, as well as the quantitative and qualitative criteria (as mentioned in the OECD Transfer Pricing Guidelines) used to identify comparable entities were detailed below in each transfer pricing analysis performed.

In the following for each type of manufacturing entity was presented each of the four steps described above. Even if a part of the information presented in certain steps is similar for all types of manufacturers it was presented in full for each type of manufacturer (i.e. even if there is a repetition of the same information). This is due to the fact that the scope of this chapter is to provide a full picture of a transfer pricing analysis for each type of manufacturer, the readers interested in only one type not being obliged to search the needed information in all the chapter, but to look specifically to the subsection of interest for it.

3.1 Toll Manufacturing Entity

This section presents the transfer pricing analysis applicable for a toll manufacturing entity. The main characteristics of a toll manufacturing entity were included in Sect. 2.1.5—Functional Analysis.

Step 1: Description of the transaction carried out between affiliated parties and presentation of the economic circumstances in which it takes place

During 2019, Paint Production manufactured paints for the affiliated entity Paint Distribution. In this respect, Paint Production uses raw materials and auxiliary materials provided by its affiliated party, during the production process Paint Distribution being the owner of these materials. The finished products (i.e. boxes with paints) were sold to Paint Distribution at a price determined based on the total costs incurred by Paint Production in order to manufacture the paints plus a mark-up. It is important to note that in case of a toll manufacturing entity, the cost base at which the mark-up is added does not include cost with raw materials or auxiliary materials, as these materials do not represent the cost of the manufacturing entity (but of the entity which acquires the finished products—i.e. Paint Distribution).

Paint Production manufactures the paints only for its affiliated entity, while Paint Distribution acquires paints only from Paint Production. The distribution entity sells the goods to third independent clients from the EU market.

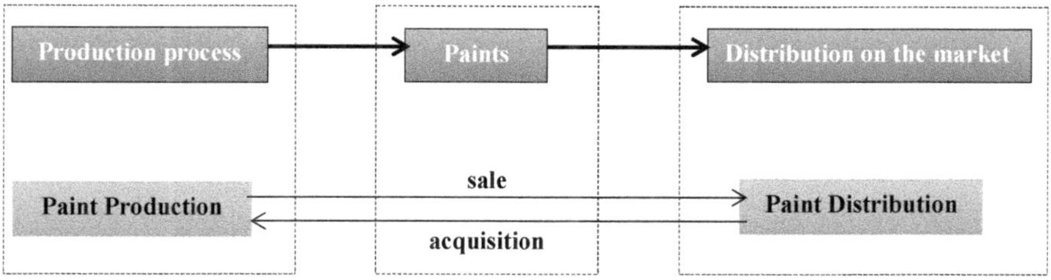

Fig. 3.1 Transaction flow. Source: Own processing

Given all the above, Fig. 3.1 presents the flow of the related-party transaction performed between Paint Production and Paint Distribution.

This step should also include a presentation of the conditions and terms under which the related-party transaction is performed, but this presentation is included in the next step of the analysis in order to ensure a clear correlation with the functions performed, risks incurred and assets used by each entity involved in the transaction. The conditions and terms of the related-party transaction should be presented based on the agreements concluded between parties in this respect, but also based on discussions with the relevant staff from the two entities and visits on the production sites.

According to paragraph 3.7 of the OECD Transfer Pricing Guidelines, July 2017 version, the analysis of the competition, industry and regulatory or economic factors that affect the related-party transaction can help in understanding the economic circumstances of that transaction.

Therefore, regarding the economic circumstances in which the related-party transaction took place, there will be supposed that during 2019 no significant trends in the industry were recorded and no competitor or regulatory factors impacted the economic circumstances from the paints market and implicitly the economic circumstances of the analyzed transaction. In practice, this affirmation should be sustained by statistics and industry analyses performed be specialized firms, but considering the purpose of this chapter (i.e. to perform a transfer pricing analysis) we limited our work form this point of view to an assumption.

Step 2: Functional analysis

Table 3.1 below presents the functional analysis related to the above transaction carried out between Paint Production and Paint Distribution, showing the functions performed, risks incurred and assets used by each entity. In relation to each function/risk/asset there were presented the contractual terms and other conditions based on which was concluded that the respective function/risk/asset should be allocated to Paint Production or Paint Distribution.

Considering the above functional analysis, there could be concluded that **Paint Production is a toll manufacturer, while Paint Distribution is a fully-fledged distributor.** Given this, Paint Production was selected as the tested party as this entity has a less complex functional profile compared to that of Paint Distribution

Table 3.1 Functional analysis—toll manufacturing entity

Details	Paint Production	Paint Distribution
Functions performed		
Acquisition of raw materials—in the production process, Paint Production uses various raw materials which are acquired by Paint Distribution from specialized suppliers. The suppliers are chosen by Paint Distribution based on various criteria and are independent entities (i.e. the suppliers are not part from the group to which Paint Production and Paint Distribution belong).	n/a	✓
Consignment of raw materials—Paint Distribution acquires the raw materials needed in the production process, this entity being the owner of the materials. Therefore, during the production process, Paint Production uses the Paint Distribution's raw materials. Practically, during the production process, Paint Production performs the consignment of raw materials.	✓	n/a
Acquisition/production planning—Paint Distribution performs periodic forecasts in relation to its sales and based on these the entity performs a planning of the products that will be ordered from Paint Production, but also an acquisition planning for the raw materials. Further on, Paint Distribution provides Paint Production with its acquisition planning including details regarding the type, quantity and delivery time of the products needed. Based on this information, Paint Production performs a production planning, in the sense of planning the needed resource (staff, equipment) in order to comply with the requirements of its affiliated entity.	✓	✓
Production of paints—The production activity is performed by Paint Production within its own plant. Within Paint Production are obtained water based and solvent based paints. The production process includes the following phases, each phase being performed at different floors from the Paint Production's plant as follows: • in the first phase, different raw materials are taken from the warehouse and put into tubes situated at the most superior floor of the manufacturing site (the fourth floor). The tubes are extend from the fourth floor to the ground floor of the factory; • at the third floor is performed the mixture of raw materials; • at the second floor is obtained the finished product; • at the first floor is performed the packing; • at the ground floor is performed the labelling.	✓	n/a
Ownership of finished products—Paint Distribution is the owner of both, the raw materials and finished products. It is considered that the production process performed by Paint Production represents in fact a provision of processing services. Therefore, Paint Production is not the owner of the finished products, as its activity consists only in processing the Paint Distribution's raw materials.	n/a	✓
Function regarding the production technology—this function is performed by Paint Distribution. The technology production, including the production recipe (i.e. mixture formula of raw materials in order to obtain various types of paints) was developed by	n/a	✓

(continued)

Table 3.1 (continued)

Details	Paint Production	Paint Distribution
Paint Distribution, the affiliated entity performing the manufacturing of products based on the orders and technological specifications provided by Paint Distribution.		
Packaging and labelling—Paint Production is responsible for proper labelling and packaging of the finished products, this being performed in its factory.	✓	n/a
Transport of finished products—Paint Distribution is in charge with the transport organization from the Paint Production's site to its warehouse.	n/a	✓
Quality control—Paint Production performs the quality control of the finished products obtained. The quality control of the finished products is also performed by Paint Distribution.	✓	✓
Warehousing—given that the production is carried out by Paint Production on a planning basis, Paint Distribution being obliged to purchase the goods within the agreed delivery time, the storage of finished products is carried out by Paint Production only for a short period of time (i.e. 1 day). Paint Production stores raw materials during the production process. Paint Distribution stores the finished products for a longer period, until they are delivered to the final customer. Specifically, Paint Distribution works with its customers both on an order basis and on a stock basis.	✓	✓
Marketing and advertising—Paint Distribution organizes marketing and promotion campaigns to identify new customers and to promote the products. This company also participates in various events and fairs.	n/a	✓
Sales and distribution—this function is performed by Paint Distribution which owns its own showrooms and shops.	n/a	✓
Risks incurred		
Market risk—is the risk associated with unfavorable business conditions that may result from increased competitiveness, unfavorable market demand, the impossibility to develop markets or the position of products and services at the consumer level. If the number of customers of Paint Distribution decreases, this would negatively affect the turnover of this company. However, this situation will not affect the turnover of Paint Production, as Paint Distribution is obliged to purchase the quantities mentioned in the procurement planning.	n/a	✓
Inventory risk—is the risk that a company records stocks of raw materials or finished products on a long period time. This risk also involve the fact that the products become physically or morally degraded, are stolen or exposed to natural disasters. Considering that Paint Production is not the owner of the raw materials and finished products, the inventory risk is incurred only by Paint Distribution.	n/a	✓
Warranty and product liability risk—if during the production process or the quality control process are discovered non-compliant	n/a	✓

(continued)

Table 3.1 (continued)

Details	Paint Production	Paint Distribution
products, the costs related to this situation are borne by Paint Distribution as the owner of the products.		
Assets used		
Tangible assets (warehousing, buildings, equipment etc.)	✓	✓
Intangible assets (trademarks, patents)	n/a	✓

Source: Own processing
✓—function is performed/risk is incurred/assets are used; n/a—function is not performed/risk is not incurred/assets are not used

(the OECD Transfer Pricing Guidelines, July 2017 version recommend that the tested party be the least complex in terms of functional analysis).

Step 3: Selection of the most appropriate transfer pricing method and of the profitability indicator

Regarding the transfer pricing analysis, there could not be used internal comparables, but only external ones. This is due to the fact that Paint Production manufactures the paints only for its affiliated entity, while Paint Distribution acquires paints only from Paint Production.

Below are detailed the reasons for accepting/rejecting each of the transfer pricing methods:

- Comparable uncontrolled price ("CUP") method—considering the fact that there is not available public information regarding the prices charged between independent entities for the sale or acquisition of paints products, the CUP method was rejecting. Practically, there is a lack of necessary information in order to apply this method;
- Cost plus method ("CPM") and Resale price method ("RPM")—as it was presented in Sect. 2.1.6—Transfer Pricing Methods, the specialized databases do not contain information related to the expenses' destination and due to this it is impossible to determine the gross mark-up obtained by comparable independent entities. In order to find a solution to this situation, in practice are used net mark-ups. Given all these aspects, both the CPM and RPM were rejected;
- Transactional net margin method ("TNMM")—considering that through this method are compared net mark-ups, TNMM was considered the most suitable in order to check if the price charged by Paint Production to Paint Distribution complies with the arm's length principle. As it was presented in Sect. 2.1.6—Transfer Pricing Methods the TNMM could be applied in a similar approach with both, the CPM and the RPM (the difference being that these two methods compare gross mark-up, while TNMM is operating with net mark-ups). Considering the fact that the tested party is the toll manufacturing entity (i.e. Paint Production), the **TNMM applied in a similar approach with the CPM was selected** in order to test the compliance with the arm's length principle of the

price charged by Paint Production to Paint Distribution. The TNMM applied in a similar approach with RPM was rejected as it would have been applied if the party tested had been Paint Distribution which is a fully-fledged distributor;
- Profit split method ("PSM")—given that the analyzed transaction does not involve interdependent activities so that a separate analysis of them cannot be performed and the two entities do not make unique contributions to the transaction, the application of the PSM was rejected.

Concluding, the TNMM applied in a similar approach with CPM was considered the most suitable method in order to test the compliance with the arm's length principle of the price charged by Paint Production to its affiliated entity Paint Distribution.

Given the selected method, the profitability indicator used in order to perform the comparability analysis is the net cost plus ("NCP"). This indicator is a net mark-up which is determined based on the following formula:

$$Net\ cost\ plus\ (NCP) = \frac{Operational\ result}{Operational\ costs} * 100$$

The selection of the profitability indicator was performed in accordance with the provisions of the OECD Transfer Pricing Guidelines, July 2017 version (detailed in Sect. 2.1.6—Transfer Pricing Methods). These provisions mention the fact that the profitability indicator should be determined as a ratio between the operational result and an indicator which is not impacted by related party transactions (in the case of Paint Production, this indicator being the operational costs).

Step 4: Comparability analysis

The comparability analysis itself involves the comparison of the net mark-up obtained by Paint Production from the paints' sale to Paint Distribution with the net mark-ups recorded by independent comparable entities which are performing similar transactions to that carried out between Paint Production and Paint Distribution.

As was described above, there could not be used internal comparables, but external ones. In this respect, according to paragraph 3.30 from the OECD Transfer Pricing Guidelines, July 2017 version the most reliable source of information may be represented by the commercial databases which include in an electronic format accounts of the companies. Therefore, there was used the Orbis database.

Search strategy applied in order to identify comparable independent companies

In order to identify comparable independent companies there were applied the following categories of criteria:

- criteria applied directly in the Orbis database: in this stage of the search was obtain a sample of potential comparable companies;
- quantitative and qualitative criteria applied: the sample of companies exported from the Orbis database was subject to further analysis by applying manual filters in the Microsoft Excel application. These filters were applied in order to ensure a

greater degree of comparability between the independent transactions identified and the analyzed transaction performed between Paint Production and Paint Distribution.

Table 3.2 below presents a detailed description of both categories of criteria (i.e. those applies in the Orbis database and the quantitative and qualitative criteria).

Considering the criteria detailed above, until the identification of the final sample of independent comparables, there were applied four search strategies. The differences between these strategies are represented by the criteria applied in relation to the geographical location and independence indicators from the Orbis database as follows:

- The first search strategy was applied on the Romanian market, using as independence indicators from the Orbis database "A−", "A" and "A+";
- The second search strategy was applied on the EU market, using as independence indicators from the Orbis database "A−", "A" and "A+";
- The third search strategy was applied on the Romanian market, using as independence indicators from the Orbis database "A−", "A", "A+" and "U";
- The fourth search strategy was applied on the EU market, using as independence indicators from the Orbis database "A−", "A", "A+" and "U".

Results obtained applying the first search strategy (Romanian market, independence indicators "A−", "A", "A+")

After the application of the first category criteria (i.e. criteria applied in the Orbis database), there was not obtained any company in the sample. Given this, the search was further expanded on the EU market.

This result, together with the criteria applied in the Orbis database can be observed in Appendix A.

Results obtained applying the second search strategy (EU market, independence indicators "A−", "A", "A+")

As could been observed in Appendix B, after the application of the first category criteria (i.e. criteria applied in the Orbis database), there was obtained a sample of 37 companies. Subsequently, on this sample there were applied the quantitative and qualitative criteria, this resulting in rejection of all companies from the sample. Table 3.3 below shows the number of companies eliminated after the application of each quantitative and qualitative criteria. The information included in this table is detailed at the level of each company in Appendix C.

Considering that no independent comparable company was identified, the search strategy was further expanded by including "U" as an independence indicator.

Results obtained applying the third search strategy (Romanian market, independence indicators "A−", "A", "A+", "U")

After the application of the first category criteria (i.e. criteria applied in the Orbis database), there was obtained only one company in the sample. Given this, the search was further expanded on the EU market.

Table 3.2 Search strategy—toll manufacturing entity

Details	Description of the applied criteria
I. Criteria applied in the Orbis database	
1. *Activity status*	
According to paragraph 3.43 from the OECD Transfer Pricing Guidelines, July 2017 version, for the purpose of the comparability analysis companies that are in a special situation (e.g. bankrupted companies etc.) are not appropriate to be considered comparable. Therefore, this criterion was applied to eliminate inactive companies, respectively companies in a special situation. The inclusion of these companies could distort the financial results of the analysis and therefore it is important to exclude them.	There were selected only active companies (i.e. companies which are not in a special situation).
2. *Geographical location*	
Regarding the geographical criterion, even if the OECD Transfer Pricing Guidelines do not provide a preference for a certain hierarchy (e.g. first should be searched local comparables and if these are not identified to extend the search on other regions), it is mentioned that „the requirement to use the most reliable information will usually, but not always, require the use of local comparables over the use of regional comparables where such local comparables are reasonably available" (OECD Transfer Pricing Guidelines, July 2017 version, paragraph 5.46: 242). Moreover, many countries included in their local transfer pricing legislation the requirement to search for comparable transactions on the local market and only if there is not identified a sufficient number of comparables to extend the search on other regions (EU market, European market etc.).	There was considered that Paint Production is a Romanian entity and therefore the search was conducted in the first instance on the Romanian market. However, given that a sufficient number of comparable independent companies was not identified on this market, the search was extended to the European Union market (there was considered that this is the market of products within the analyzed transaction). The OECD Transfer Pricing Guidelines do not include clear provisions regarding the sufficient number of comparable independent companies, but in the practice of many countries this means the identification of minimum five comparables (this number is correlated with the application of the interquartile range as a statistical tool, which requires minimum five values).
3. *Activity code*	
Using the activity code classification, there can be identified companies that undertake similar transactions to that performed between Paint Production and Paint Distribution. To this extent, there have been used the NACE Rev. 2 convention.	There have been selected companies that undertake activities that are classified under the following NACE Rev. code: *2030 "Manufacture of paints, varnishes and similar coatings, printing ink and mastics"*.
4. *Independence*	
According to paragraph 3.24 from the OECD Transfer Pricing Guidelines, July 2017 version, "a comparable uncontrolled transaction is a transaction between *two independent* parties that is comparable to the controlled transaction under examination". Given that the scope of the present analysis is to identify independent parties (entities which are not affiliated parties) involved in similar transactions to that performed between Paint Production and Paint Distribution, there were applied certain criteria in this respect. Therefore, this filter was applied to ensure the independence	

(continued)

Table 3.2 (continued)

Details	Description of the applied criteria
of the obtained set of comparable companies, in order to reduce the risk of their financials reflecting significant intra-group activities. It is important to note that the OECD Transfer Pricing Guidelines do not provide details regarding the percentage of ownership applied in order to consider two entities as affiliated. However, considering that in the practice of many countries this percentage is of 25%, for the purpose of the present analysis this one was applied. Thus, different criteria were applied to ensure the independence of the sampled companies, as follows:	
4.1 Independence indicators from the Orbis database	
There were selected from the Orbis database independence indicators "A-", "A" and "A+". This means that the selected companies have known shareholder structure and no shareholder owns more than 25% of the company's stock, either directly or indirectly Considering the fact that, based on the above strategy, no comparable companies were identified (this is detailed in the below lines), the search was extended by including companies with unknown shareholders structure (independence indicator "U" according to the Orbis database). For this companies, the independence was checked based on the information published by companies on their websites.	
4.2 Shareholders	
Companies in which any shareholder (legal entity or natural person) directly or indirectly holds a percentage of 25% or more than 25% of the shares were rejected.	
4.3 Subsidiaries	
Companies holding 25% or more of a subsidiary have been eliminated.	
4.4 Account Reporting Method	
The selected companies have financial data obtained from unconsolidated reports ("U1" indicator according to Orbis database).	
5. *Period of comparison*	
According with paragraph 3.76 from the OECD Transfer Pricing Guidelines, July 2017 version "*in order to obtain a complete understanding of the facts and circumstances surrounding the controlled transaction, it generally might be useful to examine data from both the year under examination and prior years. The analysis of such information might disclose facts that may have influenced (or should have influenced) the determination of the transfer price*". More exactly, the analysis performed over a longer period yields more reliable results to that performed on financial data associated with only one fiscal year, as this approach better captures the economic climate and other market elements that could potentially have an impact on the profitability of the selected set of comparable companies. As mentioned in Sect. 2.1.7—Comparability Analysis, transfer pricing specialists use an average over the last 3 years.	In order to analyze the conformity of the price charged by Paint Production to Paint Distribution during 2019 (when the analyzed transaction took place) the average of the profitability indicators of comparable companies from the last 3 years for which financial information is available was used, by reporting to the analyzed year. Thus, the financial data of comparable companies from 2017 to 2019 was used.

(continued)

Table 3.2 (continued)

Details	Description of the applied criteria
II. Quantitative criteria	
1. *Availability of financial data*	
This filter was applied to eliminate companies for which there is insufficient available financial data for the purposes of calculating the necessary profitability indicator used in the course of the analysis.	Companies that do not have financial data available for all of 3-year period taken into account (i.e. 2017–2019) for the purposes of the analysis were eliminated.
2. *Ratio between stocks and turnover*	
The main difference between toll manufactures and the other types of manufactures is that the toll manufacturer processes materials and raw materials that it does not own. Therefore, toll manufactures usually keep very small stocks, which are not directly related to the production process (i.e. office products, fuels, etc.) or do not keep stocks at all. Therefore, it was considered useful to exclude from the sample producers who record significant value of stocks, a characteristic which is not specific to toll manufactures. This approach is in line with the OECD Transfer Pricing Guidelines, July 2017 version, paragraph 3.43 which recommend as quantitative criteria the application of criteria related to inventories (in relative or absolute value).	Therefore, in order to exclude from the sample the companies with a functional profile other than toll manufacturer, those companies whose ratio between the level of stocks and the turnover is higher than 5% were excluded. As mentioned above, within the criterion regarding the period of comparison, the profitability indicators are computed as an average of the financial data from 2017 to 2019. Given this, when applying the criterion related to the ratio between stocks and turnover an average of data from 2017 to 2019 was also used. Regarding the threshold of 5%, this should be established based on the financial data of the tested party. Therefore, there was considered that the ratio between stocks and turnover of Paint Production is lower than 5%.
3. *Ratio between intangible assets and total assets*	
Toll manufactures own only small intangible assets that are not necessarily specific to the production process. In practice, this means that toll manufactures do not have valuable intangible assets, such as know-how, patents or licenses. In general, these types of intangible assets are in the possession of those who contract the manufactures. Therefore, it was considered useful to exclude from the sample producers who record a high level of the ratio between intangible assets and total assets, a characteristic specific to fully-fledged manufactures. This approach is in line with the OECD Transfer Pricing Guidelines, July 2017 version, paragraph 3.43 which recommend as quantitative criteria the application of intangible related criteria. Within this paragraph is mentioned that these criteria *"may be used for instance to exclude companies with valuable intangibles or significant R&D activities when the tested party does not use valuable intangible assets nor participate in significant R&D activities"*.	In this step, companies whose ratio between intangible assets and total assets is higher than 3% were excluded. As mentioned above, within the criterion regarding the period of comparison, the profitability indicators are computed as an average of the financial data from 2017 to 2019. Given this, when applying the criterion related to the ratio between intangible assets and total assets an average of data from 2017 to 2019 was also used. Regarding the threshold of 3%, this should be established based on the financial data of the tested party. Therefore, there was considered that the ratio between intangible assets and total assets of Paint Production is lower than 3%.

(continued)

Table 3.2 (continued)

Details	Description of the applied criteria
4. *Average NCP negative*	
According to paragraph 3.63 from the OECD Transfer Pricing Guidelines, July 2017 version *"Extreme results might consist of losses or unusually high profits.* *Extreme results can affect the financial indicators that are looked at in the chosen method".*	Based on this criteria there were eliminated companies that recorded a negative value of the average NCP.
III. Qualitative criteria	
1. *Availability of information regarding the activity performed*	
The purpose of this filter is to ensure the availability of sufficient information on the basis of which to select the final set of comparable companies. More exactly, in this stage of the study there is accessed the website of the companies from the sample in order to analyze its activities and other relevant information.	Companies for which there is not enough public data to analyze their activity have been eliminated. Specifically, companies that did not have an official website or had the site under construction at the time of the search (August–September 2021) were removed from the sample. Also, companies whose site did not provide sufficient information to analyze whether or not those companies are comparable to the tested party were eliminated.
2. *Independence*	
This filter is applied to ensure the independence of the selected companies, in order to eliminate the risk of their financials being impacted by intra-group activities.	Companies that are part of a group according to the website were eliminated.
3. *Comparability between activities and functional profile*	
This filter is applied to ensure the comparability of the selected companies to the tested entity with respect to their activity and functional profile. Practically, for each company remained in the sample until this stage is analyzed the information published on its official website in order to determine which is the main activity performed and the related functional profile. It is important to note that applying the TNMM there is necessary a high degree of comparison between the functional profiles, the type of products manufactured not being necessary to be identical. In relation to the products, these should have similar characteristics in order to be included in the same category of products.	For companies that were not removed from the sample by this stage of the search, a detailed analysis of the information published on their websites was performed and those companies with significant differences with respect to their type of activity or functional profile from those of the tested entity (i.e. Paint Production) were eliminated.

Source: Own processing

This result, together with the criteria applied in the Orbis database can be observed in Appendix D.

Table 3.3 Results regarding the second search strategy—toll manufacturing entity

Criteria applied	No. of checked companies	No. of rejected companies	Rejection reason according to Appendix C
Initial sample (obtained after the application of the criteria in Orbis database)	37	n/a	
Quantitative criteria			
Availability of financial data	37	10	Lack of financial data (turnover/operational result)
Ratio between stocks and turnover	27	24	Average Stocks/Turnover >5%
Ratio between intangible assets and total assets	3	1	Average Intangible assets/Total assets >3%
Average NCP negative	2	0	Negative average NCP
Qualitative criteria			
Availability of information regarding the activity performed	2	1	Lack of website/The website doesn't work
Independence	1	1	The independence criteria are not met
Comparability between activities and functional profile	0	0	Other functional profile/ Other products
No. of accepted companies	0		

Source: Own processing

Results obtained applying the fourth search strategy (EU market, independence indicators "A−", "A", "A+", "U")

As could been observed in Appendix E, after the application of the first category criteria (i.e. criteria applied in the Orbis database), there was obtained a sample of 512 companies. Subsequently, on this sample there were applied the quantitative and qualitative criteria, this resulting in a final sample of five independent comparable companies. Table 3.4 below shows the number of companies eliminated after the application of each quantitative and qualitative criteria. The information included in this table is detailed at the level of each company in Appendix C.

For each of the five companies there was computed an average profitability indicator for the period 2017–2019. As was already detailed above, the selected profitability indicator is NCP, determine based on the following formula:

$$Net\ cost\ plus\ (NCP) = \frac{Operational\ result}{Operational\ costs} * 100$$

The average NCP indicator, computed for each of the five companies is included in Appendix C.

Table 3.4 Results regarding the fourth search strategy—toll manufacturing entity

Criteria applied	No. of checked companies	No. of rejected companies	Rejection reason according to Appendix C
Initial sample (obtained after the application of the criteria in Orbis database)	512	n/a	
Quantitative criteria			
Availability of financial data	512	284	Lack of financial data (turnover/operational result)
Ratio between stocks and turnover	228	190	Average Stocks/Turnover >5%
Ratio between intangible assets and total assets	38	2	Average Intangible assets/Total assets >3%
Average NCP negative	36	5	Negative average NCP
Qualitative criteria			
Availability of information regarding the activity performed	31	20	Lack of website/The website doesn't work
Independence	11	1	The independence criteria are not met
Comparability between activities and functional profile	10	5	Other functional profile/ Other products
No. of accepted companies	5		

Source: Own processing

Table 3.5 Comparability range—toll manufacturing entity

Range	Average NCP 2017–2019
Minimum	1.13%
Quartile 1	2.94%
Median	3.83%
Quartile 3	3.91%
Maximum	9.17%

Source: Own processing

Comparability range

Based on the average NCP computed for each of the five companies for the period 2017–2019, there was determined the comparability range. In this respect, there was used the "quartile" function of the Microsoft Excel application. Table 3.5 presents the comparability range obtained.

Conclusions of the comparability analysis

According to the OECD Transfer Pricing Guidelines recommendations, the minimum and the maximum values should be excluded from the comparability range. Therefore, the comparability range is between 2.94% and 3.91% with a median of 3.83%.

Table 3.6 NCP obtained by Paint Production—toll manufacturing entity

Indicator	Row no.	Value (thousand EUR)
Revenues from the sale of paints to Paint Distribution	1	50,000
Staff costs	2	30,500
Other production expenses	3	10,000
Other operational expenses allocated to the sale of paints to Paint Distribution	4	8000
Total of the operational costs	5=2+3+4	48,500
Operational result obtained from the sale of paints to Paint Distribution	6=1−5	1500
NCP	7=6/5	3.09%

Source: Own processing

Table 3.6 below presents the computation of the NCP obtained in 2019 by Paint Production from the sale of paints to its affiliated entity Paint Distribution.

Given all the above, the NCP obtained by Paint Production from the sale of paints to its affiliated entity Paint Distribution is of 3.09%, being situated within the comparability range (i.e. between 2.94% and 3.91%). Therefore, there could be concluded that the price paid by Paint Distribution to Paint Production complies with the arm's length principle.

3.2 Contract Manufacturing Entity

This section presents the transfer pricing analysis applicable for a contract manufacturing entity. The main characteristics of a contract manufacturing entity were included in Sect. 2.1.5—Functional Analysis.

Step 1: Description of the transaction carried out between affiliated parties and presentation of the economic circumstances in which it takes place

During 2019, Paint Production manufactured paints for the affiliated entity Paint Distribution. The production process is performed based on the orders and specifications of Paint Distribution. The finished products (i.e. boxes with paints) were sold to Paint Distribution at a price determined based on the total costs incurred by Paint Production in order to manufacture the paints plus a mark-up. In case of a contract manufacturing entity, the cost base should also include the costs with raw materials and auxiliary materials, as in this case the manufacturing entity is the owner of these materials.

Paint Production manufactures the paints only for its affiliated entity, while Paint Distribution acquires paints only from Paint Production. The distribution entity sells the goods to third independent clients from the EU market. The flow of the transaction is the same with that presented in Fig. 3.1.

This step should also include a presentation of the conditions and terms under which the related-party transaction is performed, but this presentation is included in the next step of the analysis in order to ensure a clear correlation with the functions performed, risks incurred and assets used by each entity involved in the transaction. The conditions and terms of the related-party transaction should be presented based on the agreements concluded between parties in this respect, but also based on discussions with the relevant staff from the two entities and visits on the production sites.

According to paragraph 3.7 of the OECD Transfer Pricing Guidelines, July 2017 version, the analysis of the competition, industry and regulatory or economic factors that affect the related-party transaction can help in understanding the economic circumstances of that transaction.

Therefore, regarding the economic circumstances in which the related-party transaction took place, there will be supposed that during 2019 no significant trends in the industry were recorded and no competitor or regulatory factors impacted the economic circumstances from the paints market and implicitly the economic circumstances of the analyzed transaction. In practice, this affirmation should be sustained by statistics and industry analyses performed be specialized firms, but considering the purpose of this chapter (i.e. to perform a transfer pricing analysis) we limited our work from this point of view to an assumption.

Step 2: Functional analysis

Table 3.7 below presents the functional analysis related to the above transaction carried out between Paint Production and Paint Distribution, showing the functions performed, risks incurred and assets used by each entity. In relation to each function/risk/asset there were presented the contractual terms and other conditions based on which was concluded that the respective function/risk/asset should be allocated to Paint Production or Paint Distribution.

Considering the above functional analysis, there could be concluded that **Paint Production is a contract manufacturer, while Paint Distribution is a fully-fledged distributor.** Given this, Paint Production was selected as the tested party as this entity has a less complex functional profile compared to that of Paint Distribution (the OECD Transfer Pricing Guidelines, July 2017 version recommend that the tested party be the least complex in terms of functional analysis).

Step 3: Selection of the most appropriate transfer pricing method and of the profitability indicator

Regarding the transfer pricing analysis, there could not be used internal comparables, but only external ones. This is due to the fact that Paint Production manufactures the paints only for its affiliated entity, while Paint Distribution acquires paints only from Paint Production.

Below are detailed the reasons for accepting/rejecting each of the transfer pricing methods:

Table 3.7 Functional analysis—contract manufacturing entity

Details	Paint Production	Paint Distribution
Functions performed		
Acquisition of raw materials—in the production process, Paint Production uses various raw materials which are acquired by this company from specialized suppliers. The suppliers are chosen by Paint Production based on various criteria and are independent entities (i.e. the suppliers are not part from the group to which Paint Production and Paint Distribution belong).	✓	n/a
Acquisition/production planning—Paint Distribution performs periodic forecasts in relation to its sales and based on these the entity performs a planning of the acquisitions that will be performed from Paint Production. Further on, Paint Distribution provides Paint Production with its acquisition planning including details regarding the type, quantity and delivery time of the products needed. Based on this information, Paint Production performs a production planning, but also a planning for the acquisition of raw materials.	✓	✓
Production of paints—The production activity is performed by Paint Production within its own plant. Within Paint Production are obtained water based and solvent based paints. The production process includes the following phases, each phase being performed at different floors from the Paint Production's plant as follows: • in the first phase, different raw materials are taken from the warehouse and put into tubes situated at the most superior floor of the manufacturing site (the fourth floor). The tubes are extend from the fourth floor to the ground floor of the factory; • at the third floor is performed the mixture of raw materials; • at the second floor is obtained the finished product; • at the first floor is performed the packing; • at the ground floor is performed the labelling.	✓	n/a
Ownership of finished products—after the production process and until the sale, Paint Production is the owner of the finished products.	✓	n/a
Function regarding the production technology—this function is performed by Paint Distribution. The technology production, including the production recipe (i.e. mixture formula of raw materials in order to obtain various types of paints) was developed by Paint Distribution, the affiliated entity performing the manufacturing of products based on the orders and technological specifications provided by Paint Distribution.	n/a	✓
Packaging and labelling—Paint Production is responsible for proper labelling and packaging of the finished products, this being performed in its factory.	✓	n/a
Transport of finished products—Paint Distribution is in charge with the transport organization from the Paint Production's site to its warehouse.	n/a	✓
Quality control—Paint Production performs the quality control of the raw materials used in the manufacturing process and also the	✓	✓

(continued)

Table 3.7 (continued)

Details	Paint Production	Paint Distribution
quality control of the finished products obtained. In this respect, the entity developed a quality assurance procedure (for e.g. during the production process the employee in charge with the quality control checks if the production recipe is respected, if the labelling is performed in accordance with the product specifications etc.). The quality control of the finished products is also performed by Paint Distribution based on sample.		
Warehousing—given that the production is carried out by Paint Production on a planning basis, Paint Distribution being obliged to purchase the goods within the agreed delivery time, the storage of finished products is carried out by Paint Production only for a short period of time (i.e. from the end of the process production until delivery date). Paint Production stores raw materials during the production process. Paint Distribution stores the finished products for a longer period, until they are delivered to the final customer. Specifically, Paint Distribution works with its customers both on an order basis and on a stock basis.	✓	✓
Marketing and advertising—Paint Distribution organizes marketing and promotion campaigns to identify new customers and to promote the products. This company also participates in various events and fairs.	n/a	✓
Sales and distribution—this function is performed by Paint Distribution which owns its own showrooms and shops.	n/a	✓
Risks incurred		
Market risk—is the risk associated with unfavorable business conditions that may result from increased competitiveness, unfavorable market demand, the impossibility to develop markets or the position of products and services at the consumer level. If the number of customers of Paint Distribution decreases, this would negatively affect the turnover of this company. However, this situation will not affect the turnover of Paint Production, as Paint Distribution is obliged to purchase the quantities mentioned in the procurement planning.	n/a	✓
Inventory risk—is the risk that a company records stocks of raw materials or finished products on a long period time. This risk also involve the fact that the products become physically or morally degraded, are stolen or exposed to natural disasters. Considering that both companies perform the warehousing function, the inventory risk is incurred by both of them.	✓	✓
Warranty and product liability risk—this risk is incurred by Paint Production, in its capacity of production entity. More exactly, if during the production process or the quality control process are discovered non-compliant products, the costs related to this situation are borne by Paint Production. In there are discovered non-compliant products after the acceptance by Paint Distribution of the products, the risk and costs are borne by this entity.	✓	✓

(continued)

Table 3.7 (continued)

Details	Paint Production	Paint Distribution
Assets used		
Tangible assets (warehousing, buildings, equipment etc.)	✓	✓
Intangible assets (trademarks, patents)	n/a	✓

Source: Own processing
✓—function is performed/risk is incurred/assets are used; n/a—function is not performed/risk is not incurred/assets are not used

- Comparable uncontrolled price ("CUP") method—considering the fact that there is not available public information regarding the prices charged between independent entities for the sale or acquisition of paints products, the CUP method was rejecting. Practically, there is a lack of necessary information in order to apply this method;
- Cost plus method ("CPM") and Resale price method ("RPM")—as it was presented in Sect. 2.1.6—Transfer Pricing Methods, the specialized databases do not contain information related to the expenses' destination and due to this it is impossible to determine the gross mark-up obtained by comparable independent entities. In order to find a solution to this situation, in practice are used net mark-ups. Given all these aspects, both the CPM and RPM were rejected;
- Transactional net margin method ("TNMM")—considering that through this method are compared net mark-ups, TNMM was considered the most suitable in order to check if the price charged by Paint Production to Paint Distribution complies with the arm's length principle. As it was presented in Sect. 2.1.6—Transfer Pricing Methods the TNMM could be applied in a similar approach with both, the CPM and the RPM (the difference being that these two methods compare gross mark-up, while TNMM is operating with net mark-ups). Considering the fact that the tested party is the contract manufacturing entity (i.e. Paint Production), the **TNMM applied in a similar approach with the CPM was selected** in order to test the compliance with the arm's length principle of the price charged by Paint Production to Paint Distribution. The TNMM applied in a similar approach with RPM was rejected as it would have been applied if the party tested had been Paint Distribution which is a fully-fledged distributor;
- Profit split method ("PSM")—given that the analyzed transaction does not involve interdependent activities so that a separate analysis of them cannot be performed and the two entities do not make unique contributions to the transaction, the application of the PSM was rejected.

Concluding, the TNMM applied in a similar approach with CPM was considered the most suitable method in order to test the compliance with the arm's length principle of the price charged by Paint Production to its affiliated entity Paint Distribution.

Given the selected method, the profitability indicator used in order to perform the comparability analysis is the net cost plus ("NCP"). This indicator is a net mark-up which is determined based on the following formula:

$$Net\ cost\ plus\ (NCP) = \frac{Operational\ result}{Operational\ costs} * 100$$

The selection of the profitability indicator was performed in accordance with the provisions of the OECD Transfer Pricing Guidelines, July 2017 version (detailed in Sect. 2.1.6—Transfer Pricing Methods). These provisions mention the fact that the profitability indicator should be determined as a ratio between the operational result and an indicator which is not impacted by related party transactions (in the case of Paint Production, this indicator being the operational costs).

Step 4: Comparability analysis

The comparability analysis itself involves the comparison of the net mark-up obtained by Paint Production from the paints' sale to Paint Distribution with the net mark-ups recorded by independent comparable entities which are performing similar transactions to that carried out between Paint Production and Paint Distribution.

As was described above, there could not be used internal comparables, but external ones. In this respect, according to paragraph 3.30 from the OECD Transfer Pricing Guidelines, July 2017 version the most reliable source of information may be represented by the commercial databases which include in an electronic format accounts of the companies. Therefore, there was used the Orbis database.

Search strategy applied in order to identify comparable independent companies

In order to identify comparable independent companies there were applied the following categories of criteria:

- criteria applied directly in the Orbis database: in this stage of the search was obtain a sample of potential comparable companies;
- quantitative and qualitative criteria applied: the sample of companies exported from the Orbis database was subject to further analysis by applying manual filters in the Microsoft Excel application. These filters were applied in order to ensure a greater degree of comparability between the independent transactions identified and the analyzed transaction performed between Paint Production and Paint Distribution.

Table 3.8 below presents a detailed description of both categories of criteria (i.e. those applies in the Orbis database and the quantitative and qualitative criteria).

Considering the criteria detailed above, until the identification of the final sample of independent comparables, there were applied four search strategies. The differences between these strategies are represented by the criteria applied in relation to the geographical location and independence indicators from the Orbis database as follows:

Table 3.8 Search strategy—contract manufacturing entity

Details	Description of the applied criteria
I. Criteria applied in the Orbis database	
1. *Activity status*	
According to paragraph 3.43 from the OECD Transfer Pricing Guidelines, July 2017 version, for the purpose of the comparability analysis companies that are in a special situation (e.g. bankrupted companies etc.) are not appropriate to be considered comparable. Therefore, this criterion was applied to eliminate inactive companies, respectively companies in a special situation. The inclusion of these companies could distort the financial results of the analysis and therefore it is important to exclude them.	There were selected only active companies (i.e. companies which are not in a special situation).
2. *Geographical location*	
Regarding the geographical criterion, even if the OECD Transfer Pricing Guidelines do not provide a preference for a certain hierarchy (e.g. first should be searched local comparables and if these are not identified to extend the search on other regions), it is mentioned that „the requirement to use the most reliable information will usually, but not always, require the use of local comparables over the use of regional comparables where such local comparables are reasonably available" (OECD Transfer Pricing Guidelines, July 2017 version, paragraph 5.46: 242). Moreover, many countries included in their local transfer pricing legislation the requirement to search for comparable transactions on the local market and only if there is not identified a sufficient number of comparables to extend the search on other regions (EU market, European market etc.).	There was considered that Paint Production is a Romanian entity and therefore the search was conducted in the first instance on the Romanian market. However, given that a sufficient number of comparable independent companies was not identified on this market, the search was extended to the European Union market (there was considered that this is the market of products within the analyzed transaction). The OECD Transfer Pricing Guidelines do not include clear provisions regarding the sufficient number of comparable independent companies, but in the practice of many countries this means the identification of minimum five comparables (this number is correlated with the application of the interquartile range as a statistical tool, which requires minimum five values).
3. *Activity code*	
Using the activity code classification, there can be identified companies that undertake similar transactions to that performed between Paint Production and Paint Distribution. To this extent, there have been used the NACE Rev. 2 convention.	There have been selected companies that undertake activities that are classified under the following NACE Rev. code: *2030 "Manufacture of paints, varnishes and similar coatings, printing ink and mastics".*
4. *Independence*	
According to paragraph 3.24 from the OECD Transfer Pricing Guidelines, July 2017 version, "a comparable uncontrolled transaction is a transaction between *two independent* parties that is comparable to the controlled transaction under examination". Given that the scope of the present analysis is to identify independent parties (entities which are not affiliated parties) involved in similar transactions to that performed between Paint Production and Paint Distribution, there were applied certain criteria in this respect. Therefore, this filter was applied to ensure the independence	

(continued)

Table 3.8 (continued)

Details	Description of the applied criteria
of the obtained set of comparable companies, in order to reduce the risk of their financials reflecting significant intra-group activities. It is important to note that the OECD Transfer Pricing Guidelines do not provide details regarding the percentage of ownership applied in order to consider two entities as affiliated. However, considering that in the practice of many countries this percentage is of 25%, for the purpose of the present analysis this one was applied. Thus, different criteria were applied to ensure the independence of the sampled companies, as follows:	
4.1 Independence indicators from the Orbis database	
There were selected from the Orbis database independence indicators "A−", "A" and "A+". This means that the selected companies have known shareholder structure and no shareholder owns more than 25% of the company's stock, either directly or indirectly. Considering the fact that, based on the above strategy, no comparable companies were identified (this is detailed in the below lines), the search was extended by including companies with unknown shareholders structure (independence indicator "U" according to the Orbis database). For this companies, the independence was checked based on the information published by companies on their websites.	
4.2 Shareholders	
Companies in which any shareholder (legal entity or natural person) directly or indirectly holds a percentage of 25% or more than 25% of the shares were rejected.	
4.3 Subsidiaries	
Companies holding 25% or more of a subsidiary have been eliminated.	
4.4 Account Reporting Method	
The selected companies have financial data obtained from unconsolidated reports ("U1" indicator according to Orbis database).	
5. *Period of comparison*	
According with paragraph 3.76 from the OECD Transfer Pricing Guidelines, July 2017 version "*in order to obtain a complete understanding of the facts and circumstances surrounding the controlled transaction, it generally might be useful to examine data from both the year under examination and prior years. The analysis of such information might disclose facts that may have influenced (or should have influenced) the determination of the transfer price*". More exactly, the analysis performed over a longer period yields more reliable results to that performed on financial data associated with only one fiscal year, as this approach better captures the economic climate and other market elements that could potentially have an impact on the profitability of the selected set of comparable companies. As mentioned in Sect. 2.1.7—Comparability Analysis, transfer pricing specialists use an average over the last 3 years.	In order to analyze the conformity of the price charged by Paint Production to Paint Distribution during 2019 (when the analyzed transaction took place) the average of the profitability indicators of comparable companies from the last 3 years for which financial information is available was used, by reporting to the analyzed year. Thus, the financial data of comparable companies from 2017 to 2019 was used.

(continued)

Table 3.8 (continued)

Details	Description of the applied criteria
II. Quantitative criteria	
1. *Availability of financial data*	
This filter was applied to eliminate companies for which there is insufficient available financial data for the purposes of calculating the necessary profitability indicator used in the course of the analysis.	Companies that do not have financial data available for all of 3-year period taken into account (i.e. 2017–2019) for the purposes of the analysis were eliminated.
2. *Ratio between stocks and turnover*	
The main difference between contract manufactures and toll manufactures is that the letter process materials and raw materials that they do not own. Therefore, toll manufactures usually keep very small stocks, which are not directly related to the production process (i.e. office products, fuels, etc.) or do not keep stocks at all. Therefore, it was considered useful to exclude from the sample producers who record very small stocks, a characteristic specific to toll manufactures. This approach is in line with the OECD Transfer Pricing Guidelines, July 2017 version, paragraph 3.43 which recommend as quantitative criteria the application of criteria related to inventories (in relative or absolute value).	Therefore, in order to exclude from the sample the companies with a functional profile of toll manufacturer, those companies whose ratio between the level of stocks and the turnover is lower than 5% were excluded. As mentioned above, within the criterion regarding the period of comparison, the profitability indicators are computed as an average of the financial data from 2017 to 2019. Given this, when applying the criterion related to the ratio between stocks and turnover an average of data from 2017 to 2019 was also used. Regarding the threshold of 5%, this should be established based on the financial data of the tested party. Therefore, there was considered that the ratio between stocks and turnover of Paint Production is greater than 5%.
3. *Ratio between intangible assets and total assets*	
Contract manufactures own only small intangible assets that are not necessarily specific to the production process. In practice, this means that contract manufactures do not have valuable intangible assets, such as know-how, patents or licenses. In general, these types of intangible assets are in the possession of those who contract the manufactures. Therefore, it was considered useful to exclude from the sample producers who record a high level of the ratio between intangible assets and total assets, a characteristic specific to fully-fledged manufactures. This approach is in line with the OECD Transfer Pricing Guidelines, July 2017 version, paragraph 3.43 which recommend as quantitative criteria the application of intangible related criteria. Within this paragraph is mentioned that these criteria *"may be used for instance to exclude companies with valuable intangibles or significant R&D activities when the tested party does not use valuable intangible assets nor participate in significant R&D activities"*.	In this step, companies whose ratio between intangible assets and total assets is higher than 3% were excluded. As mentioned above, within the criterion regarding the period of comparison, the profitability indicators are computed as an average of the financial data from 2017 to 2019. Given this, when applying the criterion related to the ratio between intangible assets and total assets an average of data from 2017 to 2019 was also used. Regarding the threshold of 3%, this should be established based on the financial data of the tested party. Therefore, there was considered that the ratio between intangible assets and total assets of Paint Production is lower than 3%.

(continued)

Table 3.8 (continued)

Details	Description of the applied criteria
4. *Average NCP negative*	
According to paragraph 3.63 from the OECD Transfer Pricing Guidelines, July 2017 version *"Extreme results might consist of losses or unusually high profits. Extreme results can affect the financial indicators that are looked at in the chosen method".*	Based on this criteria there were eliminated companies that recorded a negative value of the average NCP.
III. Qualitative criteria	
1. *Availability of information regarding the activity performed*	
The purpose of this filter is to ensure the availability of sufficient information on the basis of which to select the final set of comparable companies. More exactly, in this stage of the study there is accessed the website of the companies from the sample in order to analyze its activities and other relevant information.	Companies for which there is not enough public data to analyze their activity have been eliminated. Specifically, companies that did not have an official website or had the site under construction at the time of the search (August–September 2021) were removed from the sample. Also, companies whose site did not provide sufficient information to analyze whether or not those companies are comparable to the tested party were eliminated.
2. *Independence*	
This filter is applied to ensure the independence of the selected companies, in order to eliminate the risk of their financials being impacted by intra-group activities.	Companies that are part of a group according to the website were eliminated.
3. *Comparability between activities and functional profile*	
This filter is applied to ensure the comparability of the selected companies to the tested entity with respect to their activity and functional profile. Practically, for each company remained in the sample until this stage is analyzed the information published on its official website in order to determine which is the main activity performed and the related functional profile. It is important to note that applying the TNMM there is necessary a high degree of comparison between the functional profiles, the type of products manufactured not being necessary to be identical. In relation to the products, these should have similar characteristics in order to be included in the same category of products.	For companies that were not removed from the sample by this stage of the search, a detailed analysis of the information published on their websites was performed and those companies with significant differences with respect to their type of activity or functional profile from those of the tested entity (i.e. Paint Production) were eliminated.

Source: Own processing

- The first search strategy was applied on the Romanian market, using as independence indicators from the Orbis database "A−", "A" and "A+";

Table 3.9 Results regarding the second search strategy—contract manufacturing entity

Criteria applied	No. of checked companies	No. of rejected companies	Rejection reason according to Appendix C
Initial sample (obtained after the application of the criteria in Orbis database)	37	n/a	
Quantitative criteria			
Availability of financial data	37	10	Lack of financial data (turnover/operational result)
Ratio between stocks and turnover	27	3	Average Stocks/Turn-over <5%
Ratio between intangible assets and total assets	24	5	Average Intangible assets/Total assets >3%
Average NCP negative	19	4	Negative average NCP
Qualitative criteria			
Availability of information regarding the activity performed	15	2	Lack of website/The website doesn't work
Independence	13	2	The independence criteria are not met
Comparability between activities and functional profile	11	10	Other functional profile/ Other products
No. of accepted companies	1		

Source: Own processing

- The second search strategy was applied on the EU market, using as independence indicators from the Orbis database "A–", "A" and "A+";
- The third search strategy was applied on the Romanian market, using as independence indicators from the Orbis database "A–", "A", "A+" and "U";
- The fourth search strategy was applied on the EU market, using as independence indicators from the Orbis database "A–", "A", "A+" and "U".

Results obtained applying the first search strategy (Romanian market, independence indicators "A–", "A", "A+")

After the application of the first category criteria (i.e. criteria applied in the Orbis database), there was not obtained any company in the sample. Given this, the search was further expanded on the EU market.

This result, together with the criteria applied in the Orbis database can be observed in Appendix A.

Results obtained applying the second search strategy (EU market, independence indicators "A–", "A", "A+")

As could been observed in Appendix B, after the application of the first category criteria (i.e. criteria applied in the Orbis database), there was obtained a sample of 37 companies. Subsequently, on this sample there were applied the quantitative and qualitative criteria, this resulting in only one independent comparable company. Table 3.9 below shows the number of companies eliminated after the application of each quantitative and qualitative criteria. The information included in this table is detailed at the level of each company in Appendix C.

Considering that the identification of only one independent comparable company is not sufficient in order to compute a comparability range of profitability indicators, the search strategy was further expanded by including "U" as an independence indicator.

Results obtained applying the third search strategy (Romanian market, independence indicators "A−", "A", "A+", "U")

After the application of the first category criteria (i.e. criteria applied in the Orbis database), there was obtained only one company in the sample. Given this, the search was further expanded on the EU market.

This result, together with the criteria applied in the Orbis database can be observed in Appendix D.

Results obtained applying the fourth search strategy (EU market, independence indicators "A−", "A", "A+", "U")

As could been observed in Appendix E, after the application of the first category criteria (i.e. criteria applied in the Orbis database), there was obtained a sample of 512 companies. Subsequently, on this sample there were applied the quantitative and qualitative criteria, this resulting in a final sample of 11 independent comparable companies. Table 3.10 below shows the number of companies eliminated after the application of each quantitative and qualitative criteria. The information included in this table is detailed at the level of each company in Appendix C.

For each of the 11 companies there was computed an average profitability indicator for the period 2017–2019. As was already detailed above, the selected profitability indicator is NCP, determine based on the following formula:

$$Net\ cost\ plus\ (NCP) = \frac{Operational\ result}{Operational\ costs} * 100$$

The average NCP indicator, computed for each of the 11 companies is included in Appendix C.

Comparability range

Based on the average NCP computed for each of the 11 companies for the period 2017–2019, there was determined the comparability range. In this respect, there was used the "quartile" function of the Microsoft Excel application. Table 3.11 presents the comparability range obtained.

Conclusions of the comparability analysis

According to the OECD Transfer Pricing Guidelines recommendations, the minimum and the maximum values should be excluded from the comparability range.

Table 3.10 Results regarding the fourth search strategy—contract manufacturing entity

Criteria applied	No. of checked companies	No. of rejected companies	Rejection reason according to Appendix C
Initial sample (obtained after the application of the criteria in Orbis database)	512	n/a	
Quantitative criteria			
Availability of financial data	512	284	Lack of financial data (turnover/operational result)
Ratio between stocks and turnover	228	34	Average Stocks/Turnover <5%
Ratio between intangible assets and total assets	194	18	Average Intangible assets/Total assets >3%
Average NCP negative	176	31	Negative average NCP
Qualitative criteria			
Availability of information regarding the activity performed	145	58	Lack of website/The website doesn't work
Independence	87	12	The independence criteria are not met
Comparability between activities and functional profile	75	64	Other functional profile/ Other products
No. of accepted companies	11		

Source: Own processing

Table 3.11 Comparability range—contract manufacturing entity

Range	Average NCP 2017–2019
Minimum	1.70%
Quartile 1	3.06%
Median	4.97%
Quartile 3	6.65%
Maximum	7.64%

Source: Own processing

Therefore, the comparability range is between 3.06% and 6.65% with a median of 4.97%.

Table 3.12 below presents the computation of the NCP obtained in 2019 by Paint Production from the sale of paints to its affiliated entity Paint Distribution.

Given all the above, the NCP obtained by Paint Production from the sale of paints to its affiliated entity Paint Distribution is of 5.33%, being situated within the comparability range (i.e. between 3.06% and 6.65%). Therefore, there could be concluded that the price paid by Paint Distribution to Paint Production complies with the arm's length principle.

Table 3.12 NCP obtained by Paint Production—contract manufacturing entity

Indicator	Row no.	Value (thousand EUR)
Revenues from the sale of paints to Paint Distribution	1	89,000
Expenses with the raw materials	2	60,000
Staff costs	3	15,000
Other production expenses	4	6500
Other operational expenses allocated to the sale of paints to Paint Distribution	5	3000
Total of the operational costs	6=2+3+4+5	84,500
Operational result obtained from the sale of paints to Paint Distribution	7=1−6	4500
NCP	8=7/6	5.33%

Source: Own processing

3.3 Fully-Fledged Manufacturing Entity

This section presents the transfer pricing analysis applicable for a fully-fledged manufacturing entity. The main characteristics of a fully-fledged manufacturing entity were included in Sect. 2.1.5—Functional Analysis.

Step 1: Description of the transaction carried out between affiliated parties and presentation of the economic circumstances in which it takes place

During 2019, Paint Production manufactured paints, owning the necessary technology in this respect and performing research and development activities in order to obtain new products and remain competitive on the market. The company was also involved in advertising activities in order to attract new customers and retain the old ones. In addition to the sales performed to its independent customers, Paint Production also sold paints to its affiliated entity Paint Distribution.

The finished products (i.e. boxes with paints) were sold to Paint Distribution at a price determined based on the total costs incurred by Paint Production in order to manufacture the paints plus a mark-up. In case of a fully-fledged manufacturing entity, the cost base should also include the costs with raw materials and auxiliary materials, but also costs related to the research and development activities performed in order to obtain the products sold to the affiliated entity.

Paint Distribution acquires paints only from Paint Production. The distribution entity sells the goods to third independent clients from the EU market. It is important to note that Paint Production sells paints only to independent customers from the non-EU market and therefore the distribution activity at the level of Group is not doubled. Due to managerial decisions, the distribution of paints on the EU market is performed through Paint Distribution. The flow of the transaction is the same with that presented in Fig. 3.1.

This step should also include a presentation of the conditions and terms under which the related-party transaction is performed, but this presentation is included in the next step of the analysis in order to ensure a clear correlation with the functions performed, risks incurred and assets used by each entity involved in the transaction. The conditions and terms of the related-party transaction should be presented based on the agreements concluded between parties in this respect, but also based on discussions with the relevant staff from the two entities and visits on the production sites.

According to paragraph 3.7 of the OECD Transfer Pricing Guidelines, July 2017 version, the analysis of the competition, industry and regulatory or economic factors that affect the related-party transaction can help in understanding the economic circumstances of that transaction.

Therefore, regarding the economic circumstances in which the related-party transaction took place, there will be supposed that during 2019 no significant trends in the industry were recorded and no competitor or regulatory factors impacted the economic circumstances from the paints market and implicitly the economic circumstances of the analyzed transaction. In practice, this affirmation should be sustained by statistics and industry analyses performed be specialized firms, but considering the purpose of this chapter (i.e. to perform a transfer pricing analysis) we limited our work from this point of view to an assumption.

Step 2: Functional analysis

Table 3.13 below presents the functional analysis related to the above transaction carried out between Paint Production and Paint Distribution, showing the functions performed, risks incurred and assets used by each entity. In relation to each function/risk/asset there were presented the contractual terms and other conditions based on which was concluded that the respective function/risk/asset should be allocated to Paint Production or Paint Distribution.

Considering the above functional analysis, there could be concluded that **Paint Production is a fully-fledged manufacturer, while Paint Distribution is a classic buy-sell distributor.**

The OECD Transfer Pricing Guidelines, July 2017 version recommend that the tested party be the least complex in terms of functional analysis. However, according with paragraph 3.18 "*as a general rule, the tested party is the one to which a transfer pricing method can be applied in the most reliable manner and for which the most reliable comparables can be found*".

Given the purpose of this chapter (i.e. to perform a transfer pricing analysis for the manufacturing entity), there will be considered that even if Paint Distribution is the least complex in terms of functional analysis, it has some problems with the accounting software and due to this is not able to extract the financial information needed to compute the profitability indicator. Therefore, choosing Paint Distribution as the tested party means that the transfer pricing method cannot be applied in the most reliable manner. As a consequence of this, the tested party will be Paint Production.

Table 3.13 Functional analysis—fully-fledged manufacturing entity

Details	Paint Production	Paint Distribution
Functions performed		
Acquisition of raw materials—in the production process, Paint Production uses various raw materials which are acquired by this company from specialized suppliers. The suppliers are chosen by Paint Production based on various criteria and are independent entities (i.e. the suppliers are not part from the group to which Paint Production and Paint Distribution belong).	✓	n/a
Acquisition/production planning—Paint Production performs production planning for the current year based on the sales volume evolutions from the previous years, but also based on the market conditions from the current year. Paint Distribution does not perform any acquisition planning regarding the products acquired from its affiliated entity, this entity acquiring only based on certain orders from its clients.	✓	n/a
Production of paints—The production activity is performed by Paint Production within its own plant. Within Paint Production are obtained water based and solvent based paints. The production process includes the following phases, each phase being performed at different floors from the Paint Production's plant as follows: • in the first phase, different raw materials are taken from the warehouse and put into tubes situated at the most superior floor of the manufacturing site (the fourth floor). The tubes are extend from the fourth floor to the ground floor of the factory; • at the third floor is performed the mixture of raw materials; • at the second floor is obtained the finished product; • at the first floor is performed the packing; • at the ground floor is performed the labelling.	✓	n/a
Ownership of finished products—after the production process and until the sale, Paint Production is the owner of the finished products.	✓	n/a
Research and development activities—Paint Production performs this type of activities in order to obtain new recipes (i.e. mixture formula of raw materials in order to obtain various types of paints).	✓	n/a
Packaging and labelling—Paint Production is responsible for proper labelling and packaging of the finished products, this being performed in its factory.	✓	n/a
Transport of finished products—Paint Distribution is in charge with the transport organization of the goods.	n/a	✓
Quality control—Paint Production performs the quality control of the raw materials used in the manufacturing process and also the quality control of the finished products obtained. In this respect, the entity developed a quality assurance procedure (for e.g. during the production process the employee in charge with the quality control checks if the production recipe is respected, if the labelling is performed in accordance with the product specifications etc.).	✓	n/a

(continued)

Table 3.13 (continued)

Details	Paint Production	Paint Distribution
Warehousing—Paint Production stores raw materials and finished products. The warehousing function is not performed by Paint Distribution as this entity works only based on orders from its clients and the transport is organized so that the goods go directly to the warehouse of the its clients.	✓	n/a
Marketing and advertising—Paint Distribution organizes marketing and promotion campaigns to identify new customers and to promote the products on the non-EU market. This company also participates in various events and fairs. Paint Production is concentrated in performing marketing and advertising activities on the EU market, but some campaigns envisage global clients.	✓	✓
Sales and distribution—in relation to the goods subject to the analyzed transaction, this function is performed by Paint Distribution.	n/a	✓
Risks incurred		
Market risk—is the risk associated with unfavorable business conditions that may result from increased competitiveness, unfavorable market demand, the impossibility to develop markets or the position of products and services at the consumer level. If the number of customers of Paint Distribution decreases, this would negatively affect the turnover of this company. This situation would also affect Paint Production.	✓	✓
Inventory risk—is the risk that a company records stocks of raw materials or finished products on a long period time. This risk also involve the fact that the products become physically or morally degraded, are stolen or exposed to natural disasters. Considering that only Paint Production perform the warehousing function, the inventory risk is incurred by this entity.	✓	n/a
Warranty and product liability risk—this risk is incurred by Paint Production, in its capacity of production entity. More exactly, if during the production process or the quality control process are discovered non-compliant products, the costs related to this situation are borne by Paint Production. In there are discovered non-compliant products after the acceptance by Paint Distribution of the products, the risk and costs are borne by this entity.	✓	✓
Research and development risk—this risk involve the failure of the research activities performed (i.e. to incur costs and not obtain any new products). The risk is incurred by Paint Production.	✓	n/a
Assets used		
Tangible assets (warehousing, buildings, equipment etc.)	✓	✓
Intangible assets (trademarks, patents)	✓	n/a

Source: Own processing
✓—function is performed/risk is incurred/assets are used; n/a—function is not performed/risk is not incurred/assets are not used

Step 3: Selection of the most appropriate transfer pricing method and of the profitability indicator

Regarding the transfer pricing analysis, there could not be used internal comparables, but only external ones. This is due to the fact that even if Paint Production sells similar products to both Paint Distribution and independent entities, the markets (EU markets vs. non-EU market) and the quantities sold are not comparable. In addition, Paint Distribution acquires paints only from Paint Production.

Below are detailed the reasons for accepting/rejecting each of the transfer pricing methods:

- Comparable uncontrolled price ("CUP") method—considering the fact that there is not available public information regarding the prices charged between independent entities for the sale or acquisition of paints products, the CUP method was rejecting. Practically, there is a lack of necessary information in order to apply this method;
- Cost plus method ("CPM") and Resale price method ("RPM")—as it was presented in Sect. 2.1.6—Transfer Pricing Methods, the specialized databases do not contain information related to the expenses' destination and due to this it is impossible to determine the gross mark-up obtained by comparable independent entities. In order to find a solution to this situation, in practice are used net mark-ups. Given all these aspects, both the CPM and RPM were rejected;
- Transactional net margin method ("TNMM")—considering that through this method are compared net mark-ups, TNMM was considered the most suitable in order to check if the price charged by Paint Production to Paint Distribution complies with the arm's length principle. As it was presented in Sect. 2.1.6—Transfer Pricing Methods the TNMM could be applied in a similar approach with both, the CPM and the RPM (the difference being that these two methods compare gross mark-up, while TNMM is operating with net mark-ups). Considering the fact that the tested party is the fully-fledged manufacturing entity (i.e. Paint Production), the **TNMM applied in a similar approach with the CPM was selected** in order to test the compliance with the arm's length principle of the price charged by Paint Production to Paint Distribution. The TNMM applied in a similar approach with RPM was rejected as it would have been applied if the party tested had been Paint Distribution which is a classic buy-sell distributor;
- Profit split method ("PSM")—given that the analyzed transaction does not involve interdependent activities so that a separate analysis of them cannot be performed and the two entities do not make unique contributions to the transaction, the application of the PSM was rejected.

Concluding, the TNMM applied in a similar approach with CPM was considered the most suitable method in order to test the compliance with the arm's length principle of the price charged by Paint Production to its affiliated entity Paint Distribution.

Given the selected method, the profitability indicator used in order to perform the comparability analysis is the net cost plus ("NCP"). This indicator is a net mark-up which is determined based on the following formula:

$$Net\ cost\ plus\ (NCP) = \frac{Operational\ result}{Operational\ costs} * 100$$

The selection of the profitability indicator was performed in accordance with the provisions of the OECD Transfer Pricing Guidelines, July 2017 version (detailed in Sect. 2.1.6—Transfer Pricing Methods). These provisions mention the fact the profitability indicator should be determined as a ratio between the operational result and an indicator which is not impacted by related party transactions (in the case of Paint Production, this indicator being the operational costs).

Step 4: Comparability analysis

The comparability analysis itself involves the comparison of the net mark-up obtained by Paint Production from the paints' sale to Paint Distribution with the net mark-ups recorded by independent comparable entities which are performing similar transactions to that carried out between Paint Production and Paint Distribution.

As was described above, there could not be used internal comparables, but external ones. In this respect, according to paragraph 3.30 from the OECD Transfer Pricing Guidelines, July 2017 version the most reliable source of information may be represented by the commercial databases which include in an electronic format accounts of the companies. Therefore, there was used the Orbis database.

Search strategy applied in order to identify comparable independent companies

In order to identify comparable independent companies there were applied the following categories of criteria:

- criteria applied directly in the Orbis database: in this stage of the search was obtain a sample of potential comparable companies;
- quantitative and qualitative criteria applied: the sample of companies exported from the Orbis database was subject to further analysis by applying manual filters in the Microsoft Excel application. These filters were applied in order to ensure a greater degree of comparability between the independent transactions identified and the analyzed transaction performed between Paint Production and Paint Distribution.

Table 3.14 below presents a detailed description of both categories of criteria (i.e. those applies in the Orbis database and the quantitative and qualitative criteria).

Considering the criteria detailed above, until the identification of the final sample of independent comparables, there were applied four search strategies. The differences between these strategies are represented by the criteria applied in relation to the geographical location and independence indicators from the Orbis database as follows:

Table 3.14 Search strategy—fully-fledged manufacturing entity

Details	Description of the applied criteria
I. Criteria applied in the Orbis database	
1. *Activity status*	
According to paragraph 3.43 from the OECD Transfer Pricing Guidelines, July 2017 version, for the purpose of the comparability analysis companies that are in a special situation (e.g. bankrupted companies etc.) are not appropriate to be considered comparable. Therefore, this criterion was applied to eliminate inactive companies, respectively companies in a special situation. The inclusion of these companies could distort the financial results of the analysis and therefore it is important to exclude them.	There were selected only active companies (i.e. companies which are not in a special situation).
2. *Geographical location*	
Regarding the geographical criterion, even if the OECD Transfer Pricing Guidelines do not provide a preference for a certain hierarchy (e.g. first should be searched local comparables and if these are not identified to extend the search on other regions), it is mentioned that „the requirement to use the most reliable information will usually, but not always, require the use of local comparables over the use of regional comparables where such local comparables are reasonably available" (OECD Transfer Pricing Guidelines, July 2017 version, paragraph 5.46: 242). Moreover, many countries included in their local transfer pricing legislation the requirement to search for comparable transactions on the local market and only if there is not identified a sufficient number of comparables to extend the search on other regions (EU market, European market etc.).	There was considered that Paint Production is a Romanian entity and therefore the search was conducted in the first instance on the Romanian market. However, given that a sufficient number of comparable independent companies was not identified on this market, the search was extended to the European Union market (there was considered that this is the market of products within the analyzed transaction). The OECD Transfer Pricing Guidelines do not include clear provisions regarding the sufficient number of comparable independent companies, but in the practice of many countries this means the identification of minimum five comparables (this number is correlated with the application of the interquartile range as a statistical tool, which requires minimum five values).
3. *Activity code*	
Using the activity code classification, there can be identified companies that undertake similar transactions to that performed between Paint Production and Paint Distribution. To this extent, there have been used the NACE Rev. 2 convention.	There have been selected companies that undertake activities that are classified under the following NACE Rev. code: *2030 "Manufacture of paints, varnishes and similar coatings, printing ink and mastics".*
4. *Independence*	
According to paragraph 3.24 from the OECD Transfer Pricing Guidelines, July 2017 version, "a comparable uncontrolled transaction is a transaction between *two independent* parties that is comparable to the controlled transaction under examination". Given that the scope of the present analysis is to identify independent parties (entities which are not affiliated parties) involved in similar transactions to that performed between Paint Production and Paint Distribution, there were applied certain criteria in this respect. Therefore, this filter was applied to ensure the independence	

(continued)

Table 3.14 (continued)

Details	Description of the applied criteria
of the obtained set of comparable companies, in order to reduce the risk of their financials reflecting significant intra-group activities. It is important to note that the OECD Transfer Pricing Guidelines do not provide details regarding the percentage of ownership applied in order to consider two entities as affiliated. However, considering that in the practice of many countries this percentage is of 25%, for the purpose of the present analysis this one was applied. Thus, different criteria were applied to ensure the independence of the sampled companies, as follows:	
4.1 Independence indicators from the Orbis database	
There were selected from the Orbis database independence indicators "A−", "A" and "A+". This means that the selected companies have known shareholder structure and no shareholder owns more than 25% of the company's stock, either directly or indirectly. Considering the fact that, based on the above strategy, no comparable companies were identified (this is detailed in the below lines), the search was extended by including companies with unknown shareholders structure (independence indicator "U" according to the Orbis database). For this companies, the independence was checked based on the information published by companies on their websites.	
4.2 Shareholders	
Companies in which any shareholder (legal entity or natural person) directly or indirectly holds a percentage of 25% or more than 25% of the shares were rejected.	
4.3 Subsidiaries	
Companies holding 25% or more of a subsidiary have been eliminated.	
4.4 Account Reporting Method	
The selected companies have financial data obtained from unconsolidated reports ("U1" indicator according to Orbis database).	
5. *Period of comparison*	
According with paragraph 3.76 from the OECD Transfer Pricing Guidelines, July 2017 version "*in order to obtain a complete understanding of the facts and circumstances surrounding the controlled transaction, it generally might be useful to examine data from both the year under examination and prior years. The analysis of such information might disclose facts that may have influenced (or should have influenced) the determination of the transfer price*". More exactly, the analysis performed over a longer period yields more reliable results to that performed on financial data associated with only one fiscal year, as this approach better captures the economic climate and other market elements that could potentially have an impact on the profitability of the selected set of comparable companies. As mentioned in Sect. 2.1.7—Comparability Analysis, transfer pricing specialists use an average over the last 3 years.	In order to analyze the conformity of the price charged by Paint Production to Paint Distribution during 2019 (when the analyzed transaction took place) the average of the profitability indicators of comparable companies from the last 3 years for which financial information is available was used, by reporting to the analyzed year. Thus, the financial data of comparable companies from 2017 to 2019 was used.
II. Quantitative criteria	

(continued)

Table 3.14 (continued)

Details	Description of the applied criteria
1. *Availability of financial data*	
This filter was applied to eliminate companies for which there is insufficient available financial data for the purposes of calculating the necessary profitability indicator used in the course of the analysis.	Companies that do not have financial data available for at all of 3-year period taken into account (i.e. 2017–2019) for the purposes of the analysis were eliminated. Specifically, if for a company there was no financial information available for all 3 years from 2017 to 2019, it was removed from the sample.
2. *Ratio between stocks and turnover*	
An important difference between toll manufactures and fully-fledged manufactures is that the toll manufacturer processes materials and raw materials that it does not own. Therefore, toll manufactures usually keep very small stocks, which are not directly related to the production process (i.e. office products, fuels, etc.) or do not keep stocks at all. Therefore, it was considered useful to exclude from the sample producers who record very small stocks, a characteristic specific to toll manufactures. This approach is in line with the OECD Transfer Pricing Guidelines, July 2017 version, paragraph 3.43 which recommend as quantitative criteria the application of criteria related to inventories (in relative or absolute value).	Therefore, in order to exclude from the sample companies with a functional profile of toll manufacturer, those companies whose ratio between the level of stocks and the turnover is lower than 5% were excluded. As mentioned above, within the criterion regarding the period of comparison, the profitability indicators are computed as an average of the financial data from 2017 to 2019. Given this, when applying the criterion related to the ratio between stocks and turnover an average of data from 2017 to 2019 was also used. Regarding the threshold of 5%, this should be established based on the financial data of the tested party. Therefore, there was considered that the ratio between stocks and turnover of Paint Production is greater than 5%.
3. *Ratio between intangible assets and total assets*	
Fully-fledged manufactures own important intangible assets that are necessarily specific to the production process. In practice, this means that fully-fledged manufactures have valuable intangible assets, such as know-how, patents or licenses. Therefore, it was considered useful to exclude from the sample producers who record a small level of the ratio between intangible assets and total assets, a characteristic which is not specific to fully-fledged manufactures. This approach is in line with the OECD Transfer Pricing Guidelines, July 2017 version, paragraph 3.43 which recommend as quantitative criteria the application of intangible related criteria. Within this paragraph is mentioned that these criteria *"may be used for instance to exclude companies with valuable intangibles or significant R&D activities when the tested party does not use valuable intangible assets nor participate in significant R&D activities"*.	In this step, companies whose ratio between intangible assets and total assets is lower than 3% were excluded. As mentioned above, within the criterion regarding the period of comparison, the profitability indicators are computed as an average of the financial data from 2017 to 2019. Given this, when applying the criterion related to the ratio between intangible assets and total assets an average of data from 2017 to 2019 was also used. Regarding the threshold of 3%, this should be established based on the financial data of the tested party. Therefore, there was considered that the ratio between intangible assets and total assets of Paint Production is higher than 3%.
4. *Average NCP negative*	

(continued)

Table 3.14 (continued)

Details	Description of the applied criteria
According to paragraph 3.63 from the OECD Transfer Pricing Guidelines, July 2017 version *"Extreme results might consist of losses or unusually high profits. Extreme results can affect the financial indicators that are looked at in the chosen method"*.	Based on this criteria there were eliminated companies that recorded a negative value of the average NCP.
III. Qualitative criteria	
1. *Availability of information regarding the activity performed*	
The purpose of this filter is to ensure the availability of sufficient information on the basis of which to select the final set of comparable companies. More exactly, in this stage of the study there is accessed the website of the companies from the sample in order to analyze its activities and other relevant information.	Companies for which there is not enough public data to analyze their activity have been eliminated. Specifically, companies that did not have an official website or had the site under construction at the time of the search (August–September 2021) were removed from the sample. Also, companies whose site did not provide sufficient information to analyze whether or not those companies are comparable to the tested party were eliminated.
2. *Independence*	
This filter is applied to ensure the independence of the selected companies, in order to eliminate the risk of their financials being impacted by intra-group activities.	Companies that are part of a group according to the website were eliminated.
3. *Comparability between activities and functional profile*	
This filter is applied to ensure the comparability of the selected companies to the tested entity with respect to their activity and functional profile. Practically, for each company remained in the sample until this stage is analyzed the information published on its official website in order to determine which is the main activity performed and the related functional profile. It is important to note that applying the TNMM there is necessary a high degree of comparison between the functional profiles, the type of products manufactured not being necessary to be identical. In relation to the products, these should have similar characteristics in order to be included in the same category of products.	For companies that were not removed from the sample by this stage of the search, a detailed analysis of the information published on their websites was performed and those companies with significant differences with respect to their type of activity or functional profile from those of the tested entity (i.e. Paint Production) were eliminated.

Source: Own processing

- The first search strategy was applied on the Romanian market, using as independence indicators from the Orbis database "A−", "A" and "A+";
- The second search strategy was applied on the EU market, using as independence indicators from the Orbis database "A−", "A" and "A+";

Table 3.15 Results regarding the second search strategy—fully-fledged manufacturing entity

Criteria applied	No. of checked companies	No. of rejected companies	Rejection reason according to Appendix C
Initial sample (obtained after the application of the criteria in Orbis database)	37	n/a	
Quantitative criteria			
Availability of financial data	37	10	Lack of financial data (turnover/operational result)
Ratio between stocks and turnover	27	3	Average Stocks/Turnover <5%
Ratio between intangible assets and total assets	24	19	Average Intangible assets/Total assets <3%
Average NCP negative	5	1	Negative average NCP
Qualitative criteria			
Availability of information regarding the activity performed	4	1	Lack of website/The website doesn't work
Independence	3	1	The independence criteria are not met
Comparability between activities and functional profile	2	1	Other functional profile/Other products
No. of accepted companies	1		

Source: Own processing

- The third search strategy was applied on the Romanian market, using as independence indicators from the Orbis database "A−", "A", "A+" and "U";
- The fourth search strategy was applied on the EU market, using as independence indicators from the Orbis database "A−", "A", "A+" and "U".

Results obtained applying the first search strategy (Romanian market, independence indicators "A−", "A", "A+")

After the application of the first category criteria (i.e. criteria applied in the Orbis database), there was not obtained any company in the sample. Given this, the search was further expanded on the EU market.

This result, together with the criteria applied in the Orbis database can be observed in Appendix A.

Results obtained applying the second search strategy (EU market, independence indicators "A−", "A", "A+")

As could been observed in Appendix B, after the application of the first category criteria (i.e. criteria applied in the Orbis database), there was obtained a sample of 37 companies. Subsequently, on this sample there were applied the quantitative and qualitative criteria, this resulting in only one independent comparable company.

Table 3.16 Results regarding the fourth search strategy—fully-fledged manufacturing entity

Criteria applied	No. of checked companies	No. of rejected companies	Rejection reason according to Appendix C
Initial sample (obtained after the application of the criteria in Orbis database)	512	n/a	
Quantitative criteria			
Availability of financial data	512	284	Lack of financial data (turnover/operational result)
Ratio between stocks and turnover	228	33	Average Stocks/Turn-over <5%
Ratio between intangible assets and total assets	195	173	Average Intangible assets/Total assets <3%
Average NCP negative	22	6	Negative average NCP
Qualitative criteria			
Availability of information regarding the activity performed	16	5	Lack of website/The website doesn't work
Independence	11	3	The independence criteria are not met
Comparability between activities and functional profile	8	3	Other functional profile/ Other products
No. of accepted companies	5		

Source: Own processing

Table 3.15 below shows the number of companies eliminated after the application of each quantitative and qualitative criteria. The information included in this table is detailed at the level of each company in Appendix C.

Considering that the identification of only one independent comparable company is not sufficient in order to compute a comparability range of profitability indicators, the search strategy was further expanded by including "U" as an independence indicator.

Results obtained applying the third search strategy (Romanian market, independence indicators "A−", "A", "A+", "U")

After the application of the first category criteria (i.e. criteria applied in the Orbis database), there was obtained only one company in the sample. Given this, the search was further expanded on the EU market.

This result, together with the criteria applied in the Orbis database can be observed in Appendix D.

Results obtained applying the fourth search strategy (EU market, independence indicators "A−", "A", "A+", "U")

As could been observed in Appendix E, after the application of the first category criteria (i.e. criteria applied in the Orbis database), there was obtained a sample of

Table 3.17 Comparability range—fully-fledged manufacturing entity

Range	Average NCP 2017–2019
Minimum	2.91%
Quartile 1	4.17%
Median	5.10%
Quartile 3	10.07%
Maximum	19.64%

Source: Own processing

512 companies. Subsequently, on this sample there were applied the quantitative and qualitative criteria, this resulting in a final sample of five independent comparable companies. Table 3.16 below shows the number of companies eliminated after the application of each quantitative and qualitative criteria. The information included in this table is detailed at the level of each company in Appendix C.

For each of the five companies there was computed an average profitability indicator for the period 2017–2019. As was already detailed above, the selected profitability indicator is NCP, determine based on the following formula:

$$Net\ cost\ plus\ (NCP) = \frac{Operational\ result}{Operational\ costs} * 100$$

The average NCP indicator, computed for each of the five companies is included in Appendix C.

Comparability range

Based on the average NCP computed for each of the five companies for the period 2017–2019, there was determined the comparability range. In this respect, there was used the "quartile" function of the Microsoft Excel application. Table 3.17 presents the comparability range obtained.

Conclusions of the comparability analysis

According to the OECD Transfer Pricing Guidelines recommendations, the minimum and the maximum values should be excluded from the comparability range. Therefore, the comparability range is between 4.17% and 10.07% with a median of 5.10%.

Table 3.18 below presents the computation of the NCP obtained in 2019 by Paint Production from the sale of paints to its affiliated entity Paint Distribution.

Given all the above, the NCP obtained by Paint Production from the sale of paints to its affiliated entity Paint Distribution is of 7.53%, being situated within the comparability range (i.e. between 4.17% and 10.07%). Therefore, there could be concluded that the price paid by Paint Distribution to Paint Production complies with the arm's length principle.

Table 3.18 NCP obtained by Paint Production—fully-fledged manufacturing entity

Indicator	Row no.	Value (thousand EUR)
Revenues from the sale of paints to Paint Distribution	1	100,000
Expenses with the raw materials	2	65,000
Staff costs	3	24,000
Other production expenses	4	3000
Other operational expenses allocated to the sale of paints to Paint Distribution	5	1000
Total of the operational costs	6=2+3+4+5	93,000
Operational result obtained from the sale of paints to Paint Distribution	7=1−6	7000
NCP	8=7/6	7.53%

Source: Own processing

3.4 Conclusions Regarding the Differences Among the Analyses

Considering the transfer pricing analyses detailed within this chapter and particularized for each type of manufacturer, there have been identified several differences among these analyses as they are presented below.

A. *Differences regarding the functional analysis*

Differences which represent the particularities of the functional analysis, specific to each type of manufacturer are summarized in Table 3.19 below.

The most complex functional profile is that of the fully-fledged manufacturer, while the toll manufacturer has the simplest functional profile.

B. *Differences regarding the criteria applied in the search strategy*

In order to reflect the particularities of each type of manufacturer and identify independent comparable companies, there were applied certain search strategies. The differences related to the search strategy are met at the level of the quantitative criteria as it is presented in Table 3.20 below.

Through these criteria are reflected in fact the particularities of the functional analysis as follows:

- The toll manufacturing entity does not own stocks of raw materials (as it performs only the consignment of them in the benefit of the affiliated entity) or finished products (as it does not have the ownership over the finished products). Therefore, this type of manufacturer should register a low value of stocks. Moreover, the toll manufacturing entity does not own production related intangible assets and therefore the level of these assets should be very low reported to the total value of the assets;

Table 3.19 Differences regarding the functional analysis

Manufacturer			
Functions/risks/assets	Toll manufacturer	Contract manufacturer	Fully-fledged manufacturer
Functions performed			
Acquisition of raw materials	n/a	✓	✓
Consignment of raw materials	✓	n/a	n/a
Acquisition/production planning	✓	✓	✓
Production of paints	✓	✓	✓
Ownership of finished products	n/a	✓	✓
Function regarding the production technology/ Research and development activities	n/a	n/a	✓
Packaging and labelling	✓	✓	✓
Transport of finished products	n/a	n/a	n/a
Quality control	✓	✓	✓
Warehousing	✓	✓	✓
Marketing and advertising	n/a	n/a	✓
Risks incurred			
Market risk	n/a	n/a	✓
Inventory risk	n/a	✓	✓
Warranty and product liability risk	n/a	✓	✓
Research and development risk	n/a	n/a	✓
Assets used			
Tangible assets (warehousing, buildings, equipment etc.)	✓	✓	✓
Intangible assets related to production (e.g. manufacturing recipes, patents)	n/a	n/a	✓

Source: Own processing

Table 3.20 Differences regarding the quantitative criteria

Quantitative criteria	Toll manufacturer	Contract manufacturer	Fully-fledged manufacturer
Ratio between stocks and turnover	<5%	>5%	>5%
Ratio between intangible assets and total assets	<3%	<3%	>3%

Source: Own processing

- The contract manufacturing entity owns stocks of raw materials (as it performs the acquisition of the raw materials needed in the production process) and finished products (as it has the ownership over the finished products). Therefore, this type of manufacturer should not register a low value of stocks. Moreover, the contract manufacturing entity does not own production related intangible assets and therefore the level of these assets should be very low reported to the total value of the assets;

Table 3.21 Differences regarding the comparability range

Range	Toll manufacturer	Contract manufacturer	Fully-fledged manufacturer
Quartile 1	2.94%	3.06%	4.17%
Median	3.83%	4.97%	5.10%
Quartile 3	3.91%	6.65%	10.07%

Source: Own processing

- The fully-fledged manufacturing entity owns stocks of raw materials (as it performs the acquisition of the raw materials needed in the production process) and finished products (as it has the ownership over the finished products). Therefore, this type of manufacturer should not register a low value of stocks. Moreover, the fully—fledged manufacturing entity owns important production related intangible assets and therefore the level of these assets should not be low reported to the total value of the assets.

C. *Differences regarding the comparability range*

After the performance of the comparability analysis, for each type of manufacturer there was obtained the comparability range summarized in Table 3.21 below.

As can be observed from the above table, the range increases gradually from the toll manufacturer until the fully-fledged manufacturer, this meaning that the profitability indicator specific to a category of manufacturer reflects the complexity of the functional analysis of that manufacturer.

Given this, through the analyses performed within this chapter it is confirmed the affirmation of Radolovic (2012) who considers that remuneration should reflect the functions performed, the risks incurred and the assets used by each company (i.e. the profit made by a contract manufacturer should be higher than the profit made by a toll manufacturer, and the profit made by a fully-fledged manufacturer should be higher than the profit made by a contract manufacturer).

References

Journals and Articles

Radolovic, J. (2012). Transfer pricing model based on multiple-factor transfer pricing model using the transactional net margin method. *Ekonomska Istrazivanja-Economic Research, 25*(1), 34–50.

Online Publications

Deloitte. (2014). *Transfer pricing industry guide*. International Tax Review. Accessed July 2021, from us-tax-tp-industry-guide-2014.pdf (deloitte.com)

OECD. (2017). *OECD transfer pricing guidelines for multinational enterprises and tax administrations 2017*. OECD. Accessed August 2021, from https://doi.org/10.1787/tpg-2017-en

Chapter 4
Recent Disputes from the Manufacturing Industry Regarding the Transfer Pricing Analysis

This chapter presents some recent disputes between manufacturing entities and tax authorities in relation to the transfer pricing analysis for manufacturing transactions. There are outlined the issues identified in each dispute. The scope is to help the readers avoid making the same errors when preparing a transfer pricing analysis.

Disputed are identified using databases such as TPcases or Bloombergtax, the chapter including a description of each selected dispute (summary of facts), the position of the tax authorities, the position of the taxpayer and the conclusions regarding the Court decision. Practically, based on this information, there is emphasized which position was the correct one (that of the taxpayer or that of the tax administration).

TPcases is an online database which contains international tax avoidance and transfer pricing case laws, being available free of charge to readers. The case laws available on this database are those published by tax authorities and local courts. Bloombergtax contains only summaries of the case laws, while TPcases includes full documents in relation to the case.

Therefore, the first five cases from this chapter are presented based on the detailed information from the documents published in TPcases, while the last two cases include only succinct information based on the summaries from Bloombergtax (i.e. https://news.bloombergtax.com/daily-tax-report/transfer-pricing-cases-of-2020-case-summaries).

When selecting the case laws from the TPcases certain criteria could be applied (the subject of the dispute: transfer pricing method, arm's length range etc.; keyword: contract manufacturing, manufacturing processes etc.). However, there was necessary a manual review of the case laws in order to identify those cases that envisage manufacturing transactions. Moreover, in most of the cases laws published on TPcases the name of the entities involved is not disclosed, there being used certain shortcuts.

I. Ignat, L. Ionescu-Feleagă, *Transfer Pricing in Manufacturing*, Contributions to Finance and Accounting, https://doi.org/10.1007/978-3-030-93889-5_4

4.1 Case No. SKM2020.224.VLR

Summary of facts

Icemachine Manufacturer A/S is a company, part of a Group which deals with processing and packaging solutions. The main activity of Icemachine Manufacturer A/S is represented by the manufacturing of production facilities dedicated for the packaging and production of different types of ice cream. The company distributes its products (i.e. ice machines) mainly through the sales companies from the Group (i.e. through affiliated entities). Through the sales companies, Icemachine Manufacturer A/S has a presence in more than 165 countries. The sales companies are responsible for the contact with customers and potential customers.

On 17 September 2010, further to a tax audit, Icemachine Manufacturer A/S submitted to the Danish Tax Agency ("SKAT") the transfer pricing documentation, covering the period 2005–2009. This documentation contained a description of the Group, a description of the company, a presentation of the market on which the company operates, a functional analysis and a transfer pricing analysis. Based on the functional analysis, Icemachine Manufacturer A/S is responsible for the research and development activities, performs the product strategy, assumes all the inventory and production risks and owns all the intellectual property rights. Therefore, Icemachine Manufacturer A/S is considered a fully-fledged manufacturing entity.

The main transaction covered by the transfer pricing file was the sale of products from Icemachine Manufacturer A/S to the sales companies. Regarding the transfer pricing analysis of this transaction, the company tested the sales companies and applied the RPM. No comparability analysis (i.e. benchmark study) was performed within the transfer pricing file. More exactly, the company presented a computation of the profitability indicator obtained by the sales companies, for this computation including all the revenues and expenses from the sale companies (and not only those related to the transaction performed with Icemachine Manufacturer A/S). Further on, without any documentation or analysis, the company concluded that the profitability indicator obtained by the sales companies is a normal one.

The position of the tax authorities

SKAT did not find the transfer pricing documentation as being adequate. Given this, SKAT considered that the company submitted a defective documentation and in this context SKAT performed estimations regarding the company's controlled transactions (i.e. the intra-group transactions regarding the sale of ice machines to the sales companies). SKAT increased the Icemachine Manufacturer A/S's taxable income by a total of DKK 353,384,000.

SKAT considered defective the transfer pricing documentation based on the following concerns:

- The company did not document the transfer pricing policy applied in relation to the sales companies;

- The transfer pricing documentation did not contain any comparability analysis and in this context, for the SKAT was not clear on what basis the company concluded that the prices practiced with the sales entities are at market level;
- The profitability indicator of the sales companies was computed considering also the transactions performed by these companies with other group entities and third parties. When performing the computation of the profitability indicator, this computation should include only figures related to the analyzed transaction. Therefore, SKAT considered that the profitability indicator obtained by each of the sales companies should include only figures from the transaction with Icemachine Manufacturer A/S. SKAT did not receive sufficient information in order to perform by itself this computation;
- The production company (i.e. Icemachine Manufacturer A/S) which performs the key functions and incurs the most important risks obtained a significantly lower profit than that obtained by the sales companies whose main activity consist in outreach sales work and issuance of invoices;
- Icemachine Manufacturer A/S recorded losses for at least 10 years, SKAT considering that these losses are the result of the fact that Icemachine Manufacturer A/S was not remunerated based on arm's length terms. Moreover, SKAT considered that an independent third party would not accept to do a business which generates consecutive losses. SKAT affirmed that Icemachine Manufacturer A/S continued the business as this generates benefits at the level of the sales companies, respectively the Group parent;
- The transfer pricing documentation does not include:
  - a complete legal structure of the Group;
  - the revenues and operating profit of the sales companies with which Icemachine Manufacturer A/S performed the intra-group transactions;
  - the value of the related party transactions performed by Icemachine Manufacturer A/S during 2005–2007;
  - a justification regarding the reasons for choosing the transfer pricing method applied and the tested party.

Considering all the above, SKAT performed its own comparability analysis using the Amadeus database, testing Icemachine Manufacturer A/S (due to the fact that the least complex part, i.e. the sales companies, did not present the necessary information for the computation of the profitability indicator), selecting NCP as the profitability indicator and applying the TNMM in a similar approach with CPM. Based on the benchmark study performed, SKAT obtained a range spanning from 3.70% to 9.02%, with a median of 6.04%.

The NCP computed by SKAT for Icemachine Manufacturer A/S for the period 2005–2009 was as follows: −9.2%; −12.5%; −10.7%; −26.1%; −21.7%. Therefore, SKAT concluded that the price received by Icemachine Manufacturer A/S from the sales companies does not comply with the arm's length principle and performed transfer pricing adjustments, bringing for each year from the period 2005–2009 the NCP of Icemachine Manufacturer A/S to the median of 6.04%.

The position of taxpayer

The Icemachine Manufacturer A/S's representative had submitted a claim that stipulated that there should not be an increase of the taxable income for the period 2005–2009. The company did not agree with the SKAT's approach invoking the following reasons:

- the company considered that it documented and justified its losses. Moreover, the company showed that it recorded profit in 2011 and considered that this profit means in fact that the losses from the previous period is due to business factors (e.g. complex product portfolio, quality issues with the product lines, failure of research and development activities) and not to the related-party transactions performed;
- the SKAT tested the manufacturing entity and not the sales companies. In this regard Icemachine Manufacturer A/S considered that this approach is contrary to the transfer pricing principle, as the manufacturer is the most complex party;
- the company considered that the benchmark performed by SKAT does not include in the final sample companies comparable from the activity and independence criteria point of view;
- Icemachine Manufacturer A/S documented that an increase of its taxable income with DKK 353,384,000 would determine in the sales companies a profit margin of −3.36% (this situation not being accepted by any independent sales company);
- the company provided SKAT with the additional documents requested and in this context considered the transfer pricing documentation as being complete.

Court decision

The Court decision was issued by the Danish Western High Court on 8 June 2020 and provides the following conclusions in relation to case no. SKM2020.224.VLR:

- in lack of sufficient information SKAT cannot select as tested party the sales companies. Therefore, the High Court agrees with the approach of SKAT in selecting Icemachine Manufacturer A/S as the tested party and applying TNMM in a similar approach with CPM;
- in relation to the benchmark performed by SKAT, the Court considered the companies from the sample as comparables from the functional profile point of view. The Court eliminated one company from the sample due to the independence criterion. This resulted in a median of the comparability range of 4.42% and an increase of the taxable income of DKK 324,925,000 (instead of DKK 353,384,000);
- the Court considered that the company did not prove that the SKAT's estimation is not in accordance with the arm's length principle. Therefore, the Court rejected the computation presented by Icemachine Manufacturer A/S in order to show that the sales companies would obtain a negative profit margin as a consequences of SKAT's estimation. This is due to the fact that the computation presented by Icemachine Manufacturer A/S is based on both figures from intra-group transactions and from transaction with independent parties. Therefore, there is not

possible to asses if the sales companies obtained a negative profit margin from the transactions performed with Icemachine ManufactureR A/S;

- the Court considered that Icemachine Manufacturer A/S did not present any extraordinary circumstances to justify its losses;
- the Court also considered that the transfer pricing documentation is deficient and it does not provide the tax authorities with the necessary information in order to asses if the intra-group transactions comply with the arm's length principle. Therefore, SKAT were entitled to perform estimations.

Concluding, the Court decided that the position of the tax authorities is a correct one.

Final remarks
Given the transfer pricing case presented above, there have been observed the following aspects:

- **continued losses**—the taxpayer did not justify its continues losses, having from this point of view an inadequate transfer pricing documentation. Therefore, it is important to take into consideration the provisions of the OECD Transfer Pricing Guidelines applicable in this respect;
- **selection of the tested party**—in lack of sufficient and relevant information needed in order to test the party with the least complex functional profile, the tested party could be the other party involved in the transaction. This approach was already accepted by the Court and is in accordance with the OECD Transfer Pricing Guidelines;
- **selection of the transfer pricing method**—in the transfer pricing file should be presented reasons for accepting or rejecting a certain method, showing that the selected method provided the most reliable results;
- **independence criterion applied in the benchmark study**—the tax authorities usually pay a big attention to this criterion. Therefore, when preparing a benchmark study it is important to be able to justify based on different proofs (e.g. print screens from Amadeus or companies' websites) that the companies from the sample are independent ones;
- **structure of the transfer pricing file**—when preparing a transfer pricing file it is important to check the local transfer pricing legislation applicable in the country for which the transfer pricing documentation is prepared and to try to cover all the information requested in terms of documentation structure.

The documents based on which was presented the above information can be found at the following link: https://tpcases.com/denmark-vs-icemachine-manufacturer-a-s-june-2020-high-court-case-no-skm2020-224-vlr/.

4.2 Case No. KHO:2020:34

Summary of facts

A Oy operates as a sales and marketing company for a Finnish Group. During 2003–2011, excepting 2008, A Oy recorded losses while the overall activity of the Group was a profitable one.

The main activity of A Oy is represented by the acquisition of products (i.e. office supplies) from the contract manufactures belonging to the Group and the sale of these products to independent customers.

In the transfer pricing file, A Oy analyzed the transfer prices applied within the intra-group transaction performed (i.e. acquisition of goods from the contract manufactures) choosing the contract manufacturers as the tested parties, applying TNMM and performing a benchmark study.

The period of dispute with the tax authorities covers the years from 2007 to 2010.

The position of the tax authorities

When processing the tax return submitted by A Oy for 2010, the tax authorities considered that the A Oy case should be further investigated as the company recorded continued losses for several years. Based on their investigations, the tax authorities concluded that the profitability of A Oy is far below the profitability recorded by independent entities performing similar activities.

Going further, the tax authorities analyzed the transfer pricing file of A Oy and considered that the tested party should be A Oy instead of the contract manufactures. The tax authorities justified this opinion through the fact that the A Oy's continued losses should be considered and testing the manufactures would not reflect the situation of A Oy. Therefore, the tax authorities performed its own transfer pricing analysis testing A Oy, applying TNMM and performing two benchmark studies (first for the period 2006–2008 and the second one for the period 2007–2009). Based on the benchmark studies performed, the tax authorities obtained a comparability range between 1.75% and 3.68% (with a median of 2.97%), respectively between 1.82% and 2.79% (with a median of 2.69%).

Given all the above, the tax authorities performed transfer pricing adjustments which lead to the increasing of the taxable income at the level of A Oy.

The position of taxpayer

A Oy maintained its position from the transfer pricing file regarding the selection of the contract manufactures as the tested parties and appealed to the Tax Adjustment Board which rejected the claim of the company.

Further on, A Oy requested to the Administrative Court the annulment of the decisions issued by the Corporate Tax Office (i.e. the tax administration) and the Tax Adjustment Board. In this regard, A Oy justified its continued losses from 2007 to 2010 through business reasons (e.g. the market price pressure which determined the sale of products to a lower margin; the decision to increase the prices which leads to a decrease in the sales volume; the loose of a product representation etc.). Moreover, A Oy sustained that it operates as a full-risk sales company.

The appeal was also rejected by the Administrative Court and A Oy proceeded to the Supreme Administrative Court. Below are detailed the decision of these two courts.

Court decision
Administrative Court

The Administrative Court considered that the functions performed and risks incurred by A Oy are common to an entity that is engaged in the distribution of goods (i.e. the Administrative Court did not considered A Oy as a full-risk sales company). Based on this, the Administrative Court decided that the tested party should not be the manufacturing entities, but A Oy.

Moreover, the Administrative Court considered that the reasons invoked by A Oy for the continued losses are situations met also by other entities that operate in the same industry and these do not represent business reasons for long-term losses.

In conclusion, the Administrative Court decided that the approach of the tax authorities is a correct one and rejected the appeal of A Oy.

Supreme Administrative Court

The Supreme Administrative Court performed a deeply analysis of the OECD Transfer Pricing Guidelines provisions related to continued losses and noted that there is stipulated the fact that continuous loss-making is not a reason to perform transfer pricing adjustments, but it is a reason to check if the related party transactions comply with the arm's length principle. Moreover, the Supreme Administrative Court found that the losses recorded by A Oy are justified by the business reasons.

Further on, the Supreme Court investigated who should be the tested party. In this respect, there was performed a comparison between the functions performed, risks incurred and assets used by each party and concluded that the functional profile of the manufacturing entities is simpler compared with that of A Oy. Therefore, the Supreme Administrative Court considered that the contract manufacturing entities should be the tested parties instead of A Oy.

The Supreme Administrative Court noted that within the transfer pricing documentation A Oy selected the manufactures as tested parties and concluded that the transactions comply with the arm's length principle. The tax authorities did not contest the comparability between the companies from the sample presented in the transfer pricing file and the activities carried out by the manufacturing entities. Given this, the Supreme Administrative Court approved the appeal of A Oy and rejected the transfer pricing adjustments performed by the tax authorities. The decision of the Supreme Administrative Court was issued in April 2020.

Final remarks
Given the transfer pricing case presented above, there have been observed the following aspects:

- **continued losses**—the taxpayer succeeded to sustain its continued losses through an unsuccessful business strategy. Through this case it is clarified the fact that continued losses do not represent a reason for the transfer pricing adjustments performed by the tax authorities. Therefore, in this context it is important for companies to have a solid justification (based on proofs) in relation to the losses recorded;

- **selection of the tested party**—when preparing a transfer pricing analysis, a significant attention should be paid to the functional analysis as based on this is chosen the tested party. Therefore, it is important for the taxpayer to be able to show in the transfer pricing file which party has the least complex functional profile;
- **selection of the transfer pricing method**—in the transfer pricing file should be presented reasons for accepting or rejecting a certain method, showing that the selected method provided the most reliable results.

The documents based on which was presented the above information can be found at the following link: https://tpcases.com/finland-vs-a-oy-april-2020-supreme-administrative-court-case-no-kho202034/.

4.3 Case No. SKM2018.173.LSR

Summary of facts

H1 A/S is the Danish parent company of the Group. In 2006, H1 A/S set up a production entity Land Y1 in order to expand its production capacity, to have a lower production cost and to be closer to various markets (reducing in this way also the freight costs).

At the request of SKAT, H1 A/S submitted the transfer pricing file covering the period 2009–2012. The analysis of SKAT was concentrated only on the transaction performed by H1 A/S with its affiliated entity Land Y1 (i.e. acquisition of goods). According with the transfer pricing file, Land Y1 manufactures goods only for H1 A/S.

Regarding the functional analysis, Land Y1 performs the production, the process control (based on guidelines provided by H1 A/S) and the bookkeeping, owning the tangible assets necessary in the production process as well as the raw materials and the finished goods. Therefore, Land Y1 is considered a contract manufacturer.

For the period 2010–2012 H1 A/S entered into a unilateral advance price agreement with the tax authorities from the country in which Land Y1 operates. Based on this agreement the price between H1 A/S and Land Y1 should be based on the TNMM, selecting as a profitability indicator the return on invested capital on capital employed ("ROCE"), computed as a ratio between the operating profit (EBIT) and the assets. Based on the benchmark study performed in the context of the advanced pricing agreement the interquartile range for ROCE is between 6.59% and 14.36% with a median of 9.09%. Therefore, in the period 2010–2012 Land Y1 charged H1 A/S for the sale of goods adding a mark-up so to obtain a ROCE of 9.1%. Quarterly and year-end adjustments (credit note/invoice) are performed in order to assure that the realized ROCE is that stipulated within the advance price agreement. Given all these, in the transfer pricing documentation was concluded that the remuneration received by Land Y1 from H1 A/S complies with the arm's length principle.

The position of the tax authorities

SKAT performed its own transfer pricing analysis considering the value chain related to the production process. Based on this, SKAT concluded that H1 A/S controls the production process being in charge with the development of products, production planning, quality control, marketing and sales and owning all the related intangible assets. Land Y1 produces only for H1 A/S, acting as a contract manufacturer.

After analyzing the advance price agreement, SKAT did not agree with the tax authorities from the country in which Land Y1 operates, considering that ROCE cannot be used as a profit level indicator. SKAT justified this opinion affirming that assets are calculated at book value and this aspect can affect the comparability within the benchmark study as companies depreciate their assets using various methods and periods. Based on the provisions of the OECD Transfer Pricing Guidelines SKAT considered that a profitability indicator based on total costs would be more relevant. Further on, SKAT computed based on the benchmark study from the advance price agreement the profitability indicator for the companies from the sample using in this respect the total costs instead of the assets.

SKAT notes that the profitability of the companies in the benchmark, which cover the years 2010–2012, measured by the new profitability indicator, shows a significantly lower spread than when measured by ROCE (this meaning that Land Y1 should obtain a smaller profitability indicator). Therefore, SKAT performed transfer pricing adjustments, increasing the taxable income of H1 A/S.

The position of taxpayer

H1 A/S appealed the SKAT's decision. H1 A/S showed that after the SKAT's adjustments, the return on invested capital obtained by Land Y1 would be between 2% and 4.1%. According to H1 A/S there should be considered what an independent company from the country in which Land Y1 operates will be demand in return for the same investments. H1 A/S describes that an independent third party will demand a return equal to the risk-free interest rate plus a risk premium that compensates for the risk that he assumes. Further on, H1 A/S compared the return on the invested capital obtained by Land Y1 with the effective interest rate and government bonds from the Land Y1's country (i.e. with the risk free rate). This analysis showed that SKAT's adjustments and the method used mean that Land Y1 achieves a return that in all years, except 2012, is lower than the risk-free interest rate. Therefore, H1 A/S concluded that an independent third-party investor would never make such an investment that yields a return below the risk-free interest rate. Based on this, H1 A/S considered that the adjustments performed by SKAT are not in accordance with the arm's length principle.

H1 A/S has subsequently calculated what the profitability indicator should be in Land Y1 to provide a return on invested capital that reflects the risk-free interest rate plus a risk premium and concluded that the increase in its taxable income should be at least reduced.

Moreover, H1 A/S considered that the rejection of ROCE by SKAT does not take into account the reinvestments in the assets of the selected comparables. H1 A/S has also stated that SKAT's use of a profitability indicator that uses the total costs also requires reliable statements of income, costs, assets and liabilities. The recognized costs thus also depend on applied accounting policies and accounting estimates.

Court decision

The National Tax Court agreed with SKAT that the differences in the depreciation periods may distort the basis of comparison.

The National Tax Court also finds that SKAT's method used is in accordance with the arm's length principle. The National Tax Tribunal does not find that the OECD Transfer Pricing Guidelines provide evidence for a methodological approach for pricing current controlled transactions of goods or services based on assessments of return requirements for financial investments. The pricing of continuously controlled transactions of goods or services must be based on a comparability analysis of similar transactions between independent companies in relation to the relevant comparability indicators.

On that basis, the National Tax Court finds that SKAT's approach is in accordance with the arm's length principle and SKAT's decision is therefore upheld.

Final remarks

Based on the above case, there could be concluded the following two main aspects:

- an unilateral **advance price agreement** is useful only in the country part of the agreement, in the other country existing the possibility that the tax authorities do not agree with the provisions of the agreement;
- when testing a contract manufacturing entity an important step is represented by the **selection of the profit level indicator**. In most of the cases, the most suitable profit level indicator applicable in this situation is NCP.

The documents based on which was presented the above information can be found at the following link: https://tpcases.com/denmark-vs-contract-manufacturing-hq-a-s-april-2018-tax-tribunal-case-no-skm2018-173-lsr/.

4.4 Case No. 5 Afs 194/2015 – 34

Summary of facts

The taxpayer subject to the tax audit is a Czech toll manufacturing entity, the products manufactured being cables. Its related party transaction consists in the provision of manufacturing services for its affiliated entity from Germany.

This transaction was analyzed by the taxpayer within the transfer pricing file. The price methodology applied by the taxpayer in order to charge its related party is based on a cost plus mark-up method. The costs used in this respect are based on a budget, with no year-end adjustments. During 2008, the taxpayer recorded a loss from its operational activity (due to a low utilization of the production capacity generated by the market conditions), this loss being the principal subject of disputes with the tax authorities.

The position of the tax authorities

The tax authorities considered that the loss recorded by the taxpayer due to a lower production capacity is translated in the fact that the taxpayer was not able to absorb the fixed production costs in the price charged to its related party. Considering the functional profile of the taxpayer, the tax authorities considered that the loss is generated by an incorrect setting of prices in relation to the affiliated entity.

Moreover, the tax authorities noted that similar independent entities did not record losses during 2008 and in this context performed their own benchmark, testing the taxpayer and applying the TNMM. Based on the results of this benchmark, the tax authorities performed transfer pricing adjustments, using in this respect the minimum value from the comparability range obtained.

The position of taxpayer

The Czech manufacturing entity sustained that the loss was a result of market conditions and appealed the decision of the tax authorities. More exactly, the taxpayer sustained that the loss is the result of the production volume decrease and not the result of setting incorrectly the prices.

Moreover, the taxpayer contested the benchmark study performed by the tax authorities, considering the selection of companies in the final sample as incorrect one.

Court decision

The Supreme Administrative Court considered that the transfer pricing method applied by the tax authorities is a correct one and justified for a toll manufacturing entity. It is important to note that the Supreme Administrative Court decided that considering the functional profile of the taxpayer, it should perform only routine activities and that the capacity utilization risk (including the market risk) should be borne by the affiliated entity and not by the taxpayer. Therefore, the only situation in which a toll manufacturing entity could record losses is that generated by the extra costs resulted from its manufacturing inefficiencies.

In conclusion, the Supreme Court approved the approach of the tax authorities and maintained the benchmark study performed by them.

Final remarks

Based on the above case, there could be concluded the following two main aspects:

- the approach of the Czech tax authorities in performing the transfer pricing adjustments at the level of the minimum value from the comparability range is a taxpayer-friendly one as in many other countries the adjustments are performed at the median value of the range;
- a toll manufacturing entity should not incur the market risk, respectively the low capacity utilization of the production.

The documents based on which was presented the above information can be found at the following link: https://tpcases.com/czech-vs-german-corp-sep-2016-supreme-administrative-court-no-5-afs-194-2015-34/.

4.5 Case No. I SA/Sz 115/20

Summary of facts

Cork Portugal SA ("CPS") was incorporated in 1995 being engaged in the production of natural cork stoppers. CPS is part of a worldwide Group which operates in the closures' sector dedicated to the wine industry. The production process of CPS can be summarized in the following steps:

- CPS acquires the cork from selected suppliers. This cork is transported weekly to the CPS's premises;
- within CPS the cork is transformed into stoppers, in this respect there being followed all the operations of the productions process: stripping, manual and automatic boring, drying, grinding, electronic and manual choice, washing and pre-drying, control of the bacteria, drying and coating;
- when destined for the American market (United States and Argentina), the stoppers are shipped from CPS and the finishing operations (humidification and treatment) are carried out in the Group companies that exist in those countries. When destined for the intra-community market, namely Spain and France, the stoppers go to the unit of CPS for finishing operations and only then are they dispatched to intra-community customers. This is because the Group in European countries only has commercial agents, entities to which it pays commissions for intermediated sales, while in the United States of America, Australia, South Africa and Argentina the Group has distribution companies, with the capacity to carry out the finishing of the stoppers before they are delivered to the final customers.

CPS sells its products to the Group companies from United States of America, Australia and South Africa through the intermediation of an Irish trading company B within the Group. More exactly, B operates as an exclusive distributor of the CPS's products for the US, Australian and South African markets. B is a company that only operates within the Group, acting as a commercial platform between CPS and the Group companies from those three markets. The transfers of goods that CPS makes to the Group companies from the three markets are based on the following aspects:

- products manufactured by CPS are sold to its counterparts in the USA (C), Australia (D) and South Africa (E), but invoiced to B. On the invoices issued by CPS the latter (i.e. B) appears as customer and C, D and E as recipients;
- the products are shipped from the CPS's premises directly to the United States, Australia or South Africa and usually transported by sea;

- the only references to B that can be found in the accounting documents that support the sales made to this entity are the indication as customer on the invoice and, sometimes, the identification as the originator of the bank transfers received;
- the date of the invoices issued by B to C/D/E is exactly the same as that of invoices issued by CPS to B. The goods, references and quantities on invoices issued by B to C/D/E are exactly the same as those on invoices issued by CPS to B.

CPS was subject to a tax audit covering the year 2010. In this respect, CPS presented to the tax authorities the transfer pricing file. The transaction subject to disputes with the tax authorities was the sales performed by CPS to its affiliated entity B. According to the transfer pricing file, this transaction was analyzed through the TNMM method, choosing as tested party CPS and selecting as profitability indicator NCP.

The benchmark study presented in the transfer pricing file was performed using the "Bureau VanDijk's" database and the APCOR (Portuguese Cork Association) database. There were selected only Portuguese companies that meet criteria related to the activity code, independence criteria, availability of financial information in period 2007–2009 and threshold of the operating results and operating income. There were selected as comparables 21 companies for which the NCP was computed for each year from the period 2007–2009, but also as an average. However, by analyzing the standard deviation of NCP, 4 companies with a higher dispersion than the average were excluded, thus defining a final sample of 17 companies comparable to CPS.

Based on the results of the benchmark study there was obtained the following comparability range computed for the values of the average NCP from 2007 to 2009:

- Maximum: 9.48%.
- 3rd Quartile: 6.82%
- Median: 5.76%
- 1st Quartile: 4.60%
- Minimum: −2.19%

According to the transfer pricing file, the NCP obtained by CPS in 2010 was 2.91% which is situated within the interval generated by the benchmark study (i.e. within the minimum value of −2.19% and the maximum value of 9.48%) and therefore the transaction performed by CPS with B complies with the arm's length principle.

The position of the tax authorities

The tax authorities accepted the approach of CPS in selecting TNMM, computing the NCP and testing CPS. The tax authorities also agreed with the benchmark study performed by CPS, but rejected the approach of CPS by considering as comparability range the minimum and maximum values of the benchmark interval. According to the tax authorities, the comparability range should be between the first and the third quartile of the benchmark interval.

The tax authorities noted that CPS claims that it acts as an industrial unit that produces stoppers for the Group, in which the commercial functions are concentrated in B. However, the tax authorities observed that the products manufactured by CPS are sold on the European and South American markets and also on the US, Australian and South African markets, with the only difference that in the first markets (Europe and South America) the products are invoiced to the respective customers, and in the second markets the products are invoiced to B. For the sales through B the transport cost and customs clearance costs are borne by CPS.

Moreover, based on a cooperation with the Irish tax authorities in order to avoid double taxation and prevent tax evasion in the area of income tax, the Portuguese tax authorities noted that:

- the existing premises at B correspond to a virtual office (i.e. a service marketed by some companies which consists of the receipt of correspondence and telephone calls associated with an address of choice, provided to clients located anywhere in the world, who only wish to formally host their company there, not effectively carry out any activity there);
- according to the financial statements obtained through the Irish tax authorities, the only supplier of B in 2010 was CPS and the only clients were C, D and E to whom the totality of its turnover was destined;
- B did not have, at that time, a material and human structure that would support the exercise of an effective economic activity;
- orders for the products are received by B from C/D/E, who are satisfied with the products they purchase from CPS, goods being shipped directly from CPS to C/D/E.

Going further, the tax authorities concluded that through the B entity the Group is trying to move profits from Portugal to Ireland. In this respect the tax authorities concluded that:

- B has neither economic substance nor commercial justification and has been used solely for tax purposes, without any effective intervention in the transactions taking place between CPS and the Group companies it supplies in US, Australia and South Africa;
- the selling price by B to C/D/E is much higher than the selling price from CPS to B bearing in mind that the value added by B to the transaction is zero. The null value added by B to the transaction is sustained by the tax authorities through the fact that the risks of the operations intermediated by B are assumed by CPS, whether they are storage, dispatch, transport, return or collection risks, the Irish company performing only the issuance and sending out of order forms, the receipt of the invoices issued by CPS and issuance of invoices to C/D/E;
- since CPS is the main generator of added value, it is not justified to obtain a NCP of 2.91%, while B obtains a margin of 12.4%;

Considering all the above, the tax authorities decided that a transfer pricing adjustment should be computed at the level of CPS in order to increase its taxable income for 2010 on the basis that CPS, in sales of goods to its related party B charged lower prices than would have been the case for similar transactions between parties not connected by special relationships. In this respect, the tax authorities considered as a comparability range the first and the third quartile of the interval presented by CPS in the transfer pricing file and computed the transfer pricing adjustments by bringing the NCP obtained by CPS in 2010 of 2.91% to the median value of the comparability range (i.e. 5.76%).

The position of taxpayer

CPS contested the tax authorities approach and understanding invoking in this respect the following reasons:

- in relation to the supposed lack of economic substance of B, CPS invoked the lack of concrete demonstration by the tax authorities concerning the commercial relationship between B and C/D/E, the profitability achieved by B, as well as the zero added value contributed by B. CPS emphasized the fact that it is important to note that the function performed by B for its customers is not merely a purchase and sale of goods. In fact, B keeps in mind the needs and stock levels of its customers, taking care to satisfy them in an efficient manner, namely by taking due account of the transport times necessary for the delivery of the acquired products—an essential aspect of good management so that the activity of such customers can proceed in a balanced manner: without interruptions due to lack of stock but with minimum storage costs—a function which is in no way performed by CPS. In other words, if B is overpaid, this can be explained by the valuation attributed to the function of assistance in the management of stock levels performed by the said company for the benefit of its customers, which does not, however, lead to any supposed movement of profits from Portugal to Ireland;
- in relation to the comparability range, CPS considered that the extreme results (i.e. the minimum and the maximum values) should not be eliminated from the interval. In this respect CPS justified that a statistical correction of the outliers was already made manually in order to exclude from the sample those observations considered extreme (in the case of four observations) that could influence the results obtained. Given this, CPS considered that the comparability range should be between the minimum and maximum value of the interval and not between the first and the third quartile;
- the value of the CPS's NCP between the minimum value and the first quartile of the interval is justified by CPS through the increase in 2010 of the cost with the raw materials.

Court decision

The case was presented by CPS for arbitration and the Arbitration Tribunal upheld the transfer pricing adjustment issued by the tax authorities.

In this respect, in May 2016 the Arbitration Court concluded that the profit sharing between CPS and B does not reflect the activities/responsibilities of each entity in the Group and the reasons why such a differentiated allocation of mark-ups over operating costs is performed (i.e. only 2.91% for CPS and 12.4% for B which carries out an activity of "management assistance"). Moreover, the Arbitration Court sustained the approach of the tax authorities by performing the transfer pricing adjustments at the level of the median value of the comparability range.

Final remarks
Based on the above case law there could be noted the following aspects:

- when performing a transfer pricing analysis, the functional analysis should demonstrate the real involvement of each party in the transaction, justifying the economic substance of each entity;
- the comparability range is considered to be situated between the first and the third quartile of the interval generated by the benchmark study.

The documents based on which was presented the above information can be found at the following link: https://tpcases.com/portugal-vs-cork-portugal-sa-may-2016-collective-arbitration-tribunal-case-no-609-2015-t/.

4.6 Case No. IT(TP)A No. 1915/Bang/2017

Toyota Kirloskar Auto Parts Private Limited ("TKA") is an entity based in India which manufactures automotive parts, using in this respect the technical know-how licensed from the related party Toyota Motor Corporation (based in Japan). The goods manufactured are sold by TKA to its related party Toyota Kirloskar Motors Limited ("TKM"), based in India.

The price of the goods sold to TKM and the royalties paid to Toyota Motor Corporation were set in combination in order to leave TKA to obtain a profitability indicator in accordance with the arm's length principle.

Going further, the tax authorities argued that the initial know-how was replaced during the time by a new know-how generated by the research and development activities performed by Toyota Motor Corporation. Moreover, the tax authorities mentioned that this know-how was exploited by TKA and considering the above transfer pricing methodology, the tax authorities argued that there would be more reasonable to apply a profit split method between TKA and Toyota Motor Corporation.

TKA considered the manufacturing and sale of goods as being a transaction different to that which involves the know-how from ToyotaMotor Corporation.

The tribunal found that TKA was not involved in research and development activities, did not make any valuable or unique contribution and that Toyota Motor Corporation was not incurred any risk in relation to the exploitation of the know-how in India.

Furthermore, the tribunal decided that the TKA's transfer pricing policy related to the combination of the know-how and goods transactions does not involve the fact that separate arm's length price was not determined for each of the two transactions. In conclusion, the tribunal rejected the approach of the tax authorities in applying the profit-split method and approved the approach of the taxpayer in testing the overall net margin (i.e. through the combination of the two transactions in discussion). The decision was issued by the Bangalore Income Tax Appellate Tribunal on 18 March 2020.

Based on this case there could be considered the following aspects:

- **use of the profit split method**—if an entity only exploit the know-how generated by other entity from the Group this does not mean that there could be applied the profit-split method;
- **combination of transactions**—there is possible to combine certain transactions in order to benchmark the overall profitability.

4.7 Case No. TS-580-ITAT-2020(MUM)-TP

Federal Mogul Anand Bearing India Ltd. is a manufacturer of automotive components, being based in India. During a tax audit performed at the level of this company, the tax authorities performed their own benchmark, based on this imposing transfer pricing adjustments and a higher taxable income at the level of Federal Mogul Anand Bearing India Ltd.

On 9 July 2020 the Court ruled in the favor of the taxpayer and rejected the benchmark performed by the tax authorities based on following reasons:

- there is no comparability in terms of size between the tested party and the comparable. More exactly, there was considered that in relation to the scale economies, a bigger company could benefit to a greater extent from these;
- the comparable was established for a longer period compared with the tested party, considering that this became a leader on the market owning more intangible assets;
- the tax authorities did not present the way in which the benchmark study was performed (i.e. the criteria applied).

Concluding, when performing a benchmark study there could be considered criteria such as the size of the comparables vs. the size of the tested party or the year of incorporation of the comparables vs. the year of incorporation of the tested party. Moreover, a taxpayer could contest a benchmark study performed by the tax authorities if for this benchmark is not presented the search strategy and the criteria applied.

Appendices

Appendix A: First Search Strategy (Romanian Market, Independence Indicators “A−”, “A”, “A+”)

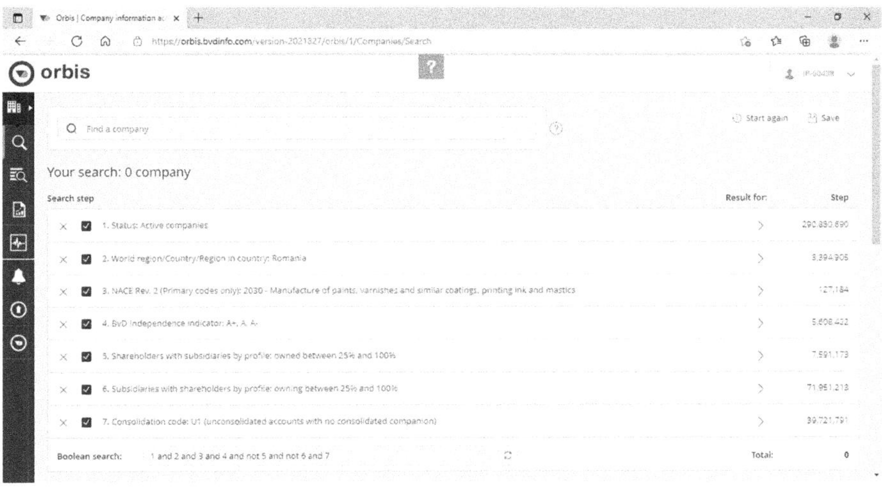

I. Ignat, L. Ionescu-Feleagă, *Transfer Pricing in Manufacturing*, Contributions to Finance and Accounting, https://doi.org/10.1007/978-3-030-93889-5

Appendix B: The Second Search Strategy (EU Market, Independence Indicators "A−", "A", "A+")

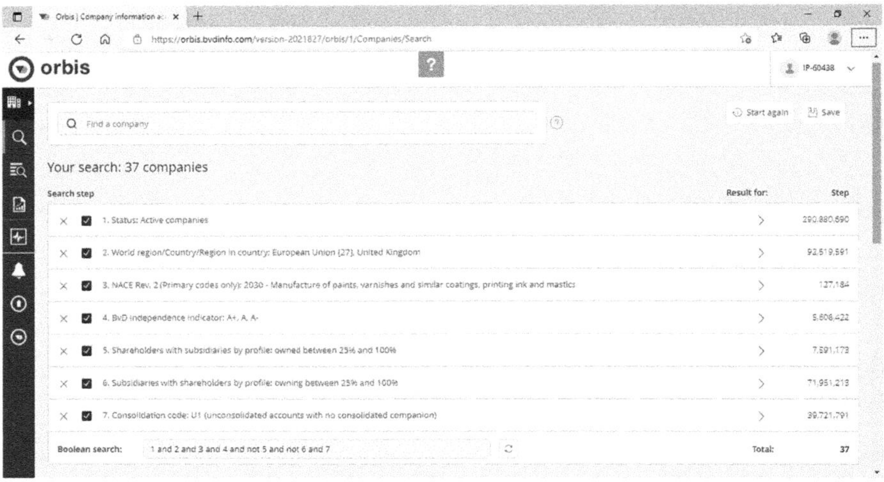

Appendix C: Details at the Level of Each Company from the Benchmark Study

No. crt.	Company name et	BvD ID number	Country	Website	BvD Independence Indicator	Average Stocks/ Turnover 2017–2019	Average Intangible assets/ Total assets 2017–2019	Average NCP 2017–2019
1.	VEBA OEL VEG GESELL-SCHAFT MIT BESCHRAENKTER HAFTUNG	DE4090092562	Germany	0	U	n/a	n/a	n/a
2.	FENZI BELGIUM	BE0866763393	Belgium	https://www.fenzigroup.com/en/fenzi-nel-mondo	U	15.24%	0.08%	6.68%
3.	FERRO MAGMALOR GESELLSCHAFT MIT BESCHRAENKTER HAFTUNG	DE3150004703	Germany	www.magmalor.de	U	n/a	n/a	n/a
4.	COLORGRAF - S.P.A.	IT00724270152	Italy	www.colorgraf.it	A+	26.15%	0.14%	1.64%
5.	HEMPEL D. O. O.	HR14448967911	Croatia	www.hempel.com	U	13.74%	0.58%	11.39%
6.	CHROMOS-SVJETLOST D. O. O.	HR72579903288	Croatia	www.chromos-svjetlost.hr	U	23.11%	0.10%	12.96%
7.	EUPINCA SA	ESA12283388	Spain	www.tkrom.com	A+	13.33%	5.88%	n/a
8.	FORTEC SP. Z O.O.	PL301500072	Poland	www.fortec.info.pl	A+	6.90%	3.49%	18.16%
9.	ROHM AND HAAS DEUTSCH-LAND PRODUKTION GMBH & CO. KG	DE6070511497	Germany	0	U	n/a	n/a	n/a
10.	PRZEDSIEBIORSTWO PRODUKCYJNO HANDLOWE UNICELL POLAND SP. Z O.O.	PL050623653	Poland	www.unicell.com.pl	U	14.98%	0.54%	12.43%
11.	SAREX BELGIUM	BE0871078311	Belgium	www.sarex.be	U	23.97%	0.00%	14.15%
12.	DRAGON POLAND SP. Z O.O. SP.K.	PL122707541	Poland	www.dragon.biz.pl	U	23.99%	0.92%	7.51%

(continued)

No. crt.	Company name et	BvD ID number	Country	Website	BvD Independence Indicator	Average Stocks/ Turnover 2017–2019	Average Intangible assets/ Total assets 2017–2019	Average NCP 2017–2019
13.	INDUSTRIAS QUIMICAS IRURENA SA	ESA20037370	Spain	www.irurenagroup.com	U	20.81%	0.47%	6.62%
14.	OLAINES KIMISKA RUPNICA BIOLARS AS	LV000324547	Latvia	www.biolar.lv	U	15.46%	0.00%	9.32%
15.	ROKOSPOL, A.S.	CZ25521446	Czech Republic	www.rokospol.cz	U	18.24%	0.20%	2.67%
16.	FUJIFILM SERICOL DEUTSCHLAND GMBH	DE4090132779	Germany	0	U	n/a	n/a	n/a
17.	AKFA S.A.	GR800594057	Greece	www.akfa-chem.com	U	7.48%	0.00%	0.18%
18.	SPRAYLAT GMBH	DE5010298512	Germany	0	U	n/a	n/a	n/a
19.	ALMACENES CELSO MIGUEZ SA	ESA36005718	Spain	www.celsomiguez.com	U	55.07%	1.91%	n/a
20.	GLOBAL POINT SP. Z O.O. SP. K.	PL360319122	Poland	www.globalpoint.pl	U	13.66%	7.89%	19.64%
21.	ZAKLAD CHEMICZNY PAWEL PAPROCKI S.J.	PL302301328	Poland	www.zakladychemiczne.com	U	6.75%	0.00%	10.99%
22.	DONECK PRONAT GYARTO ES KERESKEDELMI KFT.	HU11675853	Hungary	www.doneckpronat.com	U	9.85%	0.06%	4.94%
23.	KORCHEMIA SP. Z O.O. SP.K.	PL611034776	Poland	www.korchemia.pl	U	5.33%	0.00%	n/a
24.	INDUSTRIAS QUIMICAS EUROCOLOR SOCIEDAD ANONIMA	ESA48291645	Spain	www.pinturaseurocolor.com	A−	23.86%	0.15%	2.88%
25.	ESMALDUR SA	ESA12022224	Spain	www.esmaldur.com	A	23.18%	0.02%	2.48%
26.	KOSBUD BRACIA KOSINSCY ADAM KOSINSKI, MARIUSZ KOSINSKI, MARCIN KOSINSKI SP.J.	PL140032431	Poland	www.kosbud.com.pl	U	11.79%	0.50%	13.30%
27.	STEEL PROTECT COLOR EUROPE AB	SE5590578315	Sweden	https://spc-europe.com/	U	0.00%	0.00%	9.17%

28.	PLASTBUD SP. Z O.O.	PL691670320	Poland	www.plastbudsp.pl	A	22.44%	0.03%	12.70%
29.	CHAMPION COLOR PLUS P. LELITO SP.J.	PL192627158	Poland	www.championcolor.com	U	11.41%	0.00%	3.41%
30.	ARGACOL - TINTAS E VERNIZES, S.A.	PT501115099	Portugal	www.argatintas.pt	U	18.94%	0.09%	8.45%
31.	MEFFERT HUNGARIA FESTEKGYARTO ES KERESKEDELMI KORLATOLT FELELOSSEGU TARSASAG	HU11203025	Hungary	www.mefferthungaria.hu	U	14.17%	0.00%	3.71%
32.	SIMAB	FR415206028	France	peintures-simab.com	U	16.51%	5.83%	4.17%
33.	GVK COATING TECHNOLOGY OY	FI01359453	Finland	www.gvk.fi	U	22.05%	10.53%	5.10%
34.	AURO PFLANZENCHEMIE AKTIENGESELLSCHAFT	DE2030011470	Germany	www.auro.de	U	28.54%	2.61%	n/a
35.	SEVEN SP. Z O.O. SP.K.	PL291184632	Poland	www.seven7.pl	U	7.52%	0.58%	−7.27%
36.	NORDIC UNITED COATINGS AB	SE5592266752	Sweden	0	U	n/a	n/a	n/a
37.	AB ROA	SE5560308529	Sweden	rotmotaverken.se	U	21.31%	10.48%	7.68%
38.	CNI NYOMDA- ES CSOMAGOLOIPARI TERMEKEK KERESKEDELME ES SZOLGALTATO KORLATOLT FELELOSSEGU TARSASAG	HU12807103	Hungary	www.aninks.com	U	21.08%	0.06%	1.71%
39.	MASTER CHEMIA BUDOWLANA SP. Z O.O.	PL121104639	Poland	www.mastermas.pl	A−	5.62%	0.11%	8.16%
40.	WILCKENS PAINTS FACTORY S.A.	GR998533974	Greece	www.wilckenspaints.com	U	17.53%	0.00%	−1.67%
41.	SLOVLAK KOSECA, A.S.	SK35816651	Slovakia	www.slovlak.sk	U	50.43%	0.00%	7.64%
42.	DETECHA, CHEMICKE VYROBNI DRUZSTVO	CZ00029785	Czech Republic	www.ronseal.cz	U	30.26%	0.11%	−3.72%

(continued)

No. crt.	Company name et	BvD ID number	Country	Website	BvD Independence Indicator	Average Stocks/ Turnover 2017–2019	Average Intangible assets/ Total assets 2017–2019	Average NCP 2017–2019
43.	COLORIFICIO IMPERIAL EDILTORRES S.R.L.	IT03248560827	Italy	www.colorificioimperial.it	A+	24.12%	3.26%	2.91%
44.	PROCOAT TECNOLOGIAS SL	ESB60758497	Spain	www.procoat-tech.com	U	19.84%	0.14%	15.38%
45.	POLIFARB LODZ SP. Z O.O.	PL470581613	Poland	www.polifarb.lodz.pl	U	38.11%	0.02%	9.58%
46.	EVOCHEM S.A.	GR800397904	Greece	www.evochem.gr	U	22.10%	1.36%	3.16%
47.	LARS-ERIK JOHANSSON BILPRODUKTER AKTIEBOLAG	SE5562386523	Sweden	www.lackman.se	U	21.74%	0.00%	6.60%
48.	PALCANARIAS, SA	ESA35118132	Canary Islands (Spain)	www.palcanarias.com	U	21.19%	0.20%	5.09%
49.	PETER-LACKE HUNGARIA LAKKGYARTO, KERESKEDELMI ES SZOLGALTATO KORLATOLT FELELOSSEGU TARSASAG	HU13021353	Hungary	www.peter-lacke.com	U	18.65%	0.14%	12.10%
50.	PEARLTEC GMBH	DE8030290335	Germany	0	U	22.80%	0.00%	n/a
51.	GONFERSOL - PRODUTOS QUIMICOS, S.A.	PT508063426	Portugal	www.gonfersol.com	U	12.57%	0.02%	2.36%
52.	CHEMCOLOR BARVE, LAKI, KEMIKALIJE SEVNICA D.O.O.	SI5309115	Slovenia	www.chemcolor.si	U	42.75%	0.04%	1.25%
53.	SOLRAC COATINGS SL.	ESB65920175	Spain	www.solrac.com	U	9.50%	6.49%	1.72%
54.	EKO-KOLOR PACZOSIK KOTARBA SP.K.	PL020956148	Poland	eko-kolor.pl	U	6.65%	0.18%	n/a
55.	ARTIBAL SA	ESA22154298	Spain	www.artibal.com	U	17.42%	66.74%	10.07%
56.	DIPOLACK SL	ESB12063954	Spain	0	A–	n/a	n/a	n/a
57.	SILK COLOUR S.A.	GR094236805	Greece	www.silkcolour.gr	U	16.90%	0.04%	53.69%

58.	FESTEK BAZIS GYARTO ES KERESKEDELMI ZARTKORUEN MUKODO RESZVENYTARSASAG	HU25026331	Hungary	festekbazis.hu	U	27.46%	1.69%	5.51%
59.	TIGERLAKK LAKK- ES FESTEKGYARTO ES KERESKEDELMI KFT.	HU10454235	Hungary	www.tigerlakk.hu	U	7.16%	0.02%	16.43%
60.	PRODUCTOS PROMADE SA	ESA78760626	Spain	www.productospromade.com	U	6.92%	0.06%	7.44%
61.	N.C.I. CHEMICAL INDUSTRY LIMITED	CYC38946	Cyprus	www.ncichemicals.com	U	n/a	n/a	n/a
62.	"OTIS" GAZDASAGI SZOLGALTATO BETETI TARSASAG	HU24448044	Hungary	www.otisbt.hu	U	9.28%	0.04%	5.67%
63.	RCR BIS SP. Z O.O. SP.K.	PL300184539	Poland	www.rcr.com.pl	U	5.75%	0.00%	25.26%
64.	MITECH CHEMIA BUDOWLANA SP. Z O.O.	PL384111466	Poland	www.mitech.pl	U	n/a	0.00%	n/a
65.	SELTD REALISATIONS LIMITED	GB00871451	United Kingdom	www.prismo.co.uk	U	n/a	n/a	n/a
66.	ONEFILL TECHNOLOGIES SWEDEN AB	SE5568211048	Sweden	www.onefill.se	U	5.60%	0.00%	n/a
67.	P A D INDUSTRIE	FR502687775	France	www.orlov.finance	U	8.91%	26.77%	0.04%
68.	CALIDAD CROMATICA SL.	ESB16544926	Spain		U	0.00%	0.47%	12.62%
69.	VENGA HARTZCHEMIE SP. Z O.O. SP.J.	PL471455425	Poland	www.venga.pl	U	24.42%	0.00%	9.38%
70.	NOVOCHEMA, DRUZSTVO	SK00167886	Slovakia	www.novochema.sk	U	36.43%	0.00%	10.64%
71.	CODING AND MARKING SERVICES SARL	FR399681717	France	www.cmsink.com	U	20.29%	8.68%	n/a
72.	RESINLACK INDUSTRIAS QUIMICAS SL	ESB26403303	Spain	www.kupsa.es	U	0.00%	0.85%	7.04%
73.	AEV EUROPE KORLATOLT FELELOSSEGU TARSASAG	HU10675214	Hungary	www.koraxbp.hu	U	15.84%	0.74%	4.83%
74.	BICOLOR S.R.L.	IT03768690285	Italy	www.bicolor.it	A+	53.32%	3.84%	5.33%

(continued)

No. crt.	Company name et	BvD ID number	Country	Website	BvD Independence Indicator	Average Stocks/ Turnover 2017–2019	Average Intangible assets/ Total assets 2017–2019	Average NCP 2017–2019
75.	CERRYS RYSKALOK SP.J.	PL231074146	Poland	www.baumaster.pl	U	19.89%	0.00%	n/a
76.	TAILORS ROYAL PAINTS LLC	GR122884701000	Greece	www.royalpaints.gr	U	11.28%	0.00%	7.93%
77.	AVALON INDUSTRY AD	BG200128436	Bulgaria	www.avalon.bg	A+	35.91%	0.21%	4.16%
78.	INDUSTRIVARIUS, S.A.	PT502029587	Portugal	www.industrivarius.pt	U	15.56%	4.19%	n/a
79.	EURONAVY ENGINEERING, S.A.	PT507448693	Portugal	www. euronavyengineering. com	U	20.80%	0.00%	−2.66%
80.	CHEMCO PROIZVODNJA BARV IN LAKOV, D.O.O.	SI5560764	Slovenia	www.chemco.si	U	35.12%	0.00%	5.18%
81.	A.N.C. WATERPROOFING INDUSTRIES LIMITED	CYC26148	Cyprus	www.anc-industries.com	U	2.25%	0.00%	n/a
82.	POL - EXPO KRASOWIAK S.J.	PL368293250	Poland	0	U	19.85%	0.56%	n/a
83.	VITALVERNICI S.R.L.	IT03624820720	Italy	www.vitalvernici.it	A+	9.39%	0.09%	6.22%
84.	TINTAS LACCA, S.A.	PT501250719	Portugal	www.tintas-lacca.com	U	29.04%	0.04%	2.54%
85.	FALU VAPEN FARG AB	SE5566705892	Sweden	https://www.faluvapen.se/om-foretaget/	U	26.52%	0.00%	14.69%
86.	PINTURAS KILNHER SL	ESB98349798	Spain	kilnher.com	U	0.00%	0.00%	17.50%
87.	PIGMENT SP.J. R. BIELAK I. BIELAK	PL811099019	Poland	www.pigment.inet.pl	U	10.43%	0.00%	n/a
88.	FELTON SPRAY SL	ESB08907032	Spain	www.felton.es	U	30.60%	0.58%	1.27%
89.	DECALUVE SL	ESB60810710	Spain	www.motecsa.com	U	12.29%	0.00%	n/a
90.	AUTO LIFE GARAGE CARAIBES	FR480118140	Guadeloupe (France)	www.garage-caraibes-guadeloupe.fr	U	18.88%	24.57%	n/a
91.	BILMAT OOD	BG127008008	Bulgaria	www.bilmat-bg.com	A+	11.82%	0.00%	7.00%
92.	GYORLAKK FESTEKGYARTO ZARTKORUEN MUKODO RESZVENYTARSASAG	HU11859406	Hungary	www.gyorlakk.hu	U	40.49%	2.33%	−2.82%

93.	PINTURAS MENAPE, SL	ESB29239621	Spain	www.pinturasmenape.com	U	n/a	n/a	n/a
94.	TERAPIMA SWEDEN AB	SE5565479929	Sweden		U	54.65%	0.00%	4.22%
95.	INDUSTRIAS QUIMICAS RAISA SL	ESB46076691	Spain	www.iqraisa.com	A−	5.68%	−3.10%	4.74%
96.	ORFA SA	ESA08665390	Spain	www.orfa.es	U	n/a	n/a	n/a
97.	VERNICI I SOLVENTI SL.	ESB98495153	Spain		U	0.80%	−0.10%	7.56%
98.	DEPINSA SL	ESB59460576	Spain	www.depinsa.com	A−	19.57%	0.00%	1.15%
99.	LOS BLANCOS	BE0419985749	Belgium	0	U	21.01%	0.00%	−2.85%
100.	CB EVOLUTION	FR444765788	France	bike.skicb.com	U	2.73%	0.00%	n/a
101.	MOYPE SA	ESA30048300	Spain	www.moype.es	U	25.67%	0.05%	−0.82%
102.	PLASTBELLA SL	ESB46217444	Spain	www.plastbella.es	U	23.51%	0.00%	1.70%
103.	GALICIA DE PINTURAS SL	ESB36015949	Spain	www.galpi.com	U	63.19%	0.06%	−2.87%
104.	MORLOPIN SL.	ESB87413266	Spain	www.morlopin.com	U	14.88%	0.96%	1.13%
105.	CATALANA DE PINTURAS DEL MEDITERRANEO SL.	ESB66699869	Spain		U	0.85%	0.00%	8.29%
106.	QUIMICAS VILA HERVAS SOCIEDAD LIMITADA.	ESB98801327	Spain	www.akacolors.com	U	12.04%	0.00%	12.47%
107.	PINTURES PUIG SOCIEDAD LIMITADA.	ESB98986607	Spain	www.pinturespuig.com	U	36.83%	0.00%	n/a
108.	COLORIFICIO SARDO 4M SOCIETA' COOPERATIVA	IT02834650927	Italy	www.colorsard.it	U	15.88%	0.06%	n/a
109.	COLORI NUTINI - SOCIETA' A RESPONSABILITA' LIMITATA	IT00246670467	Italy	www.colorinutini.it	A+	47.32%	0.29%	−1.49%
110.	ASTRON KOATING SINGLE MEMBER P.C.	GR801144542	Greece	0	U	5.26%	0.00%	n/a
111.	INERGIS SP. Z O.O.	PL100940875	Poland	www.inergis.co	A+	14.05%	0.00%	2.10%
112.	ALEJANDRO ALONSO SA	ESA28579092	Spain	0	U	n/a	n/a	n/a
113.	BECKTEK INDUSTRIAL COATINGS OY	FI09353937	Finland	www.becktek.fi	U	26.38%	0.00%	9.10%
114.	WIBO FARG AKTIEBOLAG	SE5562716141	Sweden	www.wibofarg.se	U	9.68%	0.00%	4.97%
115.	TECNYRE SL	ESB17057423	Spain	www.tecnyre.com	A−	2.15%	0.00%	10.80%

(continued)

No. crt.	Company name et	BvD ID number	Country	Website	BvD Independence Indicator	Average Stocks/ Turnover 2017–2019	Average Intangible assets/ Total assets 2017–2019	Average NCP 2017–2019
116.	VALENCIANA DE ACABADOS SL	ESB96136205	Spain	www.vadea.net	U	0.81%	0.00%	8.29%
117.	REDIX T. KOSCIESZA I WSPOLNICY SP.K.	PL015339340	Poland	www.redix.pl	U	34.46%	0.00%	−0.90%
118.	MANUFACTURAS KOKOLO SL	ESB26042028	Spain	www.kokolo.es	U	37.08%	10.77%	−2.56%
119.	PEINTURE TECHNIQUE DE GUYANE	FR499131126	French Guiana (France)	0	U	n/a	n/a	n/a
120.	DK SERVICE SP. Z O.O. SP.K.	PL360643851	Poland	www.decoverni.com	U	26.77%	3.48%	2.92%
121.	COLORPOINT OSBY KEMI AB	SE5565091591	Sweden	https://colorpoint.se/en/info/about-us/	U	15.33%	0.25%	4.99%
122.	PINTURAS BRETON SLL	ESB11588431	Spain	www.pinturasbreton.com	U	23.22%	0.00%	2.16%
123.	DANACHEM S.J.	PL012566264	Poland	www.danachem.pl	U	n/a	n/a	n/a
124.	SOCIETE ANTILLAISE DE PEINTURE ET ACCESSOIRES GENERALE	FR331879601	Guadeloupe (France)	0	U	14.21%	0.00%	n/a
125.	SERVISTAND FABRICACION DE ESTANTERIAS SL.	ESB87090015	Spain	www. servistandestanterias.com	U	11.30%	0.00%	n/a
126.	REOXYL SOCIEDAD LIMITADA.	ESB98846009	Spain		U	48.89%	0.00%	2.71%
127.	HYDROTON S.A.	GR038197905000	Greece	www.hydroton.gr	U	13.46%	2.35%	15.31%
128.	PEDRERANA DE PINTURAS S. L.	ESB91591263	Spain	0	U	n/a	n/a	n/a
129.	DIGITI SIGNUM SOCIEDAD LIMITADA.	ESB12983789	Spain		U	12.58%	0.45%	1.50%
130.	QUIMICAS PENINSULARES DE CORS SL	ESB02315091	Spain		U	54.84%	0.00%	6.28%
131.	COLAS Y PINTURAS TERZA SL	ESB96120902	Spain	www.terza.es	U	8.58%	0.12%	1.46%

132.	REVESTIMIENTOS Y PINTURAS DE GALICIA SL	ESB32354250	Spain		U	29.65%	0.02%	1.82%
133.	KOLOR MIX S.A. W UPADLOSCI UKLADOWEJ	PL251018327	Poland	www.kolormix.pl	U	n/a	n/a	n/a
134.	LAINER SP. Z O.O. SP.K.	PL362221485	Poland	lainer.pl	U	16.07%	0.00%	8.91%
135.	KOPIMASK SA	ESA08367187	Spain	www.kopimask.eu	A–	47.93%	0.46%	2.74%
136.	PINTURAS Y REVESTIMIENTOS EUROSUR S.L.	ESB11413366	Spain	0	U	n/a	n/a	n/a
137.	AUTO PEINTURE DE L'OUEST	FR501203491	Reunion (France)	0	U	n/a	n/a	n/a
138.	ALAVESA DE BARNICES SA	ESA01008754	Spain	www.alaba.es	A–	52.43%	1.20%	1.48%
139.	COLOR TEHNA D.O.O.	HR23851651987	Croatia	https://colortehna.hr/index.php	U	27.99%	0.00%	1.41%
140.	DECOLOR, PROIZVODNJA IN TRGOVINA, D.O.O.	SI6612075	Slovenia	www.decolor.si	U	8.27%	0.16%	4.38%
141.	PONYSA SL	ESB36017879	Spain	www.pinturaspony.es	A+	31.09%	0.00%	–1.87%
142.	L Z N SOC COOP	ESF50976935	Spain	0	U	n/a	n/a	n/a
143.	CAMELEO SP. Z O.O. SP.K.	PL302022930	Poland	www.cameleo.pl	U	25.46%	0.00%	37.33%
144.	PRO PEINTURE AUTO	FR501586812	Guadeloupe (France)	0	U	4.76%	0.00%	n/a
145.	I G R BARNICES SL	ESB32191249	Spain	0	U	n/a	n/a	n/a
146.	TYPOCHIMIKI S.A.	GR094049655	Greece	www.typochimiki.gr	U	9.54%	0.00%	n/a
147.	MEDITERRANEA DE BARNICES Y PINTURAS SL	ESB73234551	Spain	www.mebar.es	U	99.54%	0.00%	2.97%
148.	JAURENA SA	ESA58244096	Spain	www.jaurenaart.com	U	50.71%	6.58%	n/a
149.	CAT COAT SL.	ESB63082432	Spain	0	U	n/a	n/a	n/a
150.	ETABLISSEMENTS AUGUSTE COUSSEAU ET CIE	FR061200838	France	0	U	n/a	n/a	n/a
151.	COLOR KING FESTEK KORLATOLT FELELOSSEGU TARSASAG	HU13838953	Hungary	www.gtrfutar.hu	U	123.68%	9.74%	–58.57%

(continued)

No. crt.	Company name et	BvD ID number	Country	Website	BvD Independence Indicator	Average Stocks/ Turnover 2017–2019	Average Intangible assets/ Total assets 2017–2019	Average NCP 2017–2019
152.	QUIMICAS THAI SL	ESB46137162	Spain	www.quimicasthai.com	U	37.40%	2.05%	1.03%
153.	PINTURAS CICLON SL	ESB11851581	Spain	www.pinturasciclon.com	U	23.40%	0.00%	1.44%
154.	PINTURAS TERMOPLASTICAS SUR SL	ESB70272380	Spain		U	27.98%	0.49%	6.57%
155.	PINTURAS ROBLES ANDALUCIA SL	ESB23554355	Spain	www.pinturasrobles.com	U	70.88%	0.00%	2.08%
156.	ECOLIT POLSKA SP. Z O.O. SP. K.	PL364346133	Poland	www.ecolit.pl	U	17.50%	0.00%	−8.04%
157.	ETS JOUBERT ET CIE	FR572104677	France	www.letonkinois.net	U	11.46%	0.59%	n/a
158.	DECKGARDEN HOLDING SL	ESB85309649	Spain	0	U	n/a	n/a	n/a
159.	PINTURAS JOVI RA SA	ESA46725776	Spain	www.jovira.com	U	n/a	n/a	n/a
160.	VICUR SL	ESB46106621	Spain	www.vicur.com	U	18.43%	0.02%	0.80%
161.	BARNICES DE TOLEDO SL	ESB45033362	Spain	0	U	n/a	n/a	n/a
162.	TINTALMED SOCIEDAD LIMITADA.	ESB04843132	Spain	https://tintalmed.com/productos/	U	24.09%	0.00%	7.11%
163.	UAB STATYBOS APDAILOS RANGA	LT123220686	Lithuania	www.sar.lt	U	0.00%	0.13%	2.94%
164.	ZAKLADY USLUGOWO-PRODUKCYJNE DELTA SP. Z O.O.	PL950004011	Poland	www.zupdelta.com.pl	U	9.74%	0.00%	6.29%
165.	MURO QUIMICAS S.L.	ESB91158212	Spain	www.muroquimicas.com	U	216.54%	0.00%	2.49%
166.	PINTURAS PLASTICAS PRO-GRESO SL	ESB30222160	Spain	idsapinturas.com	U	50.48%	0.01%	2.13%
167.	S.P. POLYCHROM SOLE SHAREHOLDER CO. LTD	GR998413282	Greece	0	U	8.78%	2.31%	n/a
168.	COPRIK SOCIETA' A RESPONSABILITA' LIMITATA	IT04938970284	Italy		U	3.85%	0.18%	15.82%
169.	GRAPA, S.R.O.	CZ46350055	Czech Republic	www.grapa-kh.cz	U	n/a	n/a	n/a

170.	WINK	FR440389021	France	www.welcometowink.com	U	9.48%	0.00%	1.87%
171.	AEROGRAFIC COLOR S.L.	ESB64172562	Spain	0	U	n/a	n/a	n/a
172.	PINTURAS SANABRIA SL	ESB23339856	Spain	pinturasanabria.blogspot.bg	U	n/a	n/a	n/a
173.	BACCA BYGGKEMI AB	SE5567560858	Sweden		U	25.44%	0.00%	1.12%
174.	KEMET RV OU	EE10055930	Estonia	www.kemetrv.ee	A+	14.14%	0.00%	0.36%
175.	PINTURAS FESAN SL	ESB01001205	Spain	www.fesan.info	U	n/a	n/a	n/a
176.	AXARCOLOR SLL	ESB92835438	Spain		U	72.18%	0.00%	3.17%
177.	PINTURAS LIMOLUZ SLL.	ESB21348503	Spain	0	U	n/a	n/a	n/a
178.	PINTURAS Y RESINAS TRIBO SL	ESB58893223	Spain	www.tribosa.es	U	13.14%	0.00%	9.08%
179.	ALCALA COLOR SL	ESB23415441	Spain	alcacolor.com	U	7.60%	0.00%	3.00%
180.	MATESICA - MATERIAIS SINTETICOS PARA A CONSTRUCAO, S.A.	PT500187789	Portugal	www.matesica.com	U	41.04%	62.10%	n/a
181.	PRODUCTOS GOMAFER SL	ESB26014357	Spain	www.gomafer.com	U	33.75%	0.24%	−8.26%
182.	PINTURAS YNAMELA S.L.	ESB82189358	Spain	0	U	n/a	n/a	n/a
183.	SAT CAR 6 COATING ESPANA SL.	ESB87086229	Spain	www.satcar6.es	U	30.69%	0.00%	3.87%
184.	BARNICES Y PINTURAS KARMOTEX SL	ESB91130724	Spain		U	38.05%	1.29%	7.78%
185.	PINTURAS SAENZ TORRE SL	ESB26210245	Spain	0	U	n/a	n/a	n/a
186.	PINTURAS PINMARO S.L.	ESB11798964	Spain	0	U	n/a	n/a	n/a
187.	DISOLVENTES DURAN SL	ESB78057965	Spain	disolventesduran.com	U	6.67%	0.00%	2.74%
188.	CHIMICA VE.GRA. - S.R.L.	IT00394980445	Italy	www.chimicavegra.com	A+	42.20%	0.00%	−2.91%
189.	NANOLUX KULKERESKEDELMI ES KERESKEDELMI KORLATOLT FELELOSSEGU TARSASAG	HU11631327	Hungary	www.nanolux.hu	U	19.01%	0.21%	−1.40%

(continued)

No. crt.	Company name et	BvD ID number	Country	Website	BvD Independence Indicator	Average Stocks/ Turnover 2017–2019	Average Intangible assets/ Total assets 2017–2019	Average NCP 2017–2019
190.	FENYLAKK GYARTO, KERESKEDELEMI ES SZOLGALTATO KORLATOLT FELELOSSEGU TARSASAG	HU23067002	Hungary	www.fenylakk.hu	U	16.74%	0.00%	4.02%
191.	OUTILS SOLS SYSTEMES	FR791060304	France	0	U	5.68%	0.00%	n/a
192.	SUCESORES DE ROJAS SL	ESB53835716	Spain		U	1.13%	0.86%	6.56%
193.	PRODUCTOS QUIMICOS RINALDI SA	ESA26051862	Spain	rinaldi.es	U	7.82%	0.00%	18.94%
194.	JKM PRONAT FESTEKGYARTO KERESKEDELMI ES SZOLGALTATO KORLATOLT FELELOSSEGU TARSASAG	HU10746033	Hungary	www.jkmpronat.hu	U	16.37%	0.05%	1.40%
195.	CODEC FARG AKTIEBOLAG	SE5564551223	Sweden	www.codecfarg.se	U	38.43%	0.00%	2.57%
196.	LIENZOS MOIA S.C.C.L.	ESF08731176	Spain	www.lienzosmoia.com	U	n/a	n/a	n/a
197.	JORGE ROSELL COMAS SL	ESB99083669	Spain	www.pinturasrover.com	U	12.17%	−0.04%	1.05%
198.	BARNIZADOS LUAL S.L.	ESB81767394	Spain	0	U	n/a	n/a	n/a
199.	CHEMYPLAST S.A.	GR122626202000	Greece	www.chemyplast.com	U	23.91%	0.00%	10.00%
200.	SUPREMA D.O.O.	HR28429459738	Croatia		U	31.48%	0.00%	9.95%
201.	PINTURAS DITOSA SL	ESB39341599	Spain	www.pinturasditosa.com	U	23.92%	0.00%	n/a
202.	GRUPP	FR418611307	France	www.peinture-grupp.fr	U	27.25%	14.42%	n/a
203.	MAGIBAT	FR418017919	France	0	U	15.59%	0.00%	n/a
204.	ZOLDLANCOLAT “B” KERESKEDELMI ES SZOLGALTATO KORLATOLT FELELOSSEGU TARSASAG	HU14734436	Hungary		U	8.06%	0.00%	9.87%
205.	HERACLEA PROMOLAND SL	ESB64153257	Spain	0	U	n/a	n/a	n/a
206.	INDUSTRIAL MORA DE BARNICES SL	ESB96801360	Spain	www.barnices-mora.com	U	6.85%	0.00%	16.30%

207.	IGNACIO VEGA GOROSTEGUI SA	ESA39001979	Spain	https://www.ivegor.com/en/ivegor/	U	51.05%	0.00%	2.41%
208.	PEAK CHEMICALS LIMITED	CYC11119	Cyprus	www.facebook.com/peakchemicals	A–	29.63%	3.24%	n/a
209.	PINTURAS MCQUIMIBLANC DEL VALLES SL.	ESB66486473	Spain	0	U	19.95%	0.00%	n/a
210.	VIKING FARG AB	SE5565605283	Sweden		U	17.98%	0.00%	12.76%
211.	PINTURAS MAYKA SL	ESB21190020	Spain	0	U	55.89%	0.27%	−6.74%
212.	MAYCON HELLAS CON-STRUCTION COMPANY SA GRECIA (RETHYMNO)-SUCURSALA BUCURESTI	RO30160518	Romania	0	U	0.00%	0.00%	n/a
213.	ANGAR SOCIETA' COOPERATIVA	IT04773860657	Italy		U	71.51%	0.79%	2.67%
214.	ADECO SP. Z O.O. SP.K.	PL380549906	Poland	www.adecosystem.pl	U	9.37%	n/a	n/a
215.	LABORATOIRES G BOUCHEY ONGUENT	FR576150262	France	0	U	n/a	n/a	n/a
216.	A. VINCLOVO TUB AKRILEKSAS	LT186195424	Lithuania	setta.lt	U	n/a	0.00%	n/a
217.	FRICORFAMI SL.	ESB93106177	Spain	0	U	8.63%	0.00%	n/a
218.	COLORPLAN TEXTILVEGYIPARI KORLATOLT FELELOSSEGU TARSASAG	HU10335437	Hungary	www.colorplan.hu	U	16.85%	0.11%	17.75%
219.	SOGUAPEINT	FR484788724	Guadeloupe (France)	0	U	30.08%	0.00%	n/a
220.	UVELITE AB	SE5592289135	Sweden	www.uvelite.com	U	n/a	n/a	n/a
221.	PINTURES RALLI SL	ESB25220898	Spain	www.pinturesralli.com/contacte.html	U	51.75%	−0.01%	0.91%
222.	CODIPER S. L.	ESB08753568	Spain	0	U	n/a	n/a	n/a
223.	CARPINTERIA & EBANISTERIA B HITA SL	ESB18615948	Spain	www.carpinteriabhita.com	U	6.17%	0.43%	n/a
224.	KARBON ZAPRESIC D.O.O.	HR41066473108	Croatia		U	41.91%	0.00%	4.98%

(continued)

No. crt.	Company name et	BvD ID number	Country	Website	BvD Independence Indicator	Average Stocks/ Turnover 2017–2019	Average Intangible assets/ Total assets 2017–2019	Average NCP 2017–2019
225.	MASTERCOAT SL.	ESB56001456	Spain	www.mastercoat.es	U	3.07%	0.00%	−5.18%
226.	PINTURAS JAM SL	ESB12286373	Spain	pinturas-jam-sl.business.site	U	63.89%	0.00%	−2.50%
227.	3 EN 3 OOD	BG203326551	Bulgaria	0	A+	4.66%	11.69%	6.86%
228.	SARIC	FR720704097	France	0	U	n/a	n/a	n/a
229.	NOU NORD-EST SOCIEDAD LIMITADA.	ESB55263735	Spain		U	52.90%	0.03%	2.32%
230.	PINTURAS VALCOLOR SL	ESB96673157	Spain	www.valcolor.es	U	93.78%	0.00%	4.32%
231.	H.G.D. TERUEL SL.	ESB44253268	Spain	hgdteruel.com	U	7.49%	0.00%	5.97%
232.	HARZO EUROPA KORLATOLT FELELOSSEGU TARSASAG	HU25831355	Hungary		U	n/a	0.00%	9.51%
233.	PINTURAS SIGMA SOCIEDAD LIMITADA.	ESB90125568	Spain	0	U	43.08%	0.04%	n/a
234.	INDUSTRIAS QUIMICAS UBACH SL	ESB61728002	Spain	www.ubachinkjet.com	U	7.36%	0.00%	13.90%
235.	INHIBITOR SISAK D.O.O.	HR06440204915	Croatia	www.inhibitor.hr	U	7.84%	1.21%	4.83%
236.	LIETUVOS IR OLANDIJOS UAB RAINBOW COATINGS	LT110751085	Lithuania	0	U	n/a	0.00%	n/a
237.	PINTYPOL SA	ESA26025940	Spain	pintypol-sa.telefonosynegocios.com	U	32.41%	0.36%	−0.11%
238.	CHEMICOAT SL	ESB60918034	Spain	www.pinturaschemicoat.com	U	79.82%	0.30%	0.73%
239.	REVESTIMIENTOS PINTASUR SRL	ESB41518184	Spain		U	134.83%	0.00%	3.19%
240.	SOC LEROUX	FR445820848	France	www.couleursleroux.com	U	n/a	n/a	n/a
241.	SATEENKAARI PERINNETAITO OY	FI11005085	Finland	www.sateenkaariperinnetaito.fi	U	30.27%	8.36%	−0.66%

242.	MIRO D.O.O.	HR87826925363	Croatia		U	9.99%	0.00%	1.44%
243.	LIETUVOS IR SUOMIJOS UAB SAVOLAX	LT110689032	Lithuania	www.savolax.lt	U	n/a	0.00%	n/a
244.	PINTURAS MALTIC S.A.	ESA25306580	Spain	0	U	41.25%	0.00%	n/a
245.	SUMINISTROS DE ESTAMPACION TEXTIL Y DERIVADOS SL	ESB60263647	Spain		U	22.55%	0.00%	5.77%
246.	VALUE-ADDED PRODUCTS SL	ESB85537546	Spain	www.sebacom.eu	U	n/a	n/a	n/a
247.	ADITIVOS Y COLORES SL	ESB64651953	Spain	aditivosycoloressl. wordpress.com/2012/11/19/aditivos-y-colores-s-l	U	n/a	n/a	n/a
248.	PUNTO COLOR - SOCIETA' COOPERATIVA	IT01049340571	Italy	0	U	21.44%	1.21%	n/a
249.	IBERPAINT SL	ESB01104439	Spain		U	0.00%	0.00%	36.61%
250.	TECNICAS EN PAVIMENTACION CON-TINUA SL.	ESB40577744	Spain	0	U	0.00%	0.46%	n/a
251.	ESTRELLA Y LUGAR SL	ESB78620044	Spain	www.estrellaylugar.com	U	n/a	n/a	n/a
252.	MB AUTODAZAI	LT304983202	Lithuania	0	U	n/a	n/a	n/a
253.	MANOLIN PIVACOR SOCIEDAD LIMITADA.	ESB21236195	Spain		U	49.01%	0.00%	0.91%
254.	PRODUCCION Y DISTRIBUCION DE PINTURAS Y REVESTIMIENTOS SL	ESB58894601	Spain	0	U	107.79%	0.00%	−0.93%
255.	LACAS BARNICES Y PINTURAS DISTRIBUCIONES BEJAR SL	ESB37416963	Spain		U	58.58%	0.00%	1.31%
256.	PRODUCTOS PAORGA SL	ESB91144436	Spain	www.paorga.com	A+	21.09%	21.07%	0.62%
257.	DECOBEL PINTURAS SL	ESB84705649	Spain	0	U	n/a	n/a	n/a
258.	PINTURAS PINTAJO SL.	ESB93432730	Spain	http://www.pintajo.com/	U	6.68%	0.00%	3.62%
259.	CERES INTERNATIONAL SP. Z O.O. SP.K.	PL382437175	Poland	ceres.pl	U	12.90%	n/a	n/a

(continued)

No. crt.	Company name et	BvD ID number	Country	Website	BvD Independence Indicator	Average Stocks/ Turnover 2017–2019	Average Intangible assets/ Total assets 2017–2019	Average NCP 2017–2019
260.	META TECHNIQUE	FR488652728	France	0	U	n/a	n/a	n/a
261.	FARG & BYGG I MALMO FASTIGHETS AB	SE5565541363	Sweden		U	0.00%	0.00%	18.67%
262.	SECURITY INKS SL.	ESB65809915	Spain	www.securityinks.net	U	0.00%	0.00%	1.13%
263.	DUROL FRANCE PRODUITS CHIMIQUES ET TECHNIQUES POUR PIERRES MARBRES ET POUR L INDUSTRIE	FR688501600	France	www.durol.fr	U	n/a	n/a	n/a
264.	LUCASMUR PINTURA DECORATIVA SL	ESB30394639	Spain	www.lucasmur.com	U	9.48%	0.00%	15.37%
265.	PRIPOL D.O.O.	HR30289404459	Croatia	www.pripol.hr	U	3.57%	0.00%	3.91%
266.	PUERTAS EXCLUSIVAS GARCIA SL	ESB16242463	Spain	www.puertasgarcia.com	U	n/a	n/a	n/a
267.	AUTOKOLOR-CULO, VL. JURE CULO, BJELOVAR,	HR70485207654	Croatia		U	57.17%	0.00%	14.56%
268.	EXCEL S.A.	GR094347751	Greece	0	U	n/a	n/a	n/a
269.	VIDERE REBUS COATINGS AKTIEBOLAG	SE5590193685	Sweden	www.vr-coatings.net	U	51.29%	0.00%	−62.94%
270.	XYLERO KERESKEDELMI, SZOLGALTATO KORLATOLT FELELOSSEGU TARSASAG	HU11107761	Hungary	www.xylero.hu	U	16.58%	0.00%	5.91%
271.	CARPINTERIA ANGEL MORENO SL	ESB13199146	Spain	0	U	24.73%	0.05%	n/a
272.	JOSEBA OLAETA SOCIEDAD LIMITADA.	ESB95347860	Spain	0	U	27.97%	0.00%	−4.00%
273.	PINTURA Y DECORACION BOTANA S.L.	ESB36276079	Spain	0	U	n/a	n/a	n/a
274.	TYPOCHIM P.C.	GR038798305000	Greece	www.typochim.com	U	29.53%	0.00%	11.93%
275.	UAB ARETA	LT121514543	Lithuania	www.areta.lt	U	n/a	0.00%	n/a

276.	BASELL CHEMIE KOELN GMBH	DE6190189852	Germany	0	U	n/a	n/a	n/a
277.	TOTAL CHEM CHEMICAL ZARTKORUEN MUKODO RESZVENYTARSASAG	HU26367655	Hungary	0	U	8.90%	42.84%	n/a
278.	TYFOON GROUP AB	SE5568386311	Sweden		U	34.06%	n/a	34.35%
279.	ALABASTER FARG AB	SE5590751110	Sweden	www.alabasterfarg.se	U	16.43%	0.00%	134.43%
280.	DOMCEL SP. Z O.O.	PL230502781	Poland	www.domcel.com.pl	U	n/a	n/a	n/a
281.	ESPECIALISTAS Y NUEVAS TECNOLOGIAS EN PINTURAS ALC SL.	ESB19580612	Spain	0	U	51.08%	0.00%	n/a
282.	EBANISTERIA ESNAVAL SL	ESB37504107	Spain	0	U	n/a	n/a	n/a
283.	TECNOLOGIA EN PINTURAS Y DECORACION 3000 SL	ESB64992282	Spain	0	A−	n/a	n/a	n/a
284.	PINTURAS LA ANDALUZA 84 SOCIEDAD LIMITADA.	ESB19602408	Spain	https://es.kompass.com/c/pinturas-la-andaluza-84/es990007036680/	U	1.84%	0.00%	3.83%
285.	TERMOKEMIX KENOANYAG GYARTO KORLATOLT FELELOSSEGU TARSASAG	HU14828311	Hungary		U	16.74%	0.00%	30.08%
286.	FABRICA DE PINTURAS ACOARI SLL	ESB21362207	Spain	0	U	n/a	n/a	n/a
287.	MULL UNION TRADE KORLATOLT FELELOSSEGU TARSASAG	HU14608759	Hungary	0	U	63.31%	0.00%	−7.91%
288.	PINTURAS COPINCAT SL	ESB63441216	Spain		U	40.24%	0.00%	3.50%
289.	ZATRARTE S.C.	ESF49276934	Spain	0	U	n/a	n/a	n/a
290.	INTRUSION PREPAKT S.L.	ESB78011707	Spain	0	U	n/a	n/a	n/a
291.	DOMINGUEZ IRIBARREN SL	ESB20793733	Spain		U	4.90%	0.00%	5.39%
292.	OCRES ET COULEURS DU MONT VENTOUX	FR445113376	France	0	U	n/a	n/a	n/a
293.	TOZ PENKALA INTERNATIONAL D.O.O.	HR48888905215	Croatia	0	U	0.00%	0.00%	n/a

(continued)

No. crt.	Company name et	BvD ID number	Country	Website	BvD Independence Indicator	Average Stocks/ Turnover 2017–2019	Average Intangible assets/ Total assets 2017–2019	Average NCP 2017–2019
294.	PINTURAS MORENO Y AGUADO SL.	ESB83711655	Spain	0	U	n/a	n/a	n/a
295.	OLD WOOD COLOURS & VARNISHES SOCIEDAD LIMITADA	ESB85125136	Spain	www.oldwood1700.com	U	0.12%	1.96%	27.17%
296.	UAB GLAISVITA	LT125472383	Lithuania	0	U	1.79%	0.00%	n/a
297.	PRODUCTOS OLOTINA SL	ESB17267345	Spain	www.olotina.com	U	24.34%	0.00%	13.97%
298.	INDUSTRIA COVEPIN SL.	ESB86672201	Spain		U	1.92%	0.00%	3.24%
299.	COMERCIAL QUIMICA APLICADA SA	ESA58149352	Spain	www.cequsa.net	U	146.89%	0.63%	6.30%
300.	ORGUESA&GESTIONA SOCIEDAD LIMITADA.	ESB23527443	Spain	0	U	0.00%	0.00%	n/a
301.	METAL-KORR KERESKEDELMI ES SZOLGALTATO KORLATOLT FELELOSSEGU TARSASAG	HU12337662	Hungary		U	12.13%	0.00%	9.13%
302.	L'ARTISAN PASTELLIER	FR425073442	France	artisanpastellier.com	U	n/a	n/a	n/a
303.	PINTURAS ESTHER SL	ESB73072712	Spain	estherpinturasl970. blogspot.com	U	n/a	n/a	n/a
304.	PINTURAS FRECA SL	ESB24287559	Spain		U	60.89%	0.00%	1.78%
305.	ROSANLAC SL	ESB61761805	Spain	0	U	10.83%	0.00%	n/a
306.	TAPICERIA JUAN Y ANGELES SL	ESB83363044	Spain	0	U	n/a	n/a	n/a
307.	ARPO SL	ESB36600088	Spain	aceitesdepescado.com	U	17.22%	n/a	32.03%
308.	DUGA TEHNA, D.O.O.	HR10855137365	Croatia	0	U	52.50%	0.00%	−12.40%
309.	"UVESZ" UJPESTI VEGYESZETI KORLATOLT FELELOSSEGU TARSASAG	HU10318683	Hungary	www.uvesz.hu	U	27.03%	0.00%	0.26%

310.	FABRICA DE PINTURAS TERMAR SL.	ESB11756152	Spain	0	U	0.00%	n/a	n/a
311.	"CHEMISA" IPARI ES KERESKEDELMI KORLATOLT FELELOSSEGU TARSASAG	HU11523598	Hungary	www.chemisa.hu	U	2.33%	0.00%	−10.44%
312.	OPENNANO POLSKA SP. Z O. O.	PL121486285	Poland	www.opennano.pl	U	6.78%	0.00%	n/a
313.	IMPORT EXPORT VELEZ SL.	ESB93585883	Spain	0	U	0.00%	n/a	n/a
314.	CASTIPLAS SL	ESB37036233	Spain	0	U	n/a	n/a	n/a
315.	DELIKER MANAGMENT SP. Z O.O. SP.K.	PL302553082	Poland	0	U	7.46%	7.71%	−13.36%
316.	EMAILCHIM AD	BG832084361	Bulgaria	www.emailchim.com	A+	21.19%	0.00%	−27.23%
317.	PINTURAS LA FABRICA SL	ESB04132288	Spain	pinturaskomet.com	U	5.29%	n/a	0.02%
318.	PINTURAS VERPIN SL	ESB96713664	Spain	https://pinturasverpin.com/comprar	U	311.52%	0.00%	5.32%
319.	WOODZIL AB	SE5591106322	Sweden	0	U	n/a	75.59%	n/a
320.	PINTURAS ARTESUR SLL	ESB91384495	Spain	0	U	79.91%	0.00%	n/a
321.	ADEFLOCK DEL SURESTE SLL	ESB53986642	Spain	0	U	0.00%	12.87%	3.05%
322.	PRIMEPROTECT SP. Z O.O. SP. K.	PL383306676	Poland	0	U	1.13%	n/a	n/a
323.	BARNIZADOS PARDO SL	ESB47532932	Spain	0	U	n/a	n/a	n/a
324.	HETZI ES TARSA KERESKEDELMI ES SZOLGALTATO BETETI TARSASAG	HU21243723	Hungary		U	n/a	0.14%	19.99%
325.	BITHEIS, S.R.O.	CZ63216515	Czech Republic		A−	0.00%	n/a	51.93%
326.	TORTOSA QUIMICA SL	ESB96007943	Spain		U	269.50%	0.00%	1.08%
327.	HELMET SOLUTIONS S.A.	GR998284154	Greece	0	U	n/a	n/a	n/a
328.	ELICHROM S.A.	GR122134402000	Greece	www.elichrom.eu	U	43.12%	0.00%	30.02%

(continued)

No. crt.	Company name et	BvD ID number	Country	Website	BvD Independence Indicator	Average Stocks/ Turnover 2017–2019	Average Intangible assets/ Total assets 2017–2019	Average NCP 2017–2019
329.	MUEBLES TRABAZO SL	ESB21413299	Spain	0	U	141.77%	0.00%	n/a
330.	PEDRO MATEOS GOMEZ SL	ESB49122682	Spain	0	U	n/a	n/a	n/a
331.	INTRUSION FABRIFORM S.L.	ESB92742782	Spain	0	U	n/a	n/a	n/a
332.	MONTAJES Y MANTENIMIENTO CONALSA SL	ESB83886267	Spain	www.conalsa.com	U	n/a	n/a	n/a
333.	PRZEDSIEBIORSTWO INNOWACYJNE AVANTI SP. Z O.O. SP.K.	PL380291112	Poland	0	U	1.00%	0.00%	n/a
334.	ATELIER PLASTI-TECHNIQUE	FR302558762	France	www.protex-solair-film-protection.fr	U	15.72%	48.45%	n/a
335.	REVESTIMIENTOS DECOR STONES SL	ESB91232397	Spain	0	U	n/a	n/a	n/a
336.	PINTURAS FEIMA SL	ESB45276979	Spain	pinturas-feima.pymes.com	U	42.58%	0.00%	−7.72%
337.	M & D CONSTRUCCIONS EN FUSTA SL	ESB61560959	Spain	0	U	0.00%	n/a	−1.76%
338.	PEPPAS, G., LAC, SOLE SHAREHOLDER CO. LTD	GR099917741	Greece	0	U	n/a	n/a	n/a
339.	GALVANOL IBERIA S.L.	ESB67279653	Spain	www.galvanol.es	U	48.12%	n/a	n/a
340.	RAVENGRUPPEN AB	SE5591473052	Sweden	0	U	n/a	n/a	n/a
341.	BERGSLAGSFARG AB	SE5592559172	Sweden	0	U	n/a	n/a	n/a
342.	INTERCHEMI VEGYIPARI ES KERESKEDELMI KORLATOLT FELELOSSEGU TARSASAG	HU10892749	Hungary		U	76.78%	0.00%	2.64%
343.	ISOL - QUIMICA, COMERCIO DE TINTAS, LDA	PT506209318	Portugal	0	U	n/a	n/a	n/a

344.	LAKKASZ IPARI, FEJLESZTO ES KERESKEDELMI KORLATOLT FELELOSSEGU TARSASAG	HU23446207	Hungary		U	38.31%	0.00%	7.33%
345.	KOLORES PARA METACRILATO SL	ESB80342272	Spain	0	U	155.89%	0.00%	n/a
346.	EMANUEL	HR94350287710	Croatia	0	U	n/a	n/a	n/a
347.	UMIX AB	SE5565716783	Sweden	www.umix.se	U	0.00%	0.00%	n/a
348.	BARNICES Y PINTURAS BAMU SA	ESA48183412	Spain	0	U	n/a	n/a	n/a
349.	KOPPARBERGS PIGMENT AB	SE5563714954	Sweden		U	7.83%	0.00%	5.33%
350.	ANNESTORP 3:33 AB	SE5565915120	Sweden		U	0.00%	0.00%	2.87%
351.	MERCENE COATINGS AB	SE5590821004	Sweden	0	U	n/a	108.52%	n/a
352.	KOMTEK SKAANE AB	SE5568442643	Sweden		U	0.00%	n/a	30.59%
353.	KING COLOR J.D.O.O.	HR99594483541	Croatia	0	U	0.00%	0.00%	n/a
354.	STAR G. S. ANAGNOSTOPOULOS SOLE SHAREHOLDER CO. LTD	GR095058348	Greece	www.starpaints.gr	U	n/a	n/a	n/a
355.	PINTURAS EL BULLAQUE SL	ESB45325651	Spain	0	U	261.02%	0.00%	n/a
356.	PINTURAS POLO S. COOP PEQUENA	ESF01459296	Spain	0	U	n/a	n/a	n/a
357.	CARPINTERIA CARRETERO GARCIA S.L.	ESB42190827	Spain	0	U	208.29%	0.00%	−50.52%
358.	FEROBOT LTD OOD	BG831909773	Bulgaria	0	U	112.12%	0.00%	−14.29%
359.	DALADRY AKTIEBOLAG	SE5569265704	Sweden	www.daladry.se	U	0.00%	n/a	22.14%
360.	PRODUCTOS FRAYMA SLL	ESB21391180	Spain		U	289.20%	0.00%	77.76%
361.	JUAN MELCHOR LOPEZ SALAZAR SL	ESB18411751	Spain	0	U	24.61%	0.00%	n/a
362.	CHEMI-TO GYARTO ES ERTEKESITO BT.	HU28858218	Hungary	0	U	16.11%	0.00%	n/a
363.	ESTRAXCOLOR SL	ESB46637435	Spain	0	U	10.45%	0.00%	n/a
364.	MATEPRINCS SL.	ESB71316756	Spain	www.mateprincs.com	A−	69.02%	38.50%	−82.85%

(continued)

No. crt.	Company name et	BvD ID number	Country	Website	BvD Independence Indicator	Average Stocks/ Turnover 2017–2019	Average Intangible assets/ Total assets 2017–2019	Average NCP 2017–2019
365.	PINTURAS ISMAC SOCIEDAD LIMITADA.	ESB02578359	Spain	0	U	0.00%	0.00%	n/a
366.	CTS COATING TECHNOLOGY SYSTEM ITALY SRL	IT03338260122	Italy	0	U	36.42%	2.74%	−28.70%
367.	COLOFONIAS Y DISOLVENTES SOCIEDAD LIMITADA	ESB50654383	Spain	0	U	123.47%	0.00%	−38.90%
368.	INDUSTRIAS QUIMICAS WIPHAL SLL	ESB21498399	Spain	0	U	n/a	n/a	n/a
369.	SPOLDZIELNIA SOCJALNA NOWY DZIEN	PL380327896	Poland	0	U	0.00%	0.00%	n/a
370.	SPOLDZIELCZE ZAKLADY CHEMICZNE MORS	PL000454020	Poland	www.mors.net.pl	U	4.25%	0.00%	−5.65%
371.	EURO 02 OOD	BG103778623	Bulgaria	www.evro02.com	U	5172.70%	0.00%	n/a
372.	PEINTURAL SARL	FR465800720	France		U	0.00%	1.13%	100.53%
373.	WORLD ART OUTLET S.R.L.	IT03585341203	Italy		A−	93.71%	1.24%	0.82%
374.	LACK OCH FARG HARALD JANSSON AKTIEBOLAG	SE5562453000	Sweden		U	264.88%	n/a	11.64%
375.	EPISENTUM AB	SE5590755376	Sweden		U	0.00%	n/a	4.90%
376.	CARPINGENIL SL	ESB14378855	Spain		U	1759.15%	0.00%	331.27%
377.	PINTURAS HONOR SL	ESB36001980	Spain	0	U	n/a	n/a	n/a
378.	SIOO FARGKULTUR AB	SE5569084881	Sweden		U	0.00%	n/a	64.45%
379.	PRESCRIPCIONES PROYECTOS E INVERSIONES SL	ESB97503916	Spain	0	U	0.00%	0.00%	n/a
380.	ROBERT EXACT COLOURS SLOVAKIA, S.R.O.	SK36505242	Slovakia	0	U	n/a	n/a	n/a

381.	VITENERGO KERESKEDELMI ES SZOLGALTATO KORLATOLT FELELOSSEGU TARSASAG	HU23804757	Hungary	0	U	18.27%	0.00%	−30.35%
382.	EBERTON AB	SE5590696083	Sweden	www.eberton.se	U	3.31%	n/a	8.06%
383.	PRO-FARB SP. Z O.O. SP.K.	PL364038070	Poland	0	U	0.23%	n/a	n/a
384.	NADJOB MUNKAERO-KOLCSONZO, MUNKAKOZVETITO ES MAR-KETING KORLATOLT FELELOSSEGU TARSASAG	HU23746095	Hungary	0	U	n/a	0.00%	−19.54%
385.	NANOPRO J.D.O.O.	HR96373858494	Croatia		U	0.00%	0.00%	102.87%
386.	IMPRIO AB	SE5569423055	Sweden	www.imprio.se	U	172.65%	46.86%	−57.79%
387.	XHUPS ALUSO SOCIEDAD LIMITADA	ESB43734847	Spain	0	U	n/a	n/a	n/a
388.	INDUSTRIAS RUBIO SA	ESA26019869	Spain	0	A−	n/a	n/a	n/a
389.	CYCLOMEX VEGYIPARI ES KERESKEDELMI KORLATOLT FELELOSSEGU TARSASAG	HU10627895	Hungary		U	9.82%	0.00%	0.40%
390.	COLOR PI BAC	FR838574002	France	0	U	n/a	0.00%	n/a
391.	IRIS	FR847848082	France	0	U	n/a	0.00%	n/a
392.	DREVOLUX, S.R.O. V LIKVIDACII	SK31576184	Slovakia	0	U	n/a	n/a	n/a
393.	CSB	BE0403090032	Belgium	www.csb-battery.com	U	n/a	0.00%	n/a
394.	BASIN CHEMECO	BE0403102504	Belgium	www.basin.be	U	n/a	5.48%	n/a
395.	IMPERPLEX	BE0403125763	Belgium	www.imperplex.be	U	n/a	0.00%	n/a
396.	ETABLISSEMENTEN L. MARICHAL	BE0403649761	Belgium	0	U	n/a	0.00%	n/a
397.	JORDAN EN CO	BE0403834754	Belgium	0	U	n/a	0.47%	n/a
398.	DAVID	BE0403943929	Belgium	0	U	n/a	n/a	n/a
399.	LAN 2 MIL	BE0403980254	Belgium	0	U	n/a	0.00%	n/a

(continued)

No. crt.	Company name et	BvD ID number	Country	Website	BvD Independence Indicator	Average Stocks/ Turnover 2017–2019	Average Intangible assets/ Total assets 2017–2019	Average NCP 2017–2019
400.	BRIAN INTERNATIONAL	BE0407738015	Belgium	0	U	n/a	0.00%	n/a
401.	GEHA	BE0415909373	Belgium	www.geha.com	U	n/a	n/a	n/a
402.	FRANZ JOST	BE0419125617	Belgium	franz-jost.com	U	n/a	0.46%	n/a
403.	NOVOGRAPH	BE0419686435	Belgium	0	U	n/a	0.00%	n/a
404.	PROCHIBAT	BE0423138942	Belgium	www.prochibat.be	U	n/a	0.00%	n/a
405.	BEMICOLOR	BE0425071717	Belgium	www. bemicolorpeintureengros. be	U	n/a	0.00%	n/a
406.	SUBSEA INDUSTRIES	BE0426301241	Belgium	www.subind.net	U	n/a	0.00%	n/a
407.	H.S.H. AEROSPACE FINISHES	BE0428583117	Belgium	www.hsh.be	U	n/a	0.00%	n/a
408.	DUTCH PAINTS AND TEXTILES	BE0434677586	Belgium	0	U	n/a	0.00%	n/a
409.	SICO	BE0438082583	Belgium	www.sico-inks.com	U	n/a	0.00%	n/a
410.	COPAINT	BE0444341657	Belgium	0	U	n/a	0.00%	n/a
411.	ECO - COLORS	BE0450874212	Belgium	www.ecocolors.be	U	n/a	0.24%	n/a
412.	BIOGRAPHIC	BE0452474316	Belgium	www.biographic.be	U	n/a	0.00%	n/a
413.	EVERCHEM ET DRAGOPAINT	BE0460676754	Belgium	dragopaint.be	U	n/a	0.00%	n/a
414.	M.T.C.C.	BE0461260041	Belgium	0	U	n/a	0.00%	n/a
415.	EYROFLAM	BE0461388220	Belgium	www.eyroflam.be	U	n/a	5.44%	n/a
416.	SUPERIOR PRODUCTS EUROPE	BE0461876287	Belgium	www.specoating.com	U	n/a	0.00%	n/a
417.	DOTHEE	BE0463465703	Belgium	www.dothee.be	U	n/a	1.40%	n/a
418.	EDWARDS	BE0466542482	Belgium	www.edwardsvacuum. com	U	n/a	0.00%	n/a
419.	RENKO PAINTS	BE0468319859	Belgium	www.renkopaints.be	U	n/a	0.00%	n/a
420.	JOAN-PRODUCTS	BE0476370958	Belgium	www.joanproducts.be	U	n/a	0.00%	n/a
421.	STUC AND STAFF	BE0476382836	Belgium	0	U	n/a	n/a	n/a

422.	ECO PAINT	BE0526876284	Belgium	ecopaint.be	U	n/a	1.18%	n/a
423.	NANOSKIN	BE0550572295	Belgium	www.nanoskinusa.com	U	n/a	13.74%	n/a
424.	OPEN CREATIVITY	BE0675940045	Belgium	0	U	n/a	0.00%	n/a
425.	CRALUX	BE0679475892	Belgium	0	U	n/a	0.00%	n/a
426.	UNITOP DECO	BE0683511191	Belgium	0	U	n/a	n/a	n/a
427.	BRANTON ARTS	BE0811938401	Belgium	www.williams-koch.com	U	n/a	0.00%	n/a
428.	B-COAT	BE0828102262	Belgium	b-coat.be	U	n/a	0.10%	n/a
429.	SEBEK INKS	BE0846337173	Belgium	www.sebekinks.eu	U	n/a	0.98%	n/a
430.	GE-KA SUPPLIES	BE0861114827	Belgium	www.ge-ka-supplies.com	U	n/a	0.18%	n/a
431.	SUN7.BE	BE0862830143	Belgium	www.sun7.be	U	n/a	0.00%	n/a
432.	L'OCRIER	BE0866267309	Belgium	www.locrier.com	U	n/a	0.00%	n/a
433.	HVK PRODUCTS	BE0879219084	Belgium	0	U	n/a	2.29%	n/a
434.	PROSPECTRUM COATINGS	BE0888532074	Belgium	0	U	n/a	n/a	n/a
435.	HATWEE	BE0892645666	Belgium	www.hatwee.be	U	n/a	3.58%	n/a
436.	KUS BATI	BE0893275770	Belgium	0	U	n/a	n/a	n/a
437.	KRD COATINGS GMBH	DE2150062425	Germany	www.kasiglas.de	U	n/a	n/a	n/a
438.	LACOLOR LACKFABRIKATION GMBH	DE4010037392	Germany	www.lacolor.de	U	n/a	n/a	n/a
439.	H. & W. SOETEBIER NACHF. GMBH	DE4010065377	Germany	www.hm-bautenschutz.de	U	n/a	n/a	n/a
440.	RZ CHEMIE GMBH REINIGUNGS- UND PFLEGESYSTEME	DE5030003296	Germany	www.rz-systeme.de	U	n/a	n/a	n/a
441.	MS LOESUNGSMITTEL-VERTRIEBSGESELLSCHAFT MBH	DE5130097935	Germany	0	U	n/a	n/a	n/a
442.	JOH. CARL KOCHEN GMBH & CO. KG	DE5210011935	Germany	0	U	n/a	n/a	n/a
443.	LACK- U. KLEBSTOFF-WERKE FAY GMBH & CO. KG	DE7170005519	Germany	0	U	n/a	n/a	n/a
444.	FRIEDRICH KLUMPP GMBH	DE7330091133	Germany	0	U	n/a	0.76%	n/a

(continued)

No. crt.	Company name et	BvD ID number	Country	Website	BvD Independence Indicator	Average Stocks/ Turnover 2017–2019	Average Intangible assets/ Total assets 2017–2019	Average NCP 2017–2019
445.	HUDELMAIER FARBEN GMBH	DE7330768256	Germany	www.huma-farben.de	U	n/a	n/a	n/a
446.	BAUMANN FARBEN + LACKE GMBH	DE8030106480	Germany	0	U	n/a	n/a	n/a
447.	POLYMER-CHEMIE FARBEN + LACKE GMBH	DE8030169170	Germany	0	U	n/a	n/a	n/a
448.	FARBEN DISTLER GMBH & CO. KG	DE8190628252	Germany	0	U	n/a	n/a	n/a
449.	JP COATINGS GMBH	DE8310331882	Germany	www.rz-reinigungssysteme.de	U	n/a	n/a	n/a
450.	PRODUITS MAULER SARL	FR392171351	France	www.mauler.fr	U	n/a	15.96%	n/a
451.	EURL SURGAND INDUSTRIE	FR752303347	France	www.surgand-shop.fr	U	18.94%	27.30%	n/a
452.	SIKOI	FR801913567	Reunion (France)	0	U	n/a	0.00%	n/a
453.	LES PEINTURES FRANCAISES INDUSTRIELLES	FR833219835	France	0	U	n/a	0.02%	n/a
454.	ETABLISSEMENTS TROLLIET ET COMPAGNIE	FR969508290	France	0	U	15.75%	0.00%	n/a
455.	W.S.JENKINS & COMPANY LIMITED	GB00259600	United Kingdom	www.wsjenkins.co.uk	A–	n/a	0.00%	n/a
456.	EAGLE INDUSTRIAL PAINTS LIMITED	GB00971425	United Kingdom	0	U	n/a	n/a	n/a
457.	PEELAWAY PRODUCTION LIMITED	GB07743665	United Kingdom	0	A+	n/a	0.00%	n/a
458.	ULTRIMAX COATINGS LIMITED	GB08472363	United Kingdom	www.ultrimaxcoatings.co.uk	A–	n/a	1.13%	n/a
459.	UNOVA LIMITED	GB10406638	United Kingdom	www.unovaproducts.com	A+	n/a	8.49%	n/a

460.	MANDERS COATINGS & INKS IRELAND LIMITED	IE015877	Ireland	www.manders.ie	U	n/a	0.00%	n/a
461.	AN SIOPA POITIGEARA TEORANTA	IE185254	Ireland	0	U	n/a	n/a	n/a
462.	BACSKABEL INFORMATIKAI FEJLESZTO ES SZOLGALTATO KORLATOLT FELELOSSEGU TARSASAG	HU12554104	Hungary	www.bacskabel.hu	U	n/a	0.00%	n/a
463.	HAYA MAREK BUKOWSKI I WSPOLNICY - SP.J.	PL003142255	Poland	www.haya.pl	U	n/a	n/a	n/a
464.	POLSKA FABRYKA FARB I LAKIEROW EDWARD LUTZ SP. Z O.O.	PL122786167	Poland	0	U	n/a	n/a	n/a
465.	MILKATRANS SP. Z O.O. SP.K.	PL146407725	Poland	www.milkatrans.pl	U	n/a	n/a	n/a
466.	LAKNUS SP. Z O.O. S.K.	PL146673562	Poland	redix.pl	U	0.00%	n/a	n/a
467.	POLSKI KONCERN CHEMICZNY SP. Z O.O.	PL361148154	Poland	0	A+	n/a	n/a	n/a
468.	ELVORA SP. Z O.O. SP.K.	PL364723742	Poland	0	U	n/a	n/a	n/a
469.	OSANIX SP. Z O.O. SP.K.	PL368743109	Poland	0	U	n/a	89.42%	n/a
470.	MICHOR K.MICHALSKI, S. STEFANIAK SP.J.	PL610409317	Poland	www.michor.pl	U	8.10%	0.00%	n/a
471.	SMIT COATINGS B.V.	NL05030401	Netherlands	0	U	n/a	0.00%	n/a
472.	LIEKENS B.V.	NL08074970	Netherlands	www.decoliek.nl	U	n/a	0.00%	n/a
473.	TOSAF BENELUX B.V.	NL09083996	Netherlands	www.tosaf.nl	U	n/a	1.53%	n/a
474.	SCHUITE & SCHUITE NEDER-LAND B.V.	NL09101043	Netherlands	0	U	n/a	0.00%	n/a
475.	WORLDWIDECOLOURS B.V.	NL09121004	Netherlands	www.worldwidecolours.com	U	n/a	n/a	n/a
476.	HOLCAR COATINGS B.V.	NL11065384	Netherlands	www.holcar.nl	U	n/a	0.00%	n/a
477.	ZELLER & GMELIN B.V.	NL17066528	Netherlands	www.zeller-gmelin.nl	U	n/a	0.00%	n/a
478.	LOOIJESTIJN BEHEER B.V.	NL28067574	Netherlands	0	U	n/a	0.00%	n/a

(continued)

No. crt.	Company name et	BvD ID number	Country	Website	BvD Independence Indicator	Average Stocks/ Turnover 2017–2019	Average Intangible assets/ Total assets 2017–2019	Average NCP 2017–2019
479.	DE IJSSEL COATINGS B.V.	NL29021515	Netherlands	www.de-ijssel-coatings.nl	U	n/a	0.00%	n/a
480.	A. BOK & ZONEN B.V.	NL33054596	Netherlands	www.bok-en-zn.nl	U	n/a	0.00%	n/a
481.	W. HEEREN & ZN B.V.	NL34060567	Netherlands	www.epifanes.nl	U	n/a	0.00%	n/a
482.	LAKFABRIEK KORTHALS B.V.	NL34077062	Netherlands	www.korthals.nl	U	n/a	0.00%	n/a
483.	SOEN'S MEUBELBEITSEN B.V.	NL34077100	Netherlands	www.soen.nl	U	n/a	n/a	n/a
484.	VERF- EN VERNISFABRIEKEN KOOL & CO. B.V.	NL36017231	Netherlands	www.koolmedemblik.nl	U	n/a	0.00%	n/a
485.	SPECIAL FILLS B.V.	NL37105436	Netherlands	www.specialfills.nl	U	n/a	0.00%	n/a
486.	NICE PAINTS B.V.	NL52182967	Netherlands	www.koopmansverfshop.nl	U	n/a	0.00%	n/a
487.	EARTH COATINGS B.V.	NL58537783	Netherlands	0	U	n/a	0.00%	n/a
488.	SAST!DO B.V.	NL74642642	Netherlands	0	U	n/a	n/a	n/a
489.	GLOR-ISOL B.V.	NL74659197	Netherlands	www.glor-isol.eu	U	n/a	n/a	n/a
490.	SAEDT COATINGS B.V.	NL75415054	Netherlands	0	U	n/a	n/a	n/a
491.	DOXA TECHNOLOGICAL SYSTEMS INTERNATIONAL B.V.	NL76550060	Netherlands	0	U	n/a	0.00%	n/a
492.	A ET A MADER ESPANA SA	ESA63241079	Spain	0	U	n/a	n/a	n/a
493.	CARPUVEN SL	ESB10168086	Spain	0	U	n/a	0.00%	n/a
494.	MAIDAL SL	ESB12057543	Spain	0	U	n/a	n/a	n/a
495.	EIROCRON SL	ESB12448809	Spain	0	U	n/a	0.00%	n/a
496.	GRALSA SL	ESB14415053	Spain	www.gralsa.com	U	n/a	0.00%	n/a
497.	MARTINEZ PORTILLO SL	ESB16158057	Spain	0	U	n/a	n/a	n/a

498.	CARPINTERIA ALPER ENCINASOLA SL	ESB21211107	Spain	0	U	0.61%	0.00%	n/a
499.	PREFABRICADOS Y ESTRUCTURAS TENSITERRA S.L.	ESB28704336	Spain	0	U	n/a	n/a	n/a
500.	EPC-PINTURAS SL	ESB29568482	Spain	0	U	n/a	n/a	n/a
501.	REVESTIMIENTOS PLASTICOS SL	ESB29826260	Spain	www.reyplas.com	U	n/a	n/a	n/a
502.	SAYMO COLOR S.L.	ESB30872014	Spain	0	U	n/a	0.00%	n/a
503.	SERVERA-FERRA-SERRA MADERA ESTRUCTURAL SL	ESB57620775	Spain	0	U	n/a	n/a	n/a
504.	COLORIMA S.L.	ESB61674305	Spain	0	U	n/a	n/a	n/a
505.	DISTRIBUCIO DE LAQUES DEL BAIX LLOBREGAT SL	ESB61833844	Spain	0	U	n/a	n/a	n/a
506.	TRAVAC SL	ESB78508876	Spain	0	U	n/a	0.00%	n/a
507.	COLPAINT SL	ESB81301210	Spain	0	U	n/a	n/a	n/a
508.	JOMASER SL	ESB82208778	Spain	0	U	n/a	n/a	n/a
509.	EUROLOR BRAND GMBH	AT9150126396	Austria	0	U	n/a	n/a	n/a
510.	LINOTECH AB	SE5565508446	Sweden	www.linotech.se	U	n/a	n/a	n/a
511.	AASA KARLSSON FORVALTNING AB	SE5569594384	Sweden	0	U	0.00%	0.00%	n/a
512.	SOLVENT RECYCLING SOLU-TIONS HOGBYTORP AB	SE5592718646	Sweden	0	U	n/a	n/a	n/a

No. crt.	Toll manufacturer		Contract manufacturer		Fully-fledged manufacturer	
	Rejected/ accepted	Rejection reason	Rejected/ accepted	Rejection reason	Rejected/ accepted	Rejection reason
1.	No	Lack of financial data (turnover/ operational result)	No	Lack of financial data (turnover/ operational result)	No	Lack of financial data (turnover/ operational result)
2.	No	Average Stocks/Turnover >5%	No	The independence criteria are not met	No	Average Intangibile asstes/Total assets <3%
3.	No	Lack of financial data (turnover/ operational result)	No	Lack of financial data (turnover/ operational result)	No	Lack of financial data (turnover/ operational result)
4.	No	Average Stocks/Turnover >5%	No	Other functional profile	No	Average Intangibile asstes/Total assets <3%
5.	No	Average Stocks/Turnover >5%	No	The independence criteria are not met	No	Average Intangibile asstes/Total assets <3%
6.	No	Average Stocks/Turnover >5%	No	The independence criteria are not met	No	Average Intangibile asstes/Total assets <3%
7.	No	Lack of financial data (turnover/ operational result)	No	Lack of financial data (turnover/ operational result)	No	Lack of financial data (turnover/ operational result)
8.	No	Average Stocks/Turnover >5%	No	Average Intangible assets/Total assets >3%	No	The website doesn't work
9.	No	Lack of financial data (turnover/ operational result)	No	Lack of financial data (turnover/ operational result)	No	Lack of financial data (turnover/ operational result)
10.	No	Average Stocks/Turnover >5%	No	Other functional profile	No	Average Intangibile asstes/Total assets <3%
11.	No	Average Stocks/Turnover >5%	No	Other functional profile	No	Average Intangibile asstes/Total assets <3%
12.	No	Average Stocks/Turnover >5%	No	Other products	No	Average Intangibile asstes/Total assets <3%
13.	No	Average Stocks/Turnover >5%	No	The independence criteria are not met	No	Average Intangibile asstes/Total assets <3%

14.	No	Average Stocks/Turnover >5%	No	Other functional profile	No	Average Intangibile asstes/Total assets <3%
15.	No	Average Stocks/Turnover >5%	No	The independence criteria are not met	No	Average Intangibile asstes/Total assets <3%
16.	No	Lack of financial data (turnover/ operational result)	No	Lack of financial data (turnover/ operational result)	No	Lack of financial data (turnover/ operational result)
17.	No	Average Stocks/Turnover >5%	No	The website doesn't work	No	Average Intangibile asstes/Total assets <3%
18.	No	Lack of financial data (turnover/ operational result)	No	Lack of financial data (turnover/ operational result)	No	Lack of financial data (turnover/ operational result)
19.	No	Lack of financial data (turnover/ operational result)	No	Lack of financial data (turnover/ operational result)	No	Lack of financial data (turnover/ operational result)
20.	No	Average Stocks/Turnover >5%	No	Average Intangible assets/Total assets >3%	Yes	Accepted
21.	No	Average Stocks/Turnover >5%	No	Other functional profile	No	Average Intangibile asstes/Total assets <3%
22.	No	Average Stocks/Turnover >5%	No	The website doesn't work	No	Average Intangibile asstes/Total assets <3%
23.	No	Lack of financial data (turnover/ operational result)	No	Lack of financial data (turnover/ operational result)	No	Lack of financial data (turnover/ operational result)
24.	No	Average Stocks/Turnover >5%	No	Other functional profile	No	Average Intangibile asstes/Total assets <3%
25.	No	Average Stocks/Turnover >5%	No	Other functional profile	No	Average Intangibile asstes/Total assets <3%
26.	No	Average Stocks/Turnover >5%	No	Other products	No	Average Intangibile asstes/Total assets <3%
27.	Yes	Accepted	No	Average Stocks/Turnover <5%	No	Average Stocks/Turnover <5%
28.	No	Average Stocks/Turnover >5%	No	Other functional profile	No	Average Intangibile asstes/Total assets <3%

(continued)

	Toll manufacturer		Contract manufacturer		Fully-fledged manufacturer	
No. crt.	Rejected/ accepted	Rejection reason	Rejected/ accepted	Rejection reason	Rejected/ accepted	Rejection reason
29.	No	Average Stocks/Turnover >5%	No	Other functional profile	No	Average Intangibile asstes/Total assets <3%
30.	No	Average Stocks/Turnover >5%	No	Other functional profile	No	Average Intangibile asstes/Total assets <3%
31.	No	Average Stocks/Turnover >5%	No	The website doesn't work	No	Average Intangibile asstes/Total assets <3%
32.	No	Average Stocks/Turnover >5%	No	Average Intangible assets/Total assets >3%	Yes	Accepted
33.	No	Average Stocks/Turnover >5%	No	Average Intangible assets/Total assets >3%	Yes	Accepted
34.	No	Lack of financial data (turnover/ operational result)	No	Lack of financial data (turnover/ operational result)	No	Lack of financial data (turnover/ operational result)
35.	No	Average Stocks/Turnover >5%	No	Negative average NCP	No	Average Intangibile asstes/Total assets <3%
36.	No	Lack of financial data (turnover/ operational result)	No	Lack of financial data (turnover/ operational result)	No	Lack of financial data (turnover/ operational result)
37.	No	Average Stocks/Turnover >5%	No	Average Intangible assets/Total assets >3%	No	The independence criteria are not met
38.	No	Average Stocks/Turnover >5%	No	The website doesn't work	No	Average Intangibile asstes/Total assets <3%
39.	No	Average Stocks/Turnover >5%	No	Other functional profile	No	Average Intangibile asstes/Total assets <3%
40.	No	Average Stocks/Turnover >5%	No	Negative average NCP	No	Average Intangibile asstes/Total assets <3%
41.	No	Average Stocks/Turnover >5%	Yes	Accepted	No	Average Intangibile asstes/Total assets <3%

42.	No	Average Stocks/Turnover >5%	No	Negative average NCP	No	Average Intangibile asstes/Total assets <3%
43.	No	Average Stocks/Turnover >5%	No	Average Intangible assets/Total assets >3%	Yes	Accepted
44.	No	Average Stocks/Turnover >5%	No	Other functional profile	No	Average Intangibile asstes/Total assets <3%
45.	No	Average Stocks/Turnover >5%	No	Other functional profile	No	Average Intangibile asstes/Total assets <3%
46.	No	Average Stocks/Turnover >5%	Yes	Accepted	No	Average Intangibile asstes/Total assets <3%
47.	No	Average Stocks/Turnover >5%	No	Other functional profile	No	Average Intangibile asstes/Total assets <3%
48.	No	Average Stocks/Turnover >5%	Yes	Accepted	No	Average Intangibile asstes/Total assets <3%
49.	No	Average Stocks/Turnover >5%	No	The independence criteria are not met	No	Average Intangibile asstes/Total assets <3%
50.	No	Lack of financial data (turnover/ operational result)	No	Lack of financial data (turnover/ operational result)	No	Lack of financial data (turnover/ operational result)
51.	No	Average Stocks/Turnover >5%	No	Other products	No	Average Intangibile asstes/Total assets <3%
52.	No	Average Stocks/Turnover >5%	No	Other functional profile	No	Average Intangibile asstes/Total assets <3%
53.	No	Average Stocks/Turnover >5%	No	Average Intangible assets/Total assets >3%	No	The independence criteria are not met
54.	No	Lack of financial data (turnover/ operational result)	No	Lack of financial data (turnover/ operational result)	No	Lack of financial data (turnover/ operational result)
55.	No	Average Stocks/Turnover >5%	No	Average Intangible assets/Total assets >3%	Yes	Accepted
56.	No	Lack of financial data (turnover/ operational result)	No	Lack of financial data (turnover/ operational result)	No	Lack of financial data (turnover/ operational result)

(continued)

	Toll manufacturer		Contract manufacturer		Fully-fledged manufacturer	
No. crt.	Rejected/ accepted	Rejection reason	Rejected/ accepted	Rejection reason	Rejected/ accepted	Rejection reason
57.	No	Average Stocks/Turnover >5%	No	The website doesn't work	No	Average Intangibile asstes/Total assets <3%
58.	No	Average Stocks/Turnover >5%	No	Other functional profile	No	Average Intangibile asstes/Total assets <3%
59.	No	Average Stocks/Turnover >5%	No	Other functional profile	No	Average Intangibile asstes/Total assets <3%
60.	No	Average Stocks/Turnover >5%	Yes	Accepted	No	Average Intangibile asstes/Total assets <3%
61.	No	Lack of financial data (turnover/ operational result)	No	Lack of financial data (turnover/ operational result)	No	Lack of financial data (turnover/ operational result)
62.	No	Average Stocks/Turnover >5%	No	Other products	No	Average Intangibile asstes/Total assets <3%
63.	No	Average Stocks/Turnover >5%	No	Other functional profile	No	Average Intangibile asstes/Total assets <3%
64.	No	Lack of financial data (turnover/ operational result)	No	Lack of financial data (turnover/ operational result)	No	Lack of financial data (turnover/ operational result)
65.	No	Lack of financial data (turnover/ operational result)	No	Lack of financial data (turnover/ operational result)	No	Lack of financial data (turnover/ operational result)
66.	No	Lack of financial data (turnover/ operational result)	No	Lack of financial data (turnover/ operational result)	No	Lack of financial data (turnover/ operational result)
67.	No	Average Stocks/Turnover >5%	No	Average Intangible assets/Total assets >3%	No	The website doesn't work
68.	No	Lack of website	No	Average Stocks/Turnover <5%	No	Average Stocks/Turnover <5%
69.	No	Average Stocks/Turnover >5%	No	Other products	No	Average Intangibile asstes/Total assets <3%
70.	No	Average Stocks/Turnover >5%	No	The independence criteria are not met	No	Average Intangibile asstes/Total assets <3%

71.	No	Lack of financial data (turnover/ operational result)	No	Lack of financial data (turnover/ operational result)	No	Lack of financial data (turnover/ operational result)
72.	No	Other functional profile	No	Average Stocks/Turnover <5%	No	Average Stocks/Turnover <5%
73.	No	Average Stocks/Turnover >5%	No	The website doesn't work	No	Average Intangibile asstes/Total assets <3%
74.	No	Average Stocks/Turnover >5%	No	Average Intangible assets/Total assets >3%	No	The independence criteria are not met
75.	No	Lack of financial data (turnover/ operational result)	No	Lack of financial data (turnover/ operational result)	No	Lack of financial data (turnover/ operational result)
76.	No	Average Stocks/Turnover >5%	No	The website doesn't work	No	Average Intangibile asstes/Total assets <3%
77.	No	Average Stocks/Turnover >5%	No	The independence criteria are not met	No	Average Intangibile asstes/Total assets <3%
78.	No	Lack of financial data (turnover/ operational result)	No	Lack of financial data (turnover/ operational result)	No	Lack of financial data (turnover/ operational result)
79.	No	Average Stocks/Turnover >5%	No	Negative average NCP	No	Average Intangibile asstes/Total assets <3%
80.	No	Average Stocks/Turnover >5%	No	Other functional profile	No	Average Intangibile asstes/Total assets <3%
81.	No	Lack of financial data (turnover/ operational result)	No	Lack of financial data (turnover/ operational result)	No	Lack of financial data (turnover/ operational result)
82.	No	Lack of financial data (turnover/ operational result)	No	Lack of financial data (turnover/ operational result)	No	Lack of financial data (turnover/ operational result)
83.	No	Average Stocks/Turnover >5%	No	Other products	No	Average Intangibile asstes/Total assets <3%
84.	No	Average Stocks/Turnover >5%	Yes	Accepted	No	Average Intangibile asstes/Total assets <3%
85.	No	Average Stocks/Turnover >5%	No	The independence criteria are not met	No	Average Intangibile asstes/Total assets <3%

(continued)

No. crt.	Toll manufacturer		Contract manufacturer		Fully-fledged manufacturer	
	Rejected/ accepted	Rejection reason	Rejected/ accepted	Rejection reason	Rejected/ accepted	Rejection reason
86.	No	Other functional profile	No	Average Stocks/Turnover <5%	No	Average Stocks/Turnover <5%
87.	No	Lack of financial data (turnover/ operational result)	No	Lack of financial data (turnover/ operational result)	No	Lack of financial data (turnover/ operational result)
88.	No	Average Stocks/Turnover >5%	No	Other products	No	Average Intangibile asstes/Total assets <3%
89.	No	Lack of financial data (turnover/ operational result)	No	Lack of financial data (turnover/ operational result)	No	Lack of financial data (turnover/ operational result)
90.	No	Lack of financial data (turnover/ operational result)	No	Lack of financial data (turnover/ operational result)	No	Lack of financial data (turnover/ operational result)
91.	No	Average Stocks/Turnover >5%	Yes	Accepted	No	Average Intangibile asstes/Total assets <3%
92.	No	Average Stocks/Turnover >5%	No	Negative average NCP	No	Average Intangibile asstes/Total assets <3%
93.	No	Lack of financial data (turnover/ operational result)	No	Lack of financial data (turnover/ operational result)	No	Lack of financial data (turnover/ operational result)
94.	No	Average Stocks/Turnover >5%	No	Lack of website	No	Average Intangibile asstes/Total assets <3%
95.	No	Average Stocks/Turnover >5%	No	Other products	No	Average Intangibile asstes/Total assets <3%
96.	No	Lack of financial data (turnover/ operational result)	No	Lack of financial data (turnover/ operational result)	No	Lack of financial data (turnover/ operational result)
97.	No	Lack of website	No	Average Stocks/Turnover <5%	No	Average Stocks/Turnover <5%
98.	No	Average Stocks/Turnover >5%	No	The website doesn’t work	No	Average Intangibile asstes/Total assets <3%
99.	No	Average Stocks/Turnover >5%	No	Negative average NCP	No	Average Intangibile asstes/Total assets <3%

100.	No	Lack of financial data (turnover/ operational result)	No	Lack of financial data (turnover/ operational result)	No	Lack of financial data (turnover/ operational result)
101.	No	Average Stocks/Turnover >5%	No	Negative average NCP	No	Average Intangibile asstes/Total assets <3%
102.	No	Average Stocks/Turnover >5%	Yes	Accepted	No	Average Intangibile asstes/Total assets <3%
103.	No	Average Stocks/Turnover >5%	No	Negative average NCP	No	Average Intangibile asstes/Total assets <3%
104.	No	Average Stocks/Turnover >5%	No	Other functional profile	No	Average Intangibile asstes/Total assets <3%
105.	No	Lack of website	No	Average Stocks/Turnover <5%	No	Average Stocks/Turnover <5%
106.	No	Average Stocks/Turnover >5%	No	Other functional profile	No	Average Intangibile asstes/Total assets <3%
107.	No	Lack of financial data (turnover/ operational result)	No	Lack of financial data (turnover/ operational result)	No	Lack of financial data (turnover/ operational result)
108.	No	Lack of financial data (turnover/ operational result)	No	Lack of financial data (turnover/ operational result)	No	Lack of financial data (turnover/ operational result)
109.	No	Average Stocks/Turnover >5%	No	Negative average NCP	No	Average Intangibile asstes/Total assets <3%
110.	No	Lack of financial data (turnover/ operational result)	No	Lack of financial data (turnover/ operational result)	No	Lack of financial data (turnover/ operational result)
111.	No	Average Stocks/Turnover >5%	No	Other functional profile	No	Average Intangibile asstes/Total assets <3%
112.	No	Lack of financial data (turnover/ operational result)	No	Lack of financial data (turnover/ operational result)	No	Lack of financial data (turnover/ operational result)
113.	No	Average Stocks/Turnover >5%	No	The independence criteria are not met	No	Average Intangibile asstes/Total assets <3%
114.	No	Average Stocks/Turnover >5%	Yes	Accepted	No	Average Intangibile asstes/Total assets <3%

(continued)

No. crt.	Toll manufacturer		Contract manufacturer		Fully-fledged manufacturer	
	Rejected/ accepted	Rejection reason	Rejected/ accepted	Rejection reason	Rejected/ accepted	Rejection reason
115.	No	The independence criteria are not met	No	Average Stocks/Turnover <5%	No	Average Stocks/Turnover <5%
116.	No	Other products	No	Average Stocks/Turnover <5%	No	Average Stocks/Turnover <5%
117.	No	Average Stocks/Turnover >5%	No	Negative average NCP	No	Average Intangibile asstes/Total assets <3%
118.	No	Average Stocks/Turnover >5%	No	Average Intangible assets/Total assets >3%	No	Negative average NCP
119.	No	Lack of financial data (turnover/ operational result)	No	Lack of financial data (turnover/ operational result)	No	Lack of financial data (turnover/ operational result)
120.	No	Average Stocks/Turnover >5%	No	Average Intangible assets/Total assets >3%	No	Other products
121.	No	Average Stocks/Turnover >5%	No	Other functional profile	No	Average Intangibile asstes/Total assets <3%
122.	No	Average Stocks/Turnover >5%	No	The website doesn't work	No	Average Intangibile asstes/Total assets <3%
123.	No	Lack of financial data (turnover/ operational result)	No	Lack of financial data (turnover/ operational result)	No	Lack of financial data (turnover/ operational result)
124.	No	Lack of financial data (turnover/ operational result)	No	Lack of financial data (turnover/ operational result)	No	Lack of financial data (turnover/ operational result)
125.	No	Lack of financial data (turnover/ operational result)	No	Lack of financial data (turnover/ operational result)	No	Lack of financial data (turnover/ operational result)
126.	No	Average Stocks/Turnover >5%	No	Lack of website	No	Average Intangibile asstes/Total assets <3%
127.	No	Average Stocks/Turnover >5%	No	Other functional profile	No	Average Intangibile asstes/Total assets <3%
128.	No	Lack of financial data (turnover/ operational result)	No	Lack of financial data (turnover/ operational result)	No	Lack of financial data (turnover/ operational result)

129.	No	Average Stocks/Turnover >5%	No	Lack of website	No	Average Intangibile asstes/Total assets <3%
130.	No	Average Stocks/Turnover >5%	No	Lack of website	No	Average Intangibile asstes/Total assets <3%
131.	No	Average Stocks/Turnover >5%	No	Other functional profile	No	Average Intangibile asstes/Total assets <3%
132.	No	Average Stocks/Turnover >5%	No	Lack of website	No	Average Intangibile asstes/Total assets <3%
133.	No	Lack of financial data (turnover/ operational result)	No	Lack of financial data (turnover/ operational result)	No	Lack of financial data (turnover/ operational result)
134.	No	Average Stocks/Turnover >5%	No	Other products	No	Average Intangibile asstes/Total assets <3%
135.	No	Average Stocks/Turnover >5%	No	Other products	No	Average Intangibile asstes/Total assets <3%
136.	No	Lack of financial data (turnover/ operational result)	No	Lack of financial data (turnover/ operational result)	No	Lack of financial data (turnover/ operational result)
137.	No	Lack of financial data (turnover/ operational result)	No	Lack of financial data (turnover/ operational result)	No	Lack of financial data (turnover/ operational result)
138.	No	Average Stocks/Turnover >5%	No	The independence criteria are not met	No	Average Intangibile asstes/Total assets <3%
139.	No	Average Stocks/Turnover >5%	No	Other products	No	Average Intangibile asstes/Total assets <3%
140.	No	Average Stocks/Turnover >5%	Yes	Accepted	No	Average Intangibile asstes/Total assets <3%
141.	No	Average Stocks/Turnover >5%	No	Negative average NCP	No	Average Intangibile asstes/Total assets <3%
142.	No	Lack of financial data (turnover/ operational result)	No	Lack of financial data (turnover/ operational result)	No	Lack of financial data (turnover/ operational result)
143.	No	Average Stocks/Turnover >5%	No	The website doesn't work	No	Average Intangibile asstes/Total assets <3%

(continued)

No. crt.	Toll manufacturer		Contract manufacturer		Fully-fledged manufacturer	
	Rejected/ accepted	Rejection reason	Rejected/ accepted	Rejection reason	Rejected/ accepted	Rejection reason
144.	No	Lack of financial data (turnover/ operational result)	No	Lack of financial data (turnover/ operational result)	No	Lack of financial data (turnover/ operational result)
145.	No	Lack of financial data (turnover/ operational result)	No	Lack of financial data (turnover/ operational result)	No	Lack of financial data (turnover/ operational result)
146.	No	Lack of financial data (turnover/ operational result)	No	Lack of financial data (turnover/ operational result)	No	Lack of financial data (turnover/ operational result)
147.	No	Average Stocks/Turnover >5%	Yes	Accepted	No	Average Intangibile asstes/Total assets <3%
148.	No	Lack of financial data (turnover/ operational result)	No	Lack of financial data (turnover/ operational result)	No	Lack of financial data (turnover/ operational result)
149.	No	Lack of financial data (turnover/ operational result)	No	Lack of financial data (turnover/ operational result)	No	Lack of financial data (turnover/ operational result)
150.	No	Lack of financial data (turnover/ operational result)	No	Lack of financial data (turnover/ operational result)	No	Lack of financial data (turnover/ operational result)
151.	No	Average Stocks/Turnover >5%	No	Average Intangible assets/Total assets >3%	No	Negative average NCP
152.	No	Average Stocks/Turnover >5%	No	Other products	No	Average Intangibile asstes/Total assets <3%
153.	No	Average Stocks/Turnover >5%	No	Other functional profile	No	Average Intangibile asstes/Total assets <3%
154.	No	Average Stocks/Turnover >5%	No	Lack of website	No	Average Intangibile asstes/Total assets <3%
155.	No	Average Stocks/Turnover >5%	No	Other functional profile	No	Average Intangibile asstes/Total assets <3%
156.	No	Average Stocks/Turnover >5%	No	Negative average NCP	No	Average Intangibile asstes/Total assets <3%

157.	No	Lack of financial data (turnover/ operational result)	No	Lack of financial data (turnover/ operational result)	No	Lack of financial data (turnover/ operational result)
158.	No	Lack of financial data (turnover/ operational result)	No	Lack of financial data (turnover/ operational result)	No	Lack of financial data (turnover/ operational result)
159.	No	Lack of financial data (turnover/ operational result)	No	Lack of financial data (turnover/ operational result)	No	Lack of financial data (turnover/ operational result)
160.	No	Average Stocks/Turnover >5%	No	Other functional profile	No	Average Intangibile asstes/Total assets <3%
161.	No	Lack of financial data (turnover/ operational result)	No	Lack of financial data (turnover/ operational result)	No	Lack of financial data (turnover/ operational result)
162.	No	Average Stocks/Turnover >5%	No	Other functional profile	No	Average Intangibile asstes/Total assets <3%
163.	Yes	Accepted	No	Average Stocks/Turnover <5%	No	Average Intangibile asstes/Total assets <3%
164.	No	Average Stocks/Turnover >5%	No	Other products	No	Average Intangibile asstes/Total assets <3%
165.	No	Average Stocks/Turnover >5%	No	Other functional profile	No	Average Intangibile asstes/Total assets <3%
166.	No	Average Stocks/Turnover >5%	No	The website doesn't work	No	Average Intangibile asstes/Total assets <3%
167.	No	Lack of financial data (turnover/ operational result)	No	Lack of financial data (turnover/ operational result)	No	Lack of financial data (turnover/ operational result)
168.	No	Lack of website	No	Average Stocks/Turnover <5%	No	Average Stocks/Turnover <5%
169.	No	Lack of financial data (turnover/ operational result)	No	Lack of financial data (turnover/ operational result)	No	Lack of financial data (turnover/ operational result)
170.	No	Average Stocks/Turnover >5%	No	The website doesn't work	No	Average Intangibile asstes/Total assets <3%
171.	No	Lack of financial data (turnover/ operational result)	No	Lack of financial data (turnover/ operational result)	No	Lack of financial data (turnover/ operational result)

(continued)

No. crt.	Toll manufacturer		Contract manufacturer		Fully-fledged manufacturer	
	Rejected/ accepted	Rejection reason	Rejected/ accepted	Rejection reason	Rejected/ accepted	Rejection reason
172.	No	Lack of financial data (turnover/ operational result)	No	Lack of financial data (turnover/ operational result)	No	Lack of financial data (turnover/ operational result)
173.	No	Average Stocks/Turnover >5%	No	Lack of website	No	Average Intangibile asstes/Total assets <3%
174.	No	Average Stocks/Turnover >5%	No	Other functional profile	No	Average Intangibile asstes/Total assets <3%
175.	No	Lack of financial data (turnover/ operational result)	No	Lack of financial data (turnover/ operational result)	No	Lack of financial data (turnover/ operational result)
176.	No	Average Stocks/Turnover >5%	No	Lack of website	No	Average Intangibile asstes/Total assets <3%
177.	No	Lack of financial data (turnover/ operational result)	No	Lack of financial data (turnover/ operational result)	No	Lack of financial data (turnover/ operational result)
178.	No	Average Stocks/Turnover >5%	No	The independence criteria are not met	No	Average Intangibile asstes/Total assets <3%
179.	No	Average Stocks/Turnover >5%	No	Other functional profile	No	Average Intangibile asstes/Total assets <3%
180.	No	Lack of financial data (turnover/ operational result)	No	Lack of financial data (turnover/ operational result)	No	Lack of financial data (turnover/ operational result)
181.	No	Average Stocks/Turnover >5%	No	Negative average NCP	No	Average Intangibile asstes/Total assets <3%
182.	No	Lack of financial data (turnover/ operational result)	No	Lack of financial data (turnover/ operational result)	No	Lack of financial data (turnover/ operational result)
183.	No	Average Stocks/Turnover >5%	No	Other functional profile	No	Average Intangibile asstes/Total assets <3%
184.	No	Average Stocks/Turnover >5%	No	Lack of website	No	Average Intangibile asstes/Total assets <3%

185.	No	Lack of financial data (turnover/ operational result)	No	Lack of financial data (turnover/ operational result)	No	Lack of financial data (turnover/ operational result)
186.	No	Lack of financial data (turnover/ operational result)	No	Lack of financial data (turnover/ operational result)	No	Lack of financial data (turnover/ operational result)
187.	No	Average Stocks/Turnover >5%	No	The website doesn't work	No	Average Intangibile asstes/Total assets <3%
188.	No	Average Stocks/Turnover >5%	No	Negative average NCP	No	Average Intangibile asstes/Total assets <3%
189.	No	Average Stocks/Turnover >5%	No	Negative average NCP	No	Average Intangibile asstes/Total assets <3%
190.	No	Average Stocks/Turnover >5%	No	Other functional profile	No	Average Intangibile asstes/Total assets <3%
191.	No	Lack of financial data (turnover/ operational result)	No	Lack of financial data (turnover/ operational result)	No	Lack of financial data (turnover/ operational result)
192.	No	Lack of website	No	Average Stocks/Turnover <5%	No	Average Stocks/Turnover <5%
193.	No	Average Stocks/Turnover >5%	No	Other functional profile	No	Average Intangibile asstes/Total assets <3%
194.	No	Average Stocks/Turnover >5%	No	Other functional profile	No	Average Intangibile asstes/Total assets <3%
195.	No	Average Stocks/Turnover >5%	No	Other functional profile	No	Average Intangibile asstes/Total assets <3%
196.	No	Lack of financial data (turnover/ operational result)	No	Lack of financial data (turnover/ operational result)	No	Lack of financial data (turnover/ operational result)
197.	No	Average Stocks/Turnover >5%	No	Other functional profile	No	Average Intangibile asstes/Total assets <3%
198.	No	Lack of financial data (turnover/ operational result)	No	Lack of financial data (turnover/ operational result)	No	Lack of financial data (turnover/ operational result)
199.	No	Average Stocks/Turnover >5%	No	Other products	No	Average Intangibile asstes/Total assets <3%

(continued)

No. crt.	Toll manufacturer		Contract manufacturer		Fully-fledged manufacturer	
	Rejected/ accepted	Rejection reason	Rejected/ accepted	Rejection reason	Rejected/ accepted	Rejection reason
200.	No	Average Stocks/Turnover >5%	No	Lack of website	No	Average Intangibile asstes/Total assets <3%
201.	No	Lack of financial data (turnover/ operational result)	No	Lack of financial data (turnover/ operational result)	No	Lack of financial data (turnover/ operational result)
202.	No	Lack of financial data (turnover/ operational result)	No	Lack of financial data (turnover/ operational result)	No	Lack of financial data (turnover/ operational result)
203.	No	Lack of financial data (turnover/ operational result)	No	Lack of financial data (turnover/ operational result)	No	Lack of financial data (turnover/ operational result)
204.	No	Average Stocks/Turnover >5%	No	Lack of website	No	Average Intangibile asstes/Total assets <3%
205.	No	Lack of financial data (turnover/ operational result)	No	Lack of financial data (turnover/ operational result)	No	Lack of financial data (turnover/ operational result)
206.	No	Average Stocks/Turnover >5%	No	Other functional profile	No	Average Intangibile asstes/Total assets <3%
207.	No	Average Stocks/Turnover >5%	No	Other functional profile	No	Average Intangibile asstes/Total assets <3%
208.	No	Lack of financial data (turnover/ operational result)	No	Lack of financial data (turnover/ operational result)	No	Lack of financial data (turnover/ operational result)
209.	No	Lack of financial data (turnover/ operational result)	No	Lack of financial data (turnover/ operational result)	No	Lack of financial data (turnover/ operational result)
210.	No	Average Stocks/Turnover >5%	No	Lack of website	No	Average Intangibile asstes/Total assets <3%
211.	No	Average Stocks/Turnover >5%	No	Negative average NCP	No	Average Intangibile asstes/Total assets <3%
212.	No	Lack of financial data (turnover/ operational result)	No	Lack of financial data (turnover/ operational result)	No	Lack of financial data (turnover/ operational result)

213.	No	Average Stocks/Turnover >5%	No	Lack of website	No	Average Intangibile asstes/Total assets <3%
214.	No	Lack of financial data (turnover/operational result)	No	Lack of financial data (turnover/operational result)	No	Lack of financial data (turnover/operational result)
215.	No	Lack of financial data (turnover/operational result)	No	Lack of financial data (turnover/operational result)	No	Lack of financial data (turnover/operational result)
216.	No	Lack of financial data (turnover/operational result)	No	Lack of financial data (turnover/operational result)	No	Lack of financial data (turnover/operational result)
217.	No	Lack of financial data (turnover/operational result)	No	Lack of financial data (turnover/operational result)	No	Lack of financial data (turnover/operational result)
218.	No	Average Stocks/Turnover >5%	No	Other products	No	Average Intangibile asstes/Total assets <3%
219.	No	Lack of financial data (turnover/operational result)	No	Lack of financial data (turnover/operational result)	No	Lack of financial data (turnover/operational result)
220.	No	Lack of financial data (turnover/operational result)	No	Lack of financial data (turnover/operational result)	No	Lack of financial data (turnover/operational result)
221.	No	Average Stocks/Turnover >5%	No	Other functional profile	No	Average Intangibile asstes/Total assets <3%
222.	No	Lack of financial data (turnover/operational result)	No	Lack of financial data (turnover/operational result)	No	Lack of financial data (turnover/operational result)
223.	No	Lack of financial data (turnover/operational result)	No	Lack of financial data (turnover/operational result)	No	Lack of financial data (turnover/operational result)
224.	No	Average Stocks/Turnover >5%	No	Lack of website	No	Average Intangibile asstes/Total assets <3%
225.	No	Negative average NCP	No	Average Stocks/Turnover <5%	No	Average Stocks/Turnover <5%
226.	No	Average Stocks/Turnover >5%	No	Negative average NCP	No	Average Intangibile asstes/Total assets <3%
227.	No	Average Intangible assets/Total assets >3%	No	Average Stocks/Turnover <5%	No	Average Stocks/Turnover <5%

(continued)

No. crt.	Toll manufacturer		Contract manufacturer		Fully-fledged manufacturer	
	Rejected/ accepted	Rejection reason	Rejected/ accepted	Rejection reason	Rejected/ accepted	Rejection reason
228.	No	Lack of financial data (turnover/ operational result)	No	Lack of financial data (turnover/ operational result)	No	Lack of financial data (turnover/ operational result)
229.	No	Average Stocks/Turnover >5%	No	Lack of website	No	Average Intangibile asstes/Total assets <3%
230.	No	Average Stocks/Turnover >5%	No	The website doesn't work	No	Average Intangibile asstes/Total assets <3%
231.	No	Average Stocks/Turnover >5%	No	Other products	No	Average Intangibile asstes/Total assets <3%
232.	No	Lack of website	No	Lack of website	No	Average Intangibile asstes/Total assets <3%
233.	No	Lack of financial data (turnover/ operational result)	No	Lack of financial data (turnover/ operational result)	No	Lack of financial data (turnover/ operational result)
234.	No	Average Stocks/Turnover >5%	No	Other functional profile	No	Average Intangibile asstes/Total assets <3%
235.	No	Average Stocks/Turnover >5%	No	Other products	No	Average Intangibile asstes/Total assets <3%
236.	No	Lack of financial data (turnover/ operational result)	No	Lack of financial data (turnover/ operational result)	No	Lack of financial data (turnover/ operational result)
237.	No	Average Stocks/Turnover >5%	No	Negative average NCP	No	Average Intangibile asstes/Total assets <3%
238.	No	Average Stocks/Turnover >5%	No	The website doesn't work	No	Average Intangibile asstes/Total assets <3%
239.	No	Average Stocks/Turnover >5%	No	Lack of website	No	Average Intangibile asstes/Total assets <3%
240.	No	Lack of financial data (turnover/ operational result)	No	Lack of financial data (turnover/ operational result)	No	Lack of financial data (turnover/ operational result)

241.	No	Average Stocks/Turnover >5%	No	Average Intangible assets/Total assets >3%	No	Negative average NCP
242.	No	Average Stocks/Turnover >5%	No	Lack of website	No	Average Intangibile asstes/Total assets <3%
243.	No	Lack of financial data (turnover/ operational result)	No	Lack of financial data (turnover/ operational result)	No	Lack of financial data (turnover/ operational result)
244.	No	Lack of financial data (turnover/ operational result)	No	Lack of financial data (turnover/ operational result)	No	Lack of financial data (turnover/ operational result)
245.	No	Average Stocks/Turnover >5%	No	Lack of website	No	Average Intangibile asstes/Total assets <3%
246.	No	Lack of financial data (turnover/ operational result)	No	Lack of financial data (turnover/ operational result)	No	Lack of financial data (turnover/ operational result)
247.	No	Lack of financial data (turnover/ operational result)	No	Lack of financial data (turnover/ operational result)	No	Lack of financial data (turnover/ operational result)
248.	No	Lack of financial data (turnover/ operational result)	No	Lack of financial data (turnover/ operational result)	No	Lack of financial data (turnover/ operational result)
249.	No	Lack of website	No	Average Stocks/Turnover <5%	No	Average Stocks/Turnover <5%
250.	No	Lack of financial data (turnover/ operational result)	No	Lack of financial data (turnover/ operational result)	No	Lack of financial data (turnover/ operational result)
251.	No	Lack of financial data (turnover/ operational result)	No	Lack of financial data (turnover/ operational result)	No	Lack of financial data (turnover/ operational result)
252.	No	Lack of financial data (turnover/ operational result)	No	Lack of financial data (turnover/ operational result)	No	Lack of financial data (turnover/ operational result)
253.	No	Average Stocks/Turnover >5%	No	Lack of website	No	Average Intangibile asstes/Total assets <3%
254.	No	Average Stocks/Turnover >5%	No	Negative average NCP	No	Average Intangibile asstes/Total assets <3%
255.	No	Average Stocks/Turnover >5%	No	Lack of website	No	Average Intangibile asstes/Total assets <3%

(continued)

No. crt.	Toll manufacturer		Contract manufacturer		Fully-fledged manufacturer	
	Rejected/ accepted	Rejection reason	Rejected/ accepted	Rejection reason	Rejected/ accepted	Rejection reason
256.	No	Average Stocks/Turnover >5%	No	Average Intangible assets/Total assets >3%	No	Other functional profile
257.	No	Lack of financial data (turnover/ operational result)	No	Lack of financial data (turnover/ operational result)	No	Lack of financial data (turnover/ operational result)
258.	No	Average Stocks/Turnover >5%	No	Other functional profile	No	Average Intangibile asstes/Total assets <3%
259.	No	Lack of financial data (turnover/ operational result)	No	Lack of financial data (turnover/ operational result)	No	Lack of financial data (turnover/ operational result)
260.	No	Lack of financial data (turnover/ operational result)	No	Lack of financial data (turnover/ operational result)	No	Lack of financial data (turnover/ operational result)
261.	No	Lack of website	No	Average Stocks/Turnover <5%	No	Average Stocks/Turnover <5%
262.	Yes	Accepted	No	Average Stocks/Turnover <5%	No	Average Stocks/Turnover <5%
263.	No	Lack of financial data (turnover/ operational result)	No	Lack of financial data (turnover/ operational result)	No	Lack of financial data (turnover/ operational result)
264.	No	Average Stocks/Turnover >5%	No	The website doesn’t work	No	Average Intangibile asstes/Total assets <3%
265.	Yes	Accepted	No	Average Stocks/Turnover <5%	No	Average Stocks/Turnover <5%
266.	No	Lack of financial data (turnover/ operational result)	No	Lack of financial data (turnover/ operational result)	No	Lack of financial data (turnover/ operational result)
267.	No	Average Stocks/Turnover >5%	No	Lack of website	No	Average Intangibile asstes/Total assets <3%
268.	No	Lack of financial data (turnover/ operational result)	No	Lack of financial data (turnover/ operational result)	No	Lack of financial data (turnover/ operational result)
269.	No	Average Stocks/Turnover >5%	No	Negative average NCP	No	Average Intangibile asstes/Total assets <3%
270.	No	Average Stocks/Turnover >5%	No	The website doesn't work	No	Average Intangibile asstes/Total assets <3%

271.	No	Lack of financial data (turnover/ operational result)	No	Lack of financial data (turnover/ operational result)	No	Lack of financial data (turnover/ operational result)
272.	No	Average Stocks/Turnover >5%	No	Negative average NCP	No	Average Intangibile asstes/Total assets <3%
273.	No	Lack of financial data (turnover/ operational result)	No	Lack of financial data (turnover/ operational result)	No	Lack of financial data (turnover/ operational result)
274.	No	Average Stocks/Turnover >5%	No	The website doesn't work	No	Average Intangibile asstes/Total assets <3%
275.	No	Lack of financial data (turnover/ operational result)	No	Lack of financial data (turnover/ operational result)	No	Lack of financial data (turnover/ operational result)
276.	No	Lack of financial data (turnover/ operational result)	No	Lack of financial data (turnover/ operational result)	No	Lack of financial data (turnover/ operational result)
277.	No	Lack of financial data (turnover/ operational result)	No	Lack of financial data (turnover/ operational result)	No	Lack of financial data (turnover/ operational result)
278.	No	Average Stocks/Turnover >5%	No	Lack of website	No	Lack of website
279.	No	Average Stocks/Turnover >5%	No	Other functional profile	No	Average Intangibile asstes/Total assets <3%
280.	No	Lack of financial data (turnover/ operational result)	No	Lack of financial data (turnover/ operational result)	No	Lack of financial data (turnover/ operational result)
281.	No	Lack of financial data (turnover/ operational result)	No	Lack of financial data (turnover/ operational result)	No	Lack of financial data (turnover/ operational result)
282.	No	Lack of financial data (turnover/ operational result)	No	Lack of financial data (turnover/ operational result)	No	Lack of financial data (turnover/ operational result)
283.	No	Lack of financial data (turnover/ operational result)	No	Lack of financial data (turnover/ operational result)	No	Lack of financial data (turnover/ operational result)
284.	Yes	Accepted	No	Average Stocks/Turnover <5%	No	Average Stocks/Turnover <5%
285.	No	Average Stocks/Turnover >5%	No	Lack of website	No	Average Intangibile asstes/Total assets <3%
286.	No	Lack of financial data (turnover/ operational result)	No	Lack of financial data (turnover/ operational result)	No	Lack of financial data (turnover/ operational result)

(continued)

No. crt.	Toll manufacturer		Contract manufacturer		Fully-fledged manufacturer	
	Rejected/ accepted	Rejection reason	Rejected/ accepted	Rejection reason	Rejected/ accepted	Rejection reason
287.	No	Average Stocks/Turnover >5%	No	Negative average NCP	No	Average Intangibile asstes/Total assets <3%
288.	No	Average Stocks/Turnover >5%	No	Lack of website	No	Average Intangibile asstes/Total assets <3%
289.	No	Lack of financial data (turnover/ operational result)	No	Lack of financial data (turnover/ operational result)	No	Lack of financial data (turnover/ operational result)
290.	No	Lack of financial data (turnover/ operational result)	No	Lack of financial data (turnover/ operational result)	No	Lack of financial data (turnover/ operational result)
291.	No	Lack of website	No	Average Stocks/Turnover <5%	No	Average Stocks/Turnover <5%
292.	No	Lack of financial data (turnover/ operational result)	No	Lack of financial data (turnover/ operational result)	No	Lack of financial data (turnover/ operational result)
293.	No	Lack of financial data (turnover/ operational result)	No	Lack of financial data (turnover/ operational result)	No	Lack of financial data (turnover/ operational result)
294.	No	Lack of financial data (turnover/ operational result)	No	Lack of financial data (turnover/ operational result)	No	Lack of financial data (turnover/ operational result)
295.	No	Other functional profile	No	Average Stocks/Turnover <5%	No	Average Stocks/Turnover <5%
296.	No	Lack of financial data (turnover/ operational result)	No	Lack of financial data (turnover/ operational result)	No	Lack of financial data (turnover/ operational result)
297.	No	Average Stocks/Turnover >5%	No	Other functional profile	No	Average Intangibile asstes/Total assets <3%
298.	No	Lack of website	No	Average Stocks/Turnover <5%	No	Average Stocks/Turnover <5%
299.	No	Average Stocks/Turnover >5%	Yes	Accepted	No	Average Intangibile asstes/Total assets <3%
300.	No	Lack of financial data (turnover/ operational result)	No	Lack of financial data (turnover/ operational result)	No	Lack of financial data (turnover/ operational result)
301.	No	Average Stocks/Turnover >5%	No	Lack of website	No	Average Intangibile asstes/Total assets <3%

302.	No	Lack of financial data (turnover/operational result)	No	Lack of financial data (turnover/operational result)	No	Lack of financial data (turnover/operational result)
303.	No	Lack of financial data (turnover/operational result)	No	Lack of financial data (turnover/operational result)	No	Lack of financial data (turnover/operational result)
304.	No	Average Stocks/Turnover >5%	No	Lack of website	No	Average Intangibile asstes/Total assets <3%
305.	No	Lack of financial data (turnover/operational result)	No	Lack of financial data (turnover/operational result)	No	Lack of financial data (turnover/operational result)
306.	No	Lack of financial data (turnover/operational result)	No	Lack of financial data (turnover/operational result)	No	Lack of financial data (turnover/operational result)
307.	No	Average Stocks/Turnover >5%	No	Other products	No	Other products
308.	No	Average Stocks/Turnover >5%	No	Negative average NCP	No	Average Intangibile asstes/Total assets <3%
309.	No	Average Stocks/Turnover >5%	No	The website doesn't work	No	Average Intangibile asstes/Total assets <3%
310.	No	Lack of financial data (turnover/operational result)	No	Lack of financial data (turnover/operational result)	No	Lack of financial data (turnover/operational result)
311.	No	Negative average NCP	No	Average Stocks/Turnover <5%	No	Average Stocks/Turnover <5%
312.	No	Lack of financial data (turnover/operational result)	No	Lack of financial data (turnover/operational result)	No	Lack of financial data (turnover/operational result)
313.	No	Lack of financial data (turnover/operational result)	No	Lack of financial data (turnover/operational result)	No	Lack of financial data (turnover/operational result)
314.	No	Lack of financial data (turnover/operational result)	No	Lack of financial data (turnover/operational result)	No	Lack of financial data (turnover/operational result)
315.	No	Average Stocks/Turnover >5%	No	Average Intangible assets/Total assets >3%	No	Negative average NCP
316.	No	Average Stocks/Turnover >5%	No	Negative average NCP	No	Average Intangibile asstes/Total assets <3%
317.	No	The website doesn't work	No	The website doesn't work	No	The website doesn't work

(continued)

No. crt.	Toll manufacturer		Contract manufacturer		Fully-fledged manufacturer	
	Rejected/ accepted	Rejection reason	Rejected/ accepted	Rejection reason	Rejected/ accepted	Rejection reason
318.	No	Average Stocks/Turnover >5%	No	Other functional profile	No	Average Intangibile asstes/Total assets <3%
319.	No	Lack of financial data (turnover/ operational result)	No	Lack of financial data (turnover/ operational result)	No	Lack of financial data (turnover// operational result)
320.	No	Lack of financial data (turnover/ operational result)	No	Lack of financial data (turnover/ operational result)	No	Lack of financial data (turnover/ operational result)
321.	No	Average Intangible assets/Total assets >3%	No	Average Stocks/Turnover <5%	No	Average Stocks/Turnover <5%
322.	No	Lack of financial data (turnover/ operational result)	No	Lack of financial data (turnover/ operational result)	No	Lack of financial data (turnover/ operational result)
323.	No	Lack of financial data (turnover/ operational result)	No	Lack of financial data (turnover/ operational result)	No	Lack of financial data (turnover/ operational result)
324.	No	Lack of website	No	Lack of website	No	Average Intangibile asstes/Total assets <3%
325.	No	Lack of website	No	Average Stocks/Turnover <5%	No	Average Stocks/Turnover <5%
326.	No	Average Stocks/Turnover >5%	No	Lack of website	No	Average Intangibile asstes/Total assets <3%
327.	No	Lack of financial data (turnover/ operational result)	No	Lack of financial data (turnover/ operational result)	No	Lack of financial data (turnover/ operational result)
328.	No	Average Stocks/Turnover >5%	No	The website doesn't work	No	Average Intangibile asstes/Total assets <3%
329.	No	Lack of financial data (turnover/ operational result)	No	Lack of financial data (turnover/ operational result)	No	Lack of financial data (turnover/ operational result)
330.	No	Lack of financial data (turnover/ operational result)	No	Lack of financial data (turnover/ operational result)	No	Lack of financial data (turnover/ operational result)
331.	No	Lack of financial data (turnover/ operational result)	No	Lack of financial data (turnover/ operational result)	No	Lack of financial data (turnover/ operational result)

332.	No	Lack of financial data (turnover/ operational result)	No	Lack of financial data (turnover/ operational result)	No	Lack of financial data (turnover/ operational result)
333.	No	Lack of financial data (turnover/ operational result)	No	Lack of financial data (turnover/ operational result)	No	Lack of financial data (turnover/ operational result)
334.	No	Lack of financial data (turnover/ operational result)	No	Lack of financial data (turnover/ operational result)	No	Lack of financial data (turnover/ operational result)
335.	No	Lack of financial data (turnover/ operational result)	No	Lack of financial data (turnover/ operational result)	No	Lack of financial data (turnover/ operational result)
336.	No	Average Stocks/Turnover >5%	No	Negative average NCP	No	Average Intangibile asstes/Total assets <3%
337.	No	Negative average NCP	No	Average Stocks/Turnover <5%	No	Average Stocks/Turnover <5%
338.	No	Lack of financial data (turnover/ operational result)	No	Lack of financial data (turnover/ operational result)	No	Lack of financial data (turnover/ operational result)
339.	No	Lack of financial data (turnover/ operational result)	No	Lack of financial data (turnover/ operational result)	No	Lack of financial data (turnover/ operational result)
340.	No	Lack of financial data (turnover/ operational result)	No	Lack of financial data (turnover/ operational result)	No	Lack of financial data (turnover/ operational result)
341.	No	Lack of financial data (turnover/ operational result)	No	Lack of financial data (turnover/ operational result)	No	Lack of financial data (turnover/ operational result)
342.	No	Average Stocks/Turnover >5%	No	Lack of website	No	Average Intangibile asstes/Total assets <3%
343.	No	Lack of financial data (turnover/ operational result)	No	Lack of financial data (turnover/ operational result)	No	Lack of financial data (turnover/ operational result)
344.	No	Average Stocks/Turnover >5%	No	Lack of website	No	Average Intangibile asstes/Total assets <3%
345.	No	Lack of financial data (turnover/ operational result)	No	Lack of financial data (turnover/ operational result)	No	Lack of financial data (turnover/ operational result)
346.	No	Lack of financial data (turnover/ operational result)	No	Lack of financial data (turnover/ operational result)	No	Lack of financial data (turnover/ operational result)

(continued)

No. crt.	Toll manufacturer		Contract manufacturer		Fully-fledged manufacturer	
	Rejected/ accepted	Rejection reason	Rejected/ accepted	Rejection reason	Rejected/ accepted	Rejection reason
347.	No	Lack of financial data (turnover/ operational result)	No	Lack of financial data (turnover/ operational result)	No	Lack of financial data (turnover/ operational result)
348.	No	Lack of financial data (turnover/ operational result)	No	Lack of financial data (turnover/ operational result)	No	Lack of financial data (turnover/ operational result)
349.	No	Average Stocks/Turnover >5%	No	Lack of website	No	Average Intangibile asstes/Total assets <3%
350.	No	Lack of website	No	Average Stocks/Turnover <5%	No	Average Stocks/Turnover <5%
351.	No	Lack of financial data (turnover/ operational result)	No	Lack of financial data (turnover/ operational result)	No	Lack of financial data (turnover/ operational result)
352.	No	Lack of website	No	Average Stocks/Turnover <5%	No	Average Stocks/Turnover <5%
353.	No	Lack of financial data (turnover/ operational result)	No	Lack of financial data (turnover/ operational result)	No	Lack of financial data (turnover/ operational result)
354.	No	Lack of financial data (turnover/ operational result)	No	Lack of financial data (turnover/ operational result)	No	Lack of financial data (turnover/ operational result)
355.	No	Lack of financial data (turnover/ operational result)	No	Lack of financial data (turnover/ operational result)	No	Lack of financial data (turnover/ operational result)
356.	No	Lack of financial data (turnover/ operational result)	No	Lack of financial data (turnover/ operational result)	No	Lack of financial data (turnover/ operational result)
357.	No	Average Stocks/Turnover >5%	No	Negative average NCP	No	Average Intangibile asstes/Total assets <3%
358.	No	Average Stocks/Turnover >5%	No	Negative average NCP	No	Average Intangibile asstes/Total assets <3%
359.	No	Other functional profile	No	Average Stocks/Turnover <5%	No	Average Stocks/Turnover <5%
360.	No	Average Stocks/Turnover >5%	No	Lack of website	No	Average Intangibile asstes/Total assets <3%
361.	No	Lack of financial data (turnover/ operational result)	No	Lack of financial data (turnover/ operational result)	No	Lack of financial data (turnover/ operational result)

362.	No	Lack of financial data (turnover/ operational result)	No	Lack of financial data (turnover/ operational result)	No	Lack of financial data (turnover/ operational result)
363.	No	Lack of financial data (turnover/ operational result)	No	Lack of financial data (turnover/ operational result)	No	Lack of financial data (turnover/ operational result)
364.	No	Average Stocks/Turnover >5%	No	Average Intangible assets/Total assets >3%	No	Negative average NCP
365.	No	Lack of financial data (turnover/ operational result)	No	Lack of financial data (turnover/ operational result)	No	Lack of financial data (turnover/ operational result)
366.	No	Average Stocks/Turnover >5%	No	Negative average NCP	No	Average Intangibile asstes/Total assets <3%
367.	No	Average Stocks/Turnover >5%	No	Negative average NCP	No	Average Intangibile asstes/Total assets <3%
368.	No	Lack of financial data (turnover/ operational result)	No	Lack of financial data (turnover/ operational result)	No	Lack of financial data (turnover/ operational result)
369.	No	Lack of financial data (turnover/ operational result)	No	Lack of financial data (turnover/ operational result)	No	Lack of financial data (turnover/ operational result)
370.	No	Negative average NCP	No	Average Stocks/Turnover <5%	No	Average Stocks/Turnover <5%
371.	No	Lack of financial data (turnover/ operational result)	No	Lack of financial data (turnover/ operational result)	No	Lack of financial data (turnover/ operational result)
372.	No	Lack of website	No	Average Stocks/Turnover <5%	No	Average Stocks/Turnover <5%
373.	No	Average Stocks/Turnover >5%	No	Lack of website	No	Average Intangibile asstes/Total assets <3%
374.	No	Average Stocks/Turnover >5%	No	Lack of website	No	Lack of website
375.	No	Lack of website	No	Average Stocks/Turnover <5%	No	Average Stocks/Turnover <5%
376.	No	Average Stocks/Turnover >5%	No	Lack of website	No	Average Intangibile asstes/Total assets <3%
377.	No	Lack of financial data (turnover/ operational result)	No	Lack of financial data (turnover/ operational result)	No	Lack of financial data (turnover/ operational result)
378.	No	Lack of website	No	Average Stocks/Turnover <5%	No	Average Stocks/Turnover <5%

(continued)

No. crt.	Toll manufacturer		Contract manufacturer		Fully-fledged manufacturer	
	Rejected/ accepted	Rejection reason	Rejected/ accepted	Rejection reason	Rejected/ accepted	Rejection reason
379.	No	Lack of financial data (turnover/ operational result)	No	Lack of financial data (turnover/ operational result)	No	Lack of financial data (turnover/ operational result)
380.	No	Lack of financial data (turnover/ operational result)	No	Lack of financial data (turnover/ operational result)	No	Lack of financial data (turnover/ operational result)
381.	No	Average Stocks/Turnover >5%	No	Negative average NCP	No	Average Intangibile asstes/Total assets <3%
382.	No	The website doesn't work	No	Average Stocks/Turnover <5%	No	Average Stocks/Turnover <5%
383.	No	Lack of financial data (turnover/ operational result)	No	Lack of financial data (turnover/ operational result)	No	Lack of financial data (turnover/ operational result)
384.	No	Negative average NCP	No	Negative average NCP	No	Average Intangibile asstes/Total assets <3%
385.	No	Lack of website	No	Average Stocks/Turnover <5%	No	Average Stocks/Turnover <5%
386.	No	Average Stocks/Turnover >5%	No	Average Intangible assets/Total assets >3%	No	Negative average NCP
387.	No	Lack of financial data (turnover/ operational result)	No	Lack of financial data (turnover/ operational result)	No	Lack of financial data (turnover/ operational result)
388.	No	Lack of financial data (turnover/ operational result)	No	Lack of financial data (turnover/ operational result)	No	Lack of financial data (turnover/ operational result)
389.	No	Average Stocks/Turnover >5%	No	Lack of website	No	Average Intangibile asstes/Total assets <3%
390.	No	Lack of financial data (turnover/ operational result)	No	Lack of financial data (turnover/ operational result)	No	Lack of financial data (turnover/ operational result)
391.	No	Lack of financial data (turnover/ operational result)	No	Lack of financial data (turnover/ operational result)	No	Lack of financial data (turnover/ operational result)
392.	No	Lack of financial data (turnover/ operational result)	No	Lack of financial data (turnover/ operational result)	No	Lack of financial data (turnover/ operational result)

393.	No	Lack of financial data (turnover/ operational result)	No	Lack of financial data (turnover/ operational result)	No	Lack of financial data (turnover/ operational result)
394.	No	Lack of financial data (turnover/ operational result)	No	Lack of financial data (turnover/ operational result)	No	Lack of financial data (turnover/ operational result)
395.	No	Lack of financial data (turnover/ operational result)	No	Lack of financial data (turnover/ operational result)	No	Lack of financial data (turnover/ operational result)
396.	No	Lack of financial data (turnover/ operational result)	No	Lack of financial data (turnover/ operational result)	No	Lack of financial data (turnover/ operational result)
397.	No	Lack of financial data (turnover/ operational result)	No	Lack of financial data (turnover/ operational result)	No	Lack of financial data (turnover/ operational result)
398.	No	Lack of financial data (turnover/ operational result)	No	Lack of financial data (turnover/ operational result)	No	Lack of financial data (turnover/ operational result)
399.	No	Lack of financial data (turnover/ operational result)	No	Lack of financial data (turnover/ operational result)	No	Lack of financial data (turnover/ operational result)
400.	No	Lack of financial data (turnover/ operational result)	No	Lack of financial data (turnover/ operational result)	No	Lack of financial data (turnover/ operational result)
401.	No	Lack of financial data (turnover/ operational result)	No	Lack of financial data (turnover/ operational result)	No	Lack of financial data (turnover/ operational result)
402.	No	Lack of financial data (turnover/ operational result)	No	Lack of financial data (turnover/ operational result)	No	Lack of financial data (turnover/ operational result)
403.	No	Lack of financial data (turnover/ operational result)	No	Lack of financial data (turnover/ operational result)	No	Lack of financial data (turnover/ operational result)
404.	No	Lack of financial data (turnover/ operational result)	No	Lack of financial data (turnover/ operational result)	No	Lack of financial data (turnover/ operational result)
405.	No	Lack of financial data (turnover/ operational result)	No	Lack of financial data (turnover/ operational result)	No	Lack of financial data (turnover/ operational result)
406.	No	Lack of financial data (turnover/ operational result)	No	Lack of financial data (turnover/ operational result)	No	Lack of financial data (turnover/ operational result)
407.	No	Lack of financial data (turnover/ operational result)	No	Lack of financial data (turnover/ operational result)	No	Lack of financial data (turnover/ operational result)

(continued)

No. crt.	Toll manufacturer		Contract manufacturer		Fully-fledged manufacturer	
	Rejected/ accepted	Rejection reason	Rejected/ accepted	Rejection reason	Rejected/ accepted	Rejection reason
408.	No	Lack of financial data (turnover/ operational result)	No	Lack of financial data (turnover/ operational result)	No	Lack of financial data (turnover/ operational result)
409.	No	Lack of financial data (turnover/ operational result)	No	Lack of financial data (turnover/ operational result)	No	Lack of financial data (turnover/ operational result)
410.	No	Lack of financial data (turnover/ operational result)	No	Lack of financial data (turnover/ operational result)	No	Lack of financial data (turnover/ operational result)
411.	No	Lack of financial data (turnover/ operational result)	No	Lack of financial data (turnover/ operational result)	No	Lack of financial data (turnover/ operational result)
412.	No	Lack of financial data (turnover/ operational result)	No	Lack of financial data (turnover/ operational result)	No	Lack of financial data (turnover/ operational result)
413.	No	Lack of financial data (turnover/ operational result)	No	Lack of financial data (turnover/ operational result)	No	Lack of financial data (turnover/ operational result)
414.	No	Lack of financial data (turnover/ operational result)	No	Lack of financial data (turnover/ operational result)	No	Lack of financial data (turnover/ operational result)
415.	No	Lack of financial data (turnover/ operational result)	No	Lack of financial data (turnover/ operational result)	No	Lack of financial data (turnover/ operational result)
416.	No	Lack of financial data (turnover/ operational result)	No	Lack of financial data (turnover/ operational result)	No	Lack of financial data (turnover/ operational result)
417.	No	Lack of financial data (turnover/ operational result)	No	Lack of financial data (turnover/ operational result)	No	Lack of financial data (turnover/ operational result)
418.	No	Lack of financial data (turnover/ operational result)	No	Lack of financial data (turnover/ operational result)	No	Lack of financial data (turnover/ operational result)
419.	No	Lack of financial data (turnover/ operational result)	No	Lack of financial data (turnover/ operational result)	No	Lack of financial data (turnover/ operational result)
420.	No	Lack of financial data (turnover/ operational result)	No	Lack of financial data (turnover/ operational result)	No	Lack of financial data (turnover/ operational result)

421.	No	Lack of financial data (turnover/ operational result)	No	Lack of financial data (turnover/ operational result)	No	Lack of financial data (turnover/ operational result)
422.	No	Lack of financial data (turnover/ operational result)	No	Lack of financial data (turnover/ operational result)	No	Lack of financial data (turnover/ operational result)
423.	No	Lack of financial data (turnover/ operational result)	No	Lack of financial data (turnover/ operational result)	No	Lack of financial data (turnover/ operational result)
424.	No	Lack of financial data (turnover/ operational result)	No	Lack of financial data (turnover/ operational result)	No	Lack of financial data (turnover/ operational result)
425.	No	Lack of financial data (turnover/ operational result)	No	Lack of financial data (turnover/ operational result)	No	Lack of financial data (turnover/ operational result)
426.	No	Lack of financial data (turnover/ operational result)	No	Lack of financial data (turnover/ operational result)	No	Lack of financial data (turnover/ operational result)
427.	No	Lack of financial data (turnover/ operational result)	No	Lack of financial data (turnover/ operational result)	No	Lack of financial data (turnover/ operational result)
428.	No	Lack of financial data (turnover/ operational result)	No	Lack of financial data (turnover/ operational result)	No	Lack of financial data (turnover/ operational result)
429.	No	Lack of financial data (turnover/ operational result)	No	Lack of financial data (turnover/ operational result)	No	Lack of financial data (turnover/ operational result)
430.	No	Lack of financial data (turnover/ operational result)	No	Lack of financial data (turnover/ operational result)	No	Lack of financial data (turnover/ operational result)
431.	No	Lack of financial data (turnover/ operational result)	No	Lack of financial data (turnover/ operational result)	No	Lack of financial data (turnover/ operational result)
432.	No	Lack of financial data (turnover/ operational result)	No	Lack of financial data (turnover/ operational result)	No	Lack of financial data (turnover/ operational result)
433.	No	Lack of financial data (turnover/ operational result)	No	Lack of financial data (turnover/ operational result)	No	Lack of financial data (turnover/ operational result)
434.	No	Lack of financial data (turnover/ operational result)	No	Lack of financial data (turnover/ operational result)	No	Lack of financial data (turnover/ operational result)
435.	No	Lack of financial data (turnover/ operational result)	No	Lack of financial data (turnover/ operational result)	No	Lack of financial data (turnover/ operational result)

(continued)

No. crt.	Toll manufacturer		Contract manufacturer		Fully-fledged manufacturer	
	Rejected/ accepted	Rejection reason	Rejected/ accepted	Rejection reason	Rejected/ accepted	Rejection reason
436.	No	Lack of financial data (turnover/ operational result)	No	Lack of financial data (turnover/ operational result)	No	Lack of financial data (turnover/ operational result)
437.	No	Lack of financial data (turnover/ operational result)	No	Lack of financial data (turnover/ operational result)	No	Lack of financial data (turnover/ operational result)
438.	No	Lack of financial data (turnover/ operational result)	No	Lack of financial data (turnover/ operational result)	No	Lack of financial data (turnover/ operational result)
439.	No	Lack of financial data (turnover/ operational result)	No	Lack of financial data (turnover/ operational result)	No	Lack of financial data (turnover/ operational result)
440.	No	Lack of financial data (turnover/ operational result)	No	Lack of financial data (turnover/ operational result)	No	Lack of financial data (turnover/ operational result)
441.	No	Lack of financial data (turnover/ operational result)	No	Lack of financial data (turnover/ operational result)	No	Lack of financial data (turnover/ operational result)
442.	No	Lack of financial data (turnover/ operational result)	No	Lack of financial data (turnover/ operational result)	No	Lack of financial data (turnover/ operational result)
443.	No	Lack of financial data (turnover/ operational result)	No	Lack of financial data (turnover/ operational result)	No	Lack of financial data (turnover/ operational result)
444.	No	Lack of financial data (turnover/ operational result)	No	Lack of financial data (turnover/ operational result)	No	Lack of financial data (turnover/ operational result)
445.	No	Lack of financial data (turnover/ operational result)	No	Lack of financial data (turnover/ operational result)	No	Lack of financial data (turnover/ operational result)
446.	No	Lack of financial data (turnover/ operational result)	No	Lack of financial data (turnover/ operational result)	No	Lack of financial data (turnover/ operational result)
447.	No	Lack of financial data (turnover/ operational result)	No	Lack of financial data (turnover/ operational result)	No	Lack of financial data (turnover/ operational result)
448.	No	Lack of financial data (turnover/ operational result)	No	Lack of financial data (turnover/ operational result)	No	Lack of financial data (turnover/ operational result)

449.	No	Lack of financial data (turnover/ operational result)	No	Lack of financial data (turnover/ operational result)	No	Lack of financial data (turnover/ operational result)
450.	No	Lack of financial data (turnover/ operational result)	No	Lack of financial data (turnover/ operational result)	No	Lack of financial data (turnover/ operational result)
451.	No	Lack of financial data (turnover/ operational result)	No	Lack of financial data (turnover/ operational result)	No	Lack of financial data (turnover/ operational result)
452.	No	Lack of financial data (turnover/ operational result)	No	Lack of financial data (turnover/ operational result)	No	Lack of financial data (turnover/ operational result)
453.	No	Lack of financial data (turnover/ operational result)	No	Lack of financial data (turnover/ operational result)	No	Lack of financial data (turnover/ operational result)
454.	No	Lack of financial data (turnover/ operational result)	No	Lack of financial data (turnover/ operational result)	No	Lack of financial data (turnover/ operational result)
455.	No	Lack of financial data (turnover/ operational result)	No	Lack of financial data (turnover/ operational result)	No	Lack of financial data (turnover/ operational result)
456.	No	Lack of financial data (turnover/ operational result)	No	Lack of financial data (turnover/ operational result)	No	Lack of financial data (turnover/ operational result)
457.	No	Lack of financial data (turnover/ operational result)	No	Lack of financial data (turnover/ operational result)	No	Lack of financial data (turnover/ operational result)
458.	No	Lack of financial data (turnover/ operational result)	No	Lack of financial data (turnover/ operational result)	No	Lack of financial data (turnover/ operational result)
459.	No	Lack of financial data (turnover/ operational result)	No	Lack of financial data (turnover/ operational result)	No	Lack of financial data (turnover/ operational result)
460.	No	Lack of financial data (turnover/ operational result)	No	Lack of financial data (turnover/ operational result)	No	Lack of financial data (turnover/ operational result)
461.	No	Lack of financial data (turnover/ operational result)	No	Lack of financial data (turnover/ operational result)	No	Lack of financial data (turnover/ operational result)
462.	No	Lack of financial data (turnover/ operational result)	No	Lack of financial data (turnover/ operational result)	No	Lack of financial data (turnover/ operational result)
463.	No	Lack of financial data (turnover/ operational result)	No	Lack of financial data (turnover/ operational result)	No	Lack of financial data (turnover/ operational result)

(continued)

No. crt.	Toll manufacturer		Contract manufacturer		Fully-fledged manufacturer	
	Rejected/ accepted	Rejection reason	Rejected/ accepted	Rejection reason	Rejected/ accepted	Rejection reason
464.	No	Lack of financial data (turnover/ operational result)	No	Lack of financial data (turnover/ operational result)	No	Lack of financial data (turnover/ operational result)
465.	No	Lack of financial data (turnover/ operational result)	No	Lack of financial data (turnover/ operational result)	No	Lack of financial data (turnover/ operational result)
466.	No	Lack of financial data (turnover/ operational result)	No	Lack of financial data (turnover/ operational result)	No	Lack of financial data (turnover/ operational result)
467.	No	Lack of financial data (turnover/ operational result)	No	Lack of financial data (turnover/ operational result)	No	Lack of financial data (turnover/ operational result)
468.	No	Lack of financial data (turnover/ operational result)	No	Lack of financial data (turnover/ operational result)	No	Lack of financial data (turnover/ operational result)
469.	No	Lack of financial data (turnover/ operational result)	No	Lack of financial data (turnover/ operational result)	No	Lack of financial data (turnover/ operational result)
470.	No	Lack of financial data (turnover/ operational result)	No	Lack of financial data (turnover/ operational result)	No	Lack of financial data (turnover/ operational result)
471.	No	Lack of financial data (turnover/ operational result)	No	Lack of financial data (turnover/ operational result)	No	Lack of financial data (turnover/ operational result)
472.	No	Lack of financial data (turnover/ operational result)	No	Lack of financial data (turnover/ operational result)	No	Lack of financial data (turnover/ operational result)
473.	No	Lack of financial data (turnover/ operational result)	No	Lack of financial data (turnover/ operational result)	No	Lack of financial data (turnover/ operational result)
474.	No	Lack of financial data (turnover/ operational result)	No	Lack of financial data (turnover/ operational result)	No	Lack of financial data (turnover/ operational result)
475.	No	Lack of financial data (turnover/ operational result)	No	Lack of financial data (turnover/ operational result)	No	Lack of financial data (turnover/ operational result)
476.	No	Lack of financial data (turnover/ operational result)	No	Lack of financial data (turnover/ operational result)	No	Lack of financial data (turnover/ operational result)

477.	No	Lack of financial data (turnover/ operational result)	No	Lack of financial data (turnover/ operational result)	No	Lack of financial data (turnover/ operational result)
478.	No	Lack of financial data (turnover/ operational result)	No	Lack of financial data (turnover/ operational result)	No	Lack of financial data (turnover/ operational result)
479.	No	Lack of financial data (turnover/ operational result)	No	Lack of financial data (turnover/ operational result)	No	Lack of financial data (turnover/ operational result)
480.	No	Lack of financial data (turnover/ operational result)	No	Lack of financial data (turnover/ operational result)	No	Lack of financial data (turnover/ operational result)
481.	No	Lack of financial data (turnover/ operational result)	No	Lack of financial data (turnover/ operational result)	No	Lack of financial data (turnover/ operational result)
482.	No	Lack of financial data (turnover/ operational result)	No	Lack of financial data (turnover/ operational result)	No	Lack of financial data (turnover/ operational result)
483.	No	Lack of financial data (turnover/ operational result)	No	Lack of financial data (turnover/ operational result)	No	Lack of financial data (turnover/ operational result)
484.	No	Lack of financial data (turnover/ operational result)	No	Lack of financial data (turnover/ operational result)	No	Lack of financial data (turnover/ operational result)
485.	No	Lack of financial data (turnover/ operational result)	No	Lack of financial data (turnover/ operational result)	No	Lack of financial data (turnover/ operational result)
486.	No	Lack of financial data (turnover/ operational result)	No	Lack of financial data (turnover/ operational result)	No	Lack of financial data (turnover/ operational result)
487.	No	Lack of financial data (turnover/ operational result)	No	Lack of financial data (turnover/ operational result)	No	Lack of financial data (turnover/ operational result)
488.	No	Lack of financial data (turnover/ operational result)	No	Lack of financial data (turnover/ operational result)	No	Lack of financial data (turnover/ operational result)
489.	No	Lack of financial data (turnover/ operational result)	No	Lack of financial data (turnover/ operational result)	No	Lack of financial data (turnover/ operational result)
490.	No	Lack of financial data (turnover/ operational result)	No	Lack of financial data (turnover/ operational result)	No	Lack of financial data (turnover/ operational result)
491.	No	Lack of financial data (turnover/ operational result)	No	Lack of financial data (turnover/ operational result)	No	Lack of financial data (turnover/ operational result)

(continued)

No. crt.	Toll manufacturer		Contract manufacturer		Fully-fledged manufacturer	
	Rejected/ accepted	Rejection reason	Rejected/ accepted	Rejection reason	Rejected/ accepted	Rejection reason
492.	No	Lack of financial data (turnover/ operational result)	No	Lack of financial data (turnover/ operational result)	No	Lack of financial data (turnover/ operational result)
493.	No	Lack of financial data (turnover/ operational result)	No	Lack of financial data (turnover/ operational result)	No	Lack of financial data (turnover/ operational result)
494.	No	Lack of financial data (turnover/ operational result)	No	Lack of financial data (turnover/ operational result)	No	Lack of financial data (turnover/ operational result)
495.	No	Lack of financial data (turnover/ operational result)	No	Lack of financial data (turnover/ operational result)	No	Lack of financial data (turnover/ operational result)
496.	No	Lack of financial data (turnover/ operational result)	No	Lack of financial data (turnover/ operational result)	No	Lack of financial data (turnover/ operational result)
497.	No	Lack of financial data (turnover/ operational result)	No	Lack of financial data (turnover/ operational result)	No	Lack of financial data (turnover/ operational result)
498.	No	Lack of financial data (turnover/ operational result)	No	Lack of financial data (turnover/ operational result)	No	Lack of financial data (turnover/ operational result)
499.	No	Lack of financial data (turnover/ operational result)	No	Lack of financial data (turnover/ operational result)	No	Lack of financial data (turnover/ operational result)
500.	No	Lack of financial data (turnover/ operational result)	No	Lack of financial data (turnover/ operational result)	No	Lack of financial data (turnover/ operational result)
501.	No	Lack of financial data (turnover/ operational result)	No	Lack of financial data (turnover/ operational result)	No	Lack of financial data (turnover/ operational result)
502.	No	Lack of financial data (turnover/ operational result)	No	Lack of financial data (turnover/ operational result)	No	Lack of financial data (turnover/ operational result)
503.	No	Lack of financial data (turnover/ operational result)	No	Lack of financial data (turnover/ operational result)	No	Lack of financial data (turnover/ operational result)
504.	No	Lack of financial data (turnover/ operational result)	No	Lack of financial data (turnover/ operational result)	No	Lack of financial data (turnover/ operational result)

505.	No	Lack of financial data (turnover/ operational result)	No	Lack of financial data (turnover/ operational result)	No	Lack of financial data (turnover/ operational result)
506.	No	Lack of financial data (turnover/ operational result)	No	Lack of financial data (turnover/ operational result)	No	Lack of financial data (turnover/ operational result)
507.	No	Lack of financial data (turnover/ operational result)	No	Lack of financial data (turnover/ operational result)	No	Lack of financial data (turnover/ operational result)
508.	No	Lack of financial data (turnover/ operational result)	No	Lack of financial data (turnover/ operational result)	No	Lack of financial data (turnover/ operational result)
509.	No	Lack of financial data (turnover/ operational result)	No	Lack of financial data (turnover/ operational result)	No	Lack of financial data (turnover/ operational result)
510.	No	Lack of financial data (turnover/ operational result)	No	Lack of financial data (turnover/ operational result)	No	Lack of financial data (turnover/ operational result)
511.	No	Lack of financial data (turnover/ operational result)	No	Lack of financial data (turnover/ operational result)	No	Lack of financial data (turnover/ operational result)
512.	No	Lack of financial data (turnover/ operational result)	No	Lack of financial data (turnover/ operational result)	No	Lack of financial data (turnover/ operational result)

Appendix D: The Third Search Strategy (Romanian Market, Independence Indicators "A−", "A", "A+", "U")

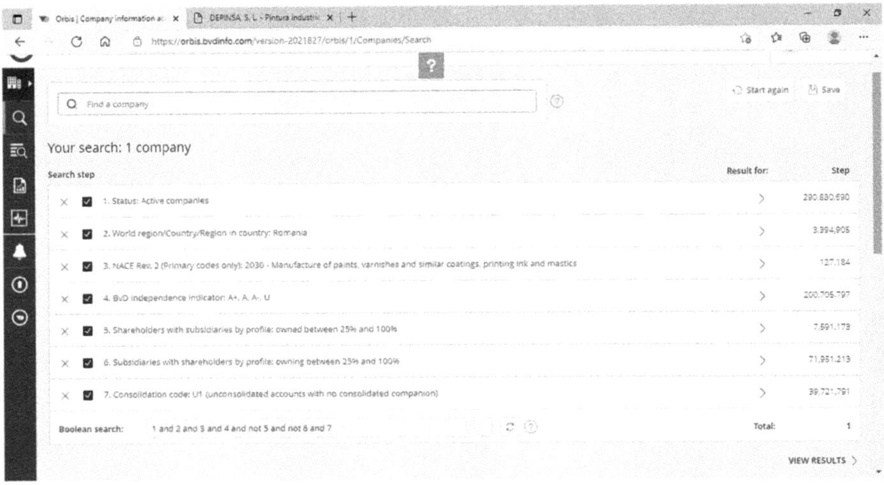

Appendix E: The Fourth Search Strategy (EU Market, Independence Indicators "A−", "A", "A+", "U")

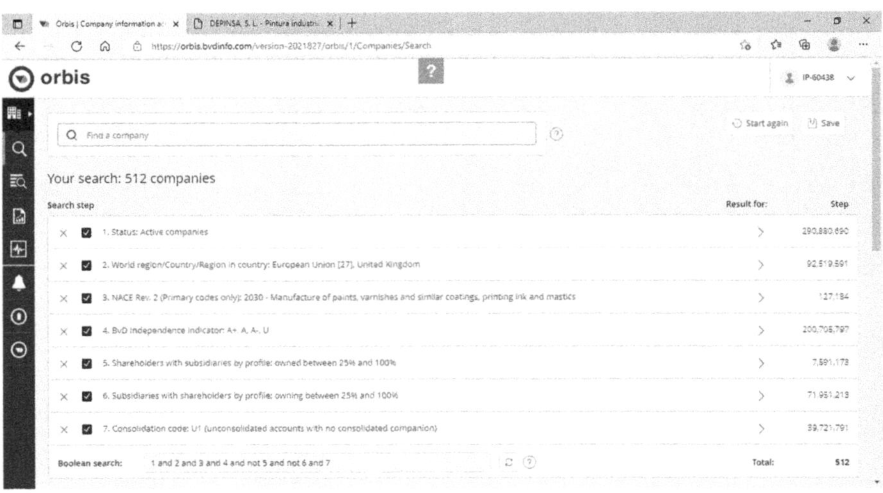

GPSR Compliance
The European Union's (EU) General Product Safety Regulation (GPSR) is a set of rules that requires consumer products to be safe and our obligations to ensure this.

If you have any concerns about our products, you can contact us on

ProductSafety@springernature.com

In case Publisher is established outside the EU, the EU authorized representative is:

Springer Nature Customer Service Center GmbH
Europaplatz 3
69115 Heidelberg, Germany

www.ingramcontent.com/pod-product-compliance
Ingram Content Group UK Ltd.
Pitfield, Milton Keynes, MK11 3LW, UK
UKHW020818290926
15470UKWH00003B/1233
* 9 7 8 3 0 3 0 9 3 8 8 8 8 *